ENGLISH SINGER

STEUART WILSON

English Singer

THE LIFE OF STEUART WILSON

MARGARET STEWART
(LADY WILSON)

GERALD DUCKWORTH & CO. LTD.
3 HENRIETTA STREET, LONDON W.C.2

First published in 1970 by
Gerald Duckworth & Company Limited
3 Henrietta Street, London W.C.2

SBN 7156 0468 6

Printed in Great Britain by
Cox & Wyman Ltd, London, Fakenham and Reading

CONTENTS

CONTENTS

LIST OF ILLUSTRATIONS

AUTHOR'S NOTE

STEUART wrote in his biography of his father J. M. Wilson, "It is not usual to 'get to know' your father better when he has passed his ninetieth year." In much the same way, I could say that it is not usual to 'get to know' your husband after his death. I had, as a child and an undergraduate, worshipped Steuart from afar, when he came to stay with my parents at Cambridge for his performances with the Cambridge University Musical Society. I had met him at Bernard Robinson's music camps and he had come to Professor Cornford's windmill in Norfolk, where members of my family and our friends were making music in the summer of 1934. But after then, we went very different ways. I went into journalism and it was not until 1962, nearly thirty years later, that we met again, he a widower, I a widow, and decided to get married.

Steuart very rarely talked about his past career and never about his unhappinesses. He threw away nearly every letter or document which might help a biographer and it is only thanks to the vigilance of his parents that a batch of his early letters from prep school and Winchester have been saved, as well as a few from Cambridge, the War fronts and Nice.

In the autumn of 1966, after long and persistent nagging, Steuart embarked on his autobiography, which he centred on his medical, rather than his musical, experiences. Called "Me and my Ulcer", it filled twenty pages of lined foolscap pages, written on both sides in the angular spiky handwriting which hardly changed during his lifetime. Much of this fragment has been included in this book.

The quest for Steuart has taken me to many different places—

to Paris, Amsterdam, Edinburgh, Gloucester, Bristol, Birmingham, Oxford and Cambridge—to the stage door at Covent Garden and into the archives of the BBC, the Arts Council, the Musicians' Benevolent Fund and many other institutions with which he was associated. I am grateful to the BBC for their help in my research and for access to scripts, to the Arts Council for letting me look through their files, to King's College Library for permission to browse through Professor Dent's papers, to the Ministry of Defence for their research into Steuart's war record, and to the International Music Council, the British Council and Dr W. Greenhouse Allt for information about Steuart's foreign trips. The list of people who have helped me is far too long to reproduce, and I am deeply indebted to everybody who so generously sent me letters, concert programmes and press cuttings, or remembered anecdotes or incidents. In particular I must mention the Executors of Clive Carey, Iris Lemare, Astra Desmond, Anneke Talma-Schilthuis, Jean Boswell, Myfanwy Jones and W. Johnstone Douglas—without whose help the book could never have been written.

I am especially grateful to Michael Kennedy, Ursula Vaughan Williams, Lady Redcliffe-Maud (Jean Hamilton) Nadine Peppard and John Firth, who read the book, either in MS or in proof and made many helpful suggestions. Thanks are also due to my brother Ludovick and other members of my family, to Hugh Wilson and Ann Pennant, who have read various chapters, and to Frank Howes who gave me great encouragement in embarking upon my task.

The responsibility for everything in the book is, however, entirely mine. I hope, as a non-practising musician, that I have not played too many false notes or missed too many beats, and I hope I have got the balance right—this was a point on which Steuart always insisted. He used to say about the dead '*Nil nisi verum*' and I have tried to give an objective and true picture of this remarkable man, whose life lasted for seventy-seven years and spanned the development of music in Britain from 1910 to 1966.

In writing, I have been generally, but not strictly chronological. I have dealt in episodes within a broad period, for example opera in the 1920s, or "Steuart at the BBC", rather than giving a faithful year by year chronicle of his activities.

PART ONE

THE MAKING OF A MUSICIAN

CHAPTER ONE

CHILDHOOD

JAMES STEUART WILSON was born on 22nd July 1889 at Clifton
College, Bristol, where his father was headmaster. At least, that
is the date on his passport. There seemed to be some doubt in
Canon Wilson's mind when he went to register the birth whether
it was the 21st or the 22nd, so Steuart always made a point of
celebrating his birthday two days running.

His father, James Maurice Wilson, lived from 1836 to 1931; his
grandfather, Edward Wilson, from 1802 to 1896; and his great
grandfather Jonathan was born in 1748 and died in 1810. Steuart
was thus able to claim that he was barely three generations away
from Bonnie Prince Charlie. The longevity of the Wilsons in the
older generations may have been due to their hardy yeoman stock.
The family were originally small farmers in Cumberland, whose
forebears had migrated south from over the Border in the eighteenth
century. The last Wilson to farm was great-great grandfather
Jonathan who lived at Westward between Carlisle and Skiddaw.
This Jonathan, according to the family annals, "was a strong man
and rode a strong horse". His feat in making his horse jump from
Duddon Brig on to the river bank 10–12 feet below is still remembered and the bank was ever after called "Jonty's Jump".

Farmer Jonathan died in 1789 and most of his descendants
became clergymen and/or schoolmasters. Steuart's grandfather
Edward was headmaster of King William's College, Isle of Man, and
became vicar of various parishes. He married Elizabeth Pears,
daughter of the Reverend James Pears, Headmaster of the Grammar
School at Charlcombe, near Bath. She was the eldest of a family all

of whose members were gifted, musical and elegant. Peter Pears, the tenor, is a descendant of this family. Steuart was the son of Peter's father's first cousin.

Steuart's father, J. M. Wilson, had the most distinguished career of the clan. He was educated at Sedbergh and St. John's College, Cambridge, where he read classics and mathematics. He became a senior wrangler in his third year, but was suddenly and inexplicably taken ill on the day the Tripos results were announced and was seized by complete amnesia. When he recovered, he found he had forgotten nearly everything he knew about higher mathematics. From Cambridge, he went to Rugby, where the then Headmaster Frederick Temple offered him a mastership in mathematics and science. He was an outstanding success as a teacher of both subjects. After twenty years at Rugby, he was made Headmaster of Clifton.

At the age of 43 he became ordained. He entered the Church in spite of very profound doctrinal differences with the authorities. The Bishop of Worcester had actually refused to ordain him, because of his views.

Wilson wrote that he had told the Bishop "that I had definitely abandoned the theory of verbal inspiration of the Bible . . . that I could not accept the general view of miracles . . . and that I held the Virgin Birth as a physical statement to be unproved and irrelevant". In the end, his former patron Frederick Temple, then Bishop of Exeter, ordained him as his Chaplain.

He was happy at Clifton, but decided that life was perhaps a trifle too comfortable and that he ought to move to a parish more in contact with the harsh realities of life. Accordingly he accepted the position of Archdeacon of Manchester and Vicar of Rochdale in 1890—this was when Steuart was nearly two. It was an exacting assignment. Rochdale was dominated by Nonconformists, who were not enthusiastic about coming to terms with the Church of England and the new Archdeacon's 'advanced' views were regarded with suspicion on all sides.

Even at that time, he had a massive white beard, which reached from his ears to his chest, and gave him a patriarchal expression. Small children used to think he must be at least Moses, if not God. This beard lasted to the last weeks of his life, when he set it alight by accident as he lay in bed.

After fifteen years at Rochdale, J. M. Wilson accepted a canonry

II. STEUART AGED FOUR

III. STEUART AND HIS BROTHER
HUGH

IV. CANON AND MRS WILSON AND THEIR FOUR SONS

at Worcester. He was then 70, but this did not stop him undertaking teaching at the King's School, as well as doing a great deal of public, social and educational work for the city. He retired from Worcester at the age of 89 in 1926—this was the year when his wife died—and moved to Steep, on the outskirts of Petersfield, where he lived until his death. His closing years belong to a later chapter.

By the time he went to Rochdale, he had a family of eight children—four by his first wife, Annie Elizabeth Moore, who died in 1878, and four by his second wife, Georgina Mary Talbot (daughter of Admiral John Talbot, who was then living in Bristol) whom he married in 1883. Mona, Edward, Maurice and Grace were Annie's children; Georgina's were Arnold, Hugh, Margaret and Steuart.

Nobody can say, thank goodness, precisely what genes enter into the make-up of a newborn child and how much character is formed by heredity and how much by environment. Steuart inherited widely different characteristics from his parents. His strong sense of right and wrong, his stubborn will-power amounting at times to obstinacy and his intellectual curiosity all came from his father. From his mother he inherited wit and charm, a love of music and a generous spirit. He always used to say that children got the parents they deserved and that he had been exceptionally lucky. This sentiment was evidently shared by his parents, for Canon Wilson wrote to his son Arnold: "I am indeed blessed in my children, every one of them —it is a matter of thankfulness to me every night."

Steuart was also lucky in his brothers and sisters, who constituted a notable and remarkably united family. His eldest half-sister Mona was prominent in the cause of women's emancipation—she herself went to Newnham in 1892—and played an active part in the 'anti-sweating' campaign* at the turn of the century, along with Sir Charles and Lady Dilke, Gertrude Tuckwell and Mary Macarthur.

She was made secretary of the Women's Trade Union League and became the first woman health insurance commissioner in 1911. She was a distinguished historian and scholar and was the author of books on William Blake, Sir Philip Sidney and Queen Victoria. Mona used to shock the residents of Petersfield by wearing trousers and smoking a clay pipe and expressing advanced socialist views. Steuart was devoted to her and to her great friend the historian G. M. Young.

* This was the movement designed to put an end to the evils of out-working which led to the establishment of Trade Boards.

The eldest son of Canon Wilson's first marriage, Edward, went to Sedbergh and Pembroke College, Cambridge, and then out to South Africa. He was killed in the First World War. 'Ted' was always rather a remote big-brother figure to Steuart. The second son, Maurice, died in early youth. The younger daughter, Grace, married a well-to-do wool merchant, Frank Padwick; they had three children and settled in Petersfield, which was to become a kind of headquarters for the whole Wilson clan.

The children of the second marriage were outstanding. Arnold, the eldest, went to Clifton and Sandhurst and had a brilliant career in the Army and in South-west Persia, where his name is still remembered with awe. He was knighted in 1920 and entered Parliament as Conservative M.P. for Hitchin in 1933. He was always completely independent in his views and was much more at home with Independent M.P.s like Eleanor Rathbone and A. P. Herbert. A.P.H., whose Divorce Bill he supported, once described him as a 'human encyclopedia'. His industry and his scholarship were prodigious. In home affairs, Arnold was a radical (which he attributed to the influence of Mona); a great social reformer, he pioneered changes in the British social insurance system long before the days of Beveridge and the Welfare State. On international matters, he was a very right-wing Tory and Imperialist (thanks, he said, to his half-brother Edward). He supported the cause of General Franco in Spain, had little use for the League of Nations and saw much that was good in the Hitler régime in Germany.

When war broke out, Arnold showed great courage and a typical Wilson ability to admit his misjudgements. He joined the R.A.F. at the age of 55. He told the House of Commons on 7th May 1940: "I have sometimes been wrong and I must accept my responsibility, like others." He told his constituents:

"From now on I am pledged to one thing and to one thing only, with my own body, with my own muscles and my own experience, such as it is, to help to bring the war to a successful conclusion. To that I am dedicated."

A few days later, 'Sir Gunner', as his crew called him, was shot down and killed in a bombing raid over Germany.

Arnold and Steuart differed in nearly every way, and Arnold was highly amused when a Kingsman once asked him whether he was any relation to Steuart—"He recognized me as his brother by my voice and added, 'Besides you have the same ideas'. Steuart and I with the same kind of ideas!!!" But they had a mutual respect and affection, and many traits in Arnold's character, for example his toughness, fearlessness and independence of spirit, were discernible in his younger brother. They collaborated happily in producing a biography* of their father in 1932.

Steuart was utterly devoted to, and inseparable from, his brother Hugh, who was nearer him in age and in spirit. They looked alike and they thought alike, and shared the same tastes and pleasure in art and poetry and in the countryside. Hugh went to Clifton and King's College Cambridge, and was an assistant master at Rugby when the War broke out. He joined up in September 1914 and was killed a year later.

Steuart's sister Margaret ('Midge') adored both her brothers. "Hugh and Steuart grow daily more wonderful," she wrote to a friend in 1907. She also followed an independent line. She decided she would take up dressmaking but met with fierce opposition— "They are reading the riot act over it at home," she wrote; her father thought it a profession below the dignity of a gentlewoman. (He was not to know that Steuart would later marry the daughter of a tailor and himself set up a dressmaking shop.) Margaret entered an Anglican convent shortly before the 1914 War and eventually joined a Mission in Melanesia. She later became a Roman Catholic.

Steuart was called James after his father and Steuart after a Pears uncle. It is strange that none of the five Wilson boys was christened Jonathan, which was a traditional family name.

Steuart was a delicate baby and for some reason was at one stage fed on asses' milk. He used to say this accounted for all his eccentricities.

Although Steuart was born in Bristol and proud of being a Bristolian, he was only two when the family moved to Lancashire and Rochdale was the first place he could remember. When his father was appointed Canon of Worcester, Steuart wrote: "Could anything beat Rochdale? It seems so funny to think of leaving it. Rochdale is so entirely home to me naturally and Worcester will be entirely the opposite kind of town . . ."

'Home' was the compact red-brick Queen Anne vicarage, standing

* *James M. Wilson*, Sidgwick & Jackson, London 1932.

B

on the crest of the slope above the town. Smoke belching up from the factory chimneys below left a black pall over the garden and there was a perpetual smell from the gasworks. The drab poverty of the mill-workers in their shawls and clogs made a deep impression on Steuart. It was this early experience of the industrial North that made him a radical for life and imbued him with a sympathy for the under-dog which he never lost.

His very first letter to his father, which I have been able to unearth, undated, and written in huge sloping letters between double lines runs:

"My dear Papa
    i love you the queen came to Manchester love to mamma goodbye James S Wilson"

On holiday in the Isle of Man, he wrote:

"If we can get a foxterrier puppy in Ramsay may we take it home on Saturday we went to Castletown and I saw the house where you were born love to you and Mamma your loving son J. S. Wilson"

And to his mother:

"Will my boots come soon I do want them very much. My other tooth came out when I was in bed. There was an enormous rat came out of a pipe in the yard this morning thank you for your letter love to Papa and you
your loving son J. Steuart Wilson"

In the late Victorian era, the idea prevailed that children should be seen and not heard and they were usually left to the tender mercies of their nurse or governess. Fortunately the Wilsons' nurse, Miss Hicks (known as Nim) was a kind and sensible woman and all the children adored her. Steuart, who often spent holidays with her on a farmhouse near Witney, always ended his letters to Nim "Your loving boy", and once Steuart's mother, rather wistfully, reported to her husband: "I cannot tell you how funny Steuart is getting. I was reading to him and to the others after dinner and we came to a very exciting adventure. I saw Steuart looking at me with great eyes of excitement and I said 'Is not your heart beating?' He shook his head and sighed dramatically—'I have no heart here to beat, it is in

Manchester with my beloved Nim. My heart and my blood are with her. All that you see before you is my little skeleton'."

Even more poignant was the story which Steuart told later, of how when his mother was very ill in 1925 and forbidden to exert herself, he found her bathing his two-year-old son. "I upbraided her, but her reply was 'You must let me; I've never been allowed to give a baby a bath'."

An early picture of Steuart at Rochdale (1892) shows him as a very beautiful, rather fragile-looking little boy, with silky golden hair in ringlets, a rather quizzical expression and a very determined chin. This chin was evidently famous, for a letter from Arnold at prep school says: "Yesterday I had a fight with a boy called Hardman. I would rather be licked by Hardman or by any boy in the school than have your chin stuck in my head. It hurts much more."

For the fullest account of the Wilson establishment at Rochdale, we may refer to a passage in Steuart's biographical sketch of his father:

"To their children in their early youth both parents were rather remote and even austere. To begin with, both of them had tasks which fully and completely occupied their minds and bodies, both at Clifton and at Rochdale.

"We lived our life upstairs, under the complete and loving despotism of our nurse, visited occasionally from outside. We went downstairs to dinner, where the conversation was seldom directed to us, and never about us, except on the occasions when my father would explain, with vivid diagrams on the tablecloth, some simple phenomena. As a rule we all sat in cheerful silence, never speaking to each other and seldom to our elders, guided by the advice given in Ecclesiasticus xxxii. 7–8:

'Speak, young man, if there be need of thee: and yet scarcely when thou art twice asked.

'Let thy speech be short, comprehending much in few words, and when ancient men are in place, use not many words.'

"But we greatly profited from, and sometimes enjoyed, the varied conversations to which we listened attentively. The guests were from many walks of life; my father was a good—my mother a supremely good—conversationalist; to hear her putting people

at their ease, and eliciting interesting points of view from un-
promising subjects, was in itself an education, as was her perfectly
genuine, if momentary, absorption in the matter in hand. At the
other end of the table my father, carving, with conscious skill and
care, the great sirloin, cross-questioning the guests with grave
courtesy, but often disconcerting directness if they had been guilty
of an exaggerated statement or an unduly broad generalization.

"My mother cared much for music, poetry and art; and the
catholicity of her interests and her natural good nature did not
entirely cloak her critical faculties; to the elder children she read
aloud whenever she had a moment to spare after meals, and
from her we imbibed some good poetry and the accepted classics
of the nursery and the schoolroom—the Bible, *Pilgrim's Progress,
Gulliver's Travels, Robinson Crusoe, The Swiss Family Robinson,
The Fairchild Family* (with many a twinkle of the eye), Sandford
and Merton, Maria Edgeworth, and, at a later stage, Walter
Scott.

"On Sundays the Collect for the day was to be learned, and a
part of the Catechism recited, and explained by her, with the
emphasis on duty rather than on dogma. In the evenings we would
assemble in the Parish Room, newly erected in the Vicarage
garden, round the grand piano, to be taught to sing—not the
childish jingles, but the great classic hymns of A and M.

"Sometimes, too, we went with her to a 'Penny Reading', over
which she presided at the Church Army Hall, to marvel at her
fervour and power of carrying her audience of mill-hands with
her, and moving them sometimes to tears with the pathos of an
oft-told tale.

"After lessons with a governess, and in later years during the
holidays, we children were expected to make ourselves useful—
to run errands, pay small bills and buy stamps, and account
carefully for the sums entrusted to us, to carry the bag of the
guest to the station. At Christmas we had to play our part at the
Waifs and Strays' Home, and occasionally at Sunday-school
outings.

"The day's work in the parish—the daily duties of my father and
mother—was always predominant, and seemed to take precedence
in their minds over domestic affairs, and we were expected, not
perhaps joyfully but dutifully, to play our part."

Steuart and his sister Margaret went to a Dame's School for girls, at 36 William Street, Rochdale. He was barely seven, but even at that age showed that he had an independent nature and was no respecter of persons.

Miss Frances G. Boycott, the headmistress, wrote weekly letters to his father and sent regular reports of his placing in form, as well as the routine end-of-term reports. One of the very earliest conduct reports on J. S. Wilson states: "Steuart has not been quite respectful in manner on all occasions, but on the whole his general conduct has improved." Later on, the verdicts became more favourable and he is described as "a reliable and helpful member of his form—except that he is careless about the 'speaking' rule, his conduct is very good."

Poor Steuart, he was ticked off twenty-one times in one single term for "speaking without leave". His best subjects were scripture, litera-ture, Latin, French and composition; his worst, arithmetic. His recitation was generally "good" though sometimes "too loud" or "drawling" and his writing was "so bad as to have made it impos-sible to read some of his examination papers."

As for music, he showed "considerable promise" at the piano, but was told he must practise harder and pay more attention to his fingering. By 1899, his teacher noted: "I am delighted with results."

CHAPTER TWO

SCHOOL DAYS

IT was not until he went to preparatory school that Steuart got the opportunity to develop his music. It seems strange that, although his mother was so gifted, there was little of the music-making at home which he himself did so much to encourage in later years. Nor was there ever any suggestion that he might become a chorister. Music usually meant finger exercises on the piano; singing was confined to hymns. But at Grove House, near Guildford, which he entered in the autumn of 1899, he was given every encouragement and opportunity, not only to work at the piano but to go to concerts in the neighbourhood. His headmaster, F. S. Pridden, and his music-loving wife showed a great deal of enlightenment in this regard.

Steuart's first teacher was "an old crock called Miss Payne who rides up from Guildford on a bicycle. She is fairly decent." Miss Payne gave him good marks. "He shows taste and much interest and has made progress," she reported in December 1899. Her successor, Mrs. Soutter, was equally impressed. "Has good ear and taste; he is doing well," she wrote.

Possibly Steuart's first public appearance on a concert platform was at the school concert in December 1902. He played Mendelssohn's *Songs Without Words*, No. 2—his own choice had been Mozart's *Turkish Patrol*, but "Mr. Pridden objected for some reason or other" —and he also played a piano duet, Moskowski's *Spanish Dances*. "The concert," he reported "went off very well indeed, everything except the clarionet solo which was dreadfully flat and out of time as well. My solo and duet went off fairly well I think."

Steuart was already enlarging his musical horizon. He wrote home that he was thinking of learning the 'Wedding March' from *Lohengrin*, and he was becoming quite a critic. He was taken to a concert in Woking and wrote: "They had two very fine trios for piano, violin and cello and two violin solos which were awfully good and two cello solos which were almost nicer. There was one piano, a waltz, which was not very nice, but not bad and some rather rotten songs by someone or other rather rotten." 'Rotten' was also his verdict on the local church service. "The choir there is something awful it could not be worse I do not think. They have a rotten organist who rushes through the psalms as if it was a gallop."

Steuart was a normal little boy and his letters home are full of the items of news that every prep school boy gives in the compulsory Sunday letter home. News of the weather, of what he ate and, above all, full accounts of football and cricket matches fill the standard four pages, written laboriously but with a somewhat limited vocabulary. "We had a ripping game . . . we had a ripping tea afterwards with unlimited cups of hot coffee and buns. It was ripping coming back" . . . "We played a 2nd XI match on Wednesday against Cobham but we got beaten by 4 goals to none. I played in goal, but I was not much of a success as you can see."

His letters were always punctiliously addressed to 'Dear Papa', or 'Dear Mamma' and always ended

"I remain, Your loving son

J. S. Wilson"

His father kept a critical eye on Steuart's general progress and on his composition. He enjoined him to "take all pains with your lessons, as well as your games" and criticized his spelling. "There are two slips of spelling in your last letter" he wrote "One is Monogram which you spell Monagram; the other is the difficult word Sergeant. You call it Seargent, getting the *a* in the wrong place." Steuart was evidently conscious of the criticisms because in one letter he wrote "If I say that this is a bad letter, you will write and say it is a very good one; if I say it is a good one you will say it is not. So I leave it to you." He also went out of his way to show his spelling prowess. In describing a dancing lesson, he tackled some very difficult words and got them right: "I was put with a chap who can no more dance than a dissipated dyspeptic poker with three joints and all in the wrong place."

Steuart was able to make the most of the long school vacations. One red-letter holiday was when he went to London, at Mona's invitation, for the Coronation of King Edward VII in June 1902. This, he forecast, would be "a sight well worth seeing and one that one will remember for a lifetime." The Coronation was postponed owing to the King's illness but Steuart still made the jaunt to London. During his visit, he was taken to the House of Commons where he met the great Dilke and heard a debate about the Licensing Bill, which must have been extremely dreary for him. He went to several theatres, including *Ben Hur* at Drury Lane, and to Madame Tussaud's and, to crown it all:

"We went in the twopenny tube which is a spiffing thing. You go in a lift down and then into some well-lighted not smelling clean carriages driven by electricity."

Most summer holidays were spent with his dear Nim on a farm near Witney, but in 1902 he was sent to France to 'cram' with a family at Ambrières, near Caen.

His main concern at prep school was about what public school he would go to. Canon Wilson had a preference for Rugby but Steuart himself was attracted by Clifton, where his brother Hugh was at school. Mr Pridden wrote that Steuart would have a good chance of getting into any school, Eton and Winchester included. Steuart himself had definite ideas of where he did *not* want to go. "I don't want to go to Charterhouse at all, it always gives me an idea of a slack place and besides I have a prejudice against it. Eton too seems such a very swagger place with all Dukes and snobs in it."

Mr. Pridden's confidence in Steuart was justified. He won a scholarship to Winchester in July 1903. "Best paper, Divinity; worst paper Arithmetic (very weak)." He left Grove House that term with glowing testimonials. He had been captain of the school in his last year and the headmaster wrote to his father:

"Steuart will probably be able to excel at anything he takes up. He should become, with his decided character, in addition to all else, quite an exceptional man. He is certainly one of the most independent as well as the most capable boys of 13 I can remember. I often wonder what the future has in store for him—as a man he will certainly be a match for most people."

Steuart left his prep school a 'boy'. He arrived at Winchester on 16th September 1903 as a 'man'. (All Winchester boys are called men). He was bidden attend at 6 p.m. promptly so that he could be 'inducted' by the Headmaster, then the Rev. Dr. M. R. Burge. He was carrying a hat-box with his night gear, his large trunk with his belongings having been dispatched by train from Worcester.

He was utterly baffled by the procedure of initiation as one of the College's seventy scholars. He wrote to his father:

"At six all the new men sallied to Burge's house and had our names, ages and addresses taken down in a great kind of ledger. First of all I took my things up to my 'shop' or dormitory and discovered, or rather was discovered by my 'pater' who had to instruct his 'son' in all the various 'notions' or slang terms, phrases etc. which are legion—each one more meaningless, senseless and absurd than the last."

'Notions' need some explanation. They are the curious traditional language and slang which were (and still are) in use at Winchester, and are utterly incomprehensible to the outsider. Thus preparation time was called 'toy time' and a prep school 'tother'; 'tug' meant commonplace. A boy—sorry, man—would talk about his 'pitch-up' when he referred to his parents and would ask for a 'tozzie' when he wanted sixpence. These are a few of the examples quoted by Francis Toye in his autobiography. One other example sent me by an old Wykehamist: Q: "Who's the 'cuddest' man in College?" Correct answer: "J. S. Wilson." Translation: 'most handsome'.

Every new arrival was given a fortnight to master this vocabulary under the guidance of his 'pater'. If he failed consistently, he might be given a 'tunding' (beating). 'Notions' were not all. He had to learn where he might or might not walk, what he might or might not wear, the words of Domum (the school song) the topography of the school and, in general, the correct way to behave towards his elders and betters. Steuart did not relate how he fared in the 'notions' test, nor who his 'pater' was, but he wrote of the problem about 'Where e'er you walk'.

"All College buildings face out on to a large quad called Chamber Court. At night everybody goes round on the stone paving, only Prefects, 18 in number, being allowed to walk in the middle part called Middle Sands."

Another unwritten rule was that only the prefects were entitled to warm themselves in front of the big open fire, the smaller fry being left to shiver on the outskirts. Arnold Toynbee, one of Steuart's contemporaries, remembers seeing him standing among a group of men who were considerably his seniors, warming himself with his back to the fire:

"Steuart was looking thoroughly at home in that formidable company, and this struck me at the time and made a permanent mark on my memory. At that date College was a highly hierarchical community, but here was an exceptional junior who had the self-assurance to assert himself and was getting away with it."

Steuart disliked fagging intensely and hated having to be anybody's servant; but he never complained at the time about the rigours of the régime, nor did I ever hear him refer to them in later life. He had, after all, been brought up to be tough, to walk and cycle for hours on end, to sleep out in the open and to take cold baths, and neither the vicarage at Rochdale nor Grove House were exactly temples of luxury.

Arnold Toynbee recalls one freezing December morning, when the Rifle Corps was being drilled by Lance-Corporal J. S. Wilson, all the men in the squad were frozen to the marrow, but "Steuart alone did not appear to feel any discomfort." He was as impervious to physical discomfort as he was to physical fear.

Nor, to my knowledge, did he ever grumble about the food which, according to Francis Toye, was "execrable, badly cooked and inconceivably monotonous," and to D. N. Pritt (another of Steuart's contemporaries) "edible but dreary." Steuart never cared much in those days what he ate, or how it was cooked, so long as there was plenty of it.

"You get a huge hunk of bread and as much butter as you want, also as much tea. Meat always for breakfast at 8.15, dinner at 1.15, tea at 6.15, supper at 8.15."

He did, however, complain vociferously about a particularly noxious concoction 'egg flip' which was served on Hatch Thoke. This was the day in November which, in his words, commemorated "the death or birth, I do not know which" of the founder, William of Wykeham. "We drink egg flip in school, which is made out of College 'swipes' (small beer) eggs, hot water and brandy. As regards such drinks I am strictly teetotal for anything which has College swipes in it must be beastly."

To say that the education was biased towards the Classics would be an understatement. According to D. N. Pritt, Latin and Greek took up 95 per cent of the curriculum, with about one hour a week for History and another hour for French and German. Chapel was, of course, compulsory, with attendance twice a day and extra long services on Sundays and Feast Days.

At Canon Wilson's request, special arrangements were made for Steuart to continue his music. This meant the piano; there was no instruction in singing, harmony or any other of the elements of music.

Music was not given high priority at Winchester and it did not reach a very high standard in those days. There was the mass singing of glees and rollicking songs on Hatch Thoke; there was the Glee Club and there was college Chapel. The music master and organist in Steuart's day was Dr. E. T. Sweeting, formerly organist of St. John's College, Cambridge. Steuart wrote home: "About music, I have one lesson of about one hour once every week and I practise whenever I can. There are four pianos I can get at, so I can get in a good deal." He reported his great disappointment with the music in the Cathedral:

"I was very much struck with the great poorness of the Chants. Nothing to compare with some, in fact, most of the Chants in the Clifton book. Sweeting, the organist, is very fond of having the Chants and hymns sung very softly, which I do not like at all. The Cathedral organist wants them loud, so he plays the organ while the choir sings pp. The effect is that of course the choir are entirely drowned."

His first music report in December 1903, says: "Possesses considerable ability and works well." But a year later: "Has made distinct progress but he *must* try to be more accurate." However, in 1906, the master comments: "He is thoroughly interested and interesting to teach." There is only one mention of his singing—July 1907: "He has a very promising voice."

His 'character' reports, whether from the Headmaster Dr. Burge or the Second Master, M. J. Rendall, were invariably favourable and must have given his parents great joy. Rendall, in particular, was glowing. It was well-known to Wykehamists that 'M.J.R.' tended to have his favourites and was 'drawn towards those who were brilliant, attractive and vital.'* All three adjectives applied to Steuart and as early as December 1903, at the end of his first half, Rendall wrote:

> "He towers over his contemporaries and suggests physically and otherwise, marked strength. All I have seen of him is good—no doubt he possesses 'character'."

Rendall bestowed on Steuart the most laudatory adjectives in his vocabulary . . . "Manly and straight" . . . "Manly and honourable" . . . "A capital fellow" . . . "Cheery and trustworthy" . . . "A strong, earnest, attractive nature" . . . "Free from all taint of the prig" . . .

He did not foresee much hope of academic distinction, but was certain that Steuart would go far. "He gives us all a feeling of strong sense and strong character, which will tell in life." But, he added: "There is just the danger that his independence of view may take the form of obstinacy. He has not always been happy 'under authority'." Shape of things to come! And in his very last letter to Canon Wilson in August 1908, when Steuart had just left College, Rendall wrote: "His leading characteristic is firmness of conviction which might be obstinacy if his aims were less high. But I think the things for which he contends so stoutly are good and he has won general respect. Clearly he has some power of leading." This was a remarkably percipient summary of Steuart's character. Firmness of conviction, high aims and a dogged determination to fight for the things he believed in were typical of him throughout his life.

For Rendall, as for all who heard him, Steuart's singing was sheer joy. He wrote:

> "Steuart Wilson formed a small choir of College men to sing Church music in Chamber Court on church festivals and other occasions. Here I heard for the first time the magnificent Dutch Easter carol *This joyful Eastertide* which Steuart often sang for my benefit as a solo after that date."

He sang regularly in the cathedral, at the monthly services for the benefit of the whole school; his voice was rivalled in power and volume only by that of a bass lay-clerk whom he nicknamed 'Thunderguts'.

* *Rendall of Winchester.* By J. D'E. Firth. Oxford University Press, 1954.

Many of his contemporaries have given me vivid, and revealing, recollections of Steuart at Winchester. Thus Arnold Toynbee: "Steuart soon gathered a group round him. His personality was attractive and commanding. One of his attractions was the mock-ruffianly air that he knew how to assume." He was extremely athletic and according to D. N. Pritt, 'excelled' at that ferocious game, Winchester football.

G. E. Law was impressed by Steuart's "total and sometimes daunting sincerity . . . If you made any remark to him or asked any question, he looked straight at you and gave you a direct and un-compromising answer." This characteristic, shown in his teens, was to prove shattering in later years, when he entered organizations in which compromise and obliqueness were expected. It was also characteristic of Steuart that he took up the cudgels on behalf of an underporter, who had been sacked without being given any reason.

This man, Steuart told his father, was "a perfect Shakespearean character, a kind of second Falstaff" and he (Steuart) suspected that he had been sacked because he spent too long telling stories of his Army life to the boys. Could Canon Wilson possibly find work at Worcester for this man? "He is badly off and if we could direct his steps anywhere it would be a great benefit." The suggestion did not come off, like so many of the causes which Steuart was to take up later, but the fact that he made the effort was significant.

G. E. Law, summed up Steuart thus: "He was gay, carefree and with a slight tendency to iconoclasm. He had great respect for what he considered worthy, but a startlingly critical outlook on the less admirable." This attitude was illustrated in a review which Steuart wrote for the College magazine *The Wykehamist* of a Domum Day Concert. He pulled no punches, and said exactly what he thought of the performance. Not only was he rebuked by the authorities for not paying sufficient tribute to the efforts of the performers and the organizers, but the Editor, E. M. Barlow, was 'put on the mat' for employing so tactless a music critic.

There were no signs at Winchester that Steuart had any thoughts of taking up music. Professional musicians in those days were looked down upon, unless they happened to be organists or German opera singers, and tenors were less than the dust. At one point, it was suggested that Steuart should desert the Classics for History, but he objected:

"It is to me an entirely mistaken idea that I have even the makings of an historian . . . I cannot carry facts and dates in the very least. Apparently, I possess the doubtful virtue of being able to 'gas' without committing myself to any statement of fact. This is a desirable acquisition no doubt, but it is not an argument for History particularly."

There was some idea that Steuart might try for the Indian Civil Service, which was the destination of most Wykehamists of the day. Steuart did not agree—it would need too much mathematics, a subject at which "he would never be anything but hopeless". So, he asked his father, "Why not the Army?" He wanted to follow in the footsteps of his brother Arnold, who had gone straight from Clifton to Sandhurst, and he enjoyed his afternoons with the Rifle Corps. "I know that the pay in the I.C.S. is better but the risks of being stranded at 23 or so with nothing worth considering left to do are, you will admit, considerable."

For a public-school boy of 17, a career was a remote prospect and Steuart was not really serious about the Army, or unduly concerned about his future. He did not have to worry about earning his living and he still had four to five years ahead of him *in statu pupillari*. The main task in his final year at school was to concentrate on winning a scholarship to the University.

Many people look back in later years on their schooldays as the happiest time of their lives, forgetting how acutely miserable they were for most of the time. Steuart, however, was genuinely happy at Winchester and said so while he was there. "It *is* the best place in the world," he wrote home. "However I shall leave this place I cannot imagine."

CHAPTER THREE

CAMBRIDGE

T HE records of King's College show that Steuart came up from Winchester as an Honorary Exhibitioner in Classics in October 1908 and that he obtained a Second in the May examinations of 1909 and 1910, but only a Third in his Tripos. This was a great disappointment to his former Winchester masters, his Cambridge tutors and his father, who had entertained high hopes of his success. But Steuart took it calmly. His lack of academic distinction was entirely due to the fact that he spent all his time at Cambridge making music, to the neglect of his classical studies.

In October 1908, Hugh Wilson wrote to his friend Geoffrey Keynes:

"Steuart is there (Cambridge) now and likely to be all that I expected him to be—an important person where I was a spectator and a leader where I was barely fit to follow. It keeps that part of Cambridge which meant everything to me, to know that he is enjoying it so ably as I hear from many sides."

Steuart made an immediate impression upon everybody who came into contact with him. He was at that time extremely beautiful, and attractive to both men and women. From the photographs of his early King's days and from the portrait of him by his friend Geoffroy-Dechaume, he looked like a Greek god— very tall and willowy, but with an athletic physique; fair hair, a straight nose, deep-set eyes, a determined chin and that crooked smile which was to melt so many hearts. Sir Arthur Bliss, his contemporary at Cambridge, said "he was very striking-looking indeed—rather like an eagle of some kind."

Quite apart from his good looks, he had charm, humour and was already developing into a compelling personality.

Unfortunately Steuart lost the good habit of writing home regularly which he had acquired at his prep school, and his letters from Cambridge are few and far between. We know that he first had rooms in M 5, Chetwynd Court, known as the 'Drain' or the 'Lane', near those of Maynard Keynes who had recently become a Fellow. The next year he moved to A 12 on the top floor of Wilkins Building, overlooking King's Parade. Here his neighbour was the eminent philosopher and don, Oscar Browning. Some later letters are written from No. 8 Bene't Street.

Steuart's tutor was W. H. Macaulay, a great Cambridge figure who taught engineering. There were five lecturers on the College Classical staff: J. E. Nixon, M. S. Dimsdale, N. Wedd, H. H. Sills and J. T. Sheppard. Dr. Nixon who was then advanced in years was a remarkable 'Cambridge character' and Steuart used to tell many anecdotes about him. One concerned the time when he fell off his tricycle and broke a lot of bones. When he was well again, he took a friend out to show him the place where it had happened, again fell off his tricycle and broke yet more bones.

Despite the eminence of the teaching staff, Steuart became increasingly bored with the Classics. He wrote to his father (30th October 1910):

"Classical work does not really equip one for anything in particular. And I can't help feeling that I have no real feeling for the niceties of Classical language beyond the point at which I have arrived. All this sounds very negative and so it is, I am in short thoroughly bored with my actual work of Classics and I cannot attack it with any enthusiasm or any pleasure. I am afraid that is the real truth of the matter and I am so constituted unfortunately that I cannot work hard at things which *per se* bore me, and do not lead to any definite end. You will say that it is an unfortunate moment at which to discover it, and I think it is, very unfortunate. Well the upshot of it, in my own mind at least, seems at the moment clear and to be this, that I must change my whole ideas."

He was, he wrote, seriously thinking of giving up the Classics and taking up Medicine:

"It is a new subject to me, does not require any previous specialized training, and when you are equipped and trained, you can always find employment, there is always someone who wants your knowledge. It is difficult and arduous, that I know . . . No doubt this seems to you to be perfectly lunatic: but I have been thinking over it for a month or so now and have asked a good many questions of various people. I could I believe pass the first stage in a year, i.e. by next Christmas, the next by the following Christmas and then two years or two and a half in a hospital in London. I hope you will consider this seriously as I am quite serious about it—not that I wish to accuse you of flippancy! But it is such a complete volte-face that it is difficult to view it seriously at first."

One of the people he consulted was Geoffrey Keynes, who was then a medical student at Pembroke. Sir Geoffrey remembers clearly how he and Steuart walked up and down the Backs one morning, talking about the pros and cons of such a move. But Canon Wilson poured cold water on the scheme and Steuart abandoned the idea. He wrote to his father (6th November 1910):

"There is obviously no more to be said on either side. Your objections seem to me to be quite sound. There is one thing to which I am rather inclined to take exception; you say that the life would be a harder one than my upbringing and education fits me for. I do not think, or I hope rather, that is not true. It would seem an unfortunate result of a Liberal education to unfit one entirely for hard work: I think rather that the whole object of making one's education a pleasant and cultured thing is to enable one to endure hard work later on without becoming fossilized in any way: it ought to be surely the whole object of it to plant seeds in the mind that will flourish and help one, rather than hinder one."

His decision to drop the idea of becoming a doctor did not mean that he became any more enthusiastic about Classics. Far from it:

"It still seems clear to me, however, that unless something is done in Cambridge to alter the Classical Schools, no one will read Classics in future. I for one could not recommend it as useful or

c

interesting to anyone but a first-class man. It means three years of uninspiring work which fits one ultimately for nothing."

His parents advised him to take up teaching, which was a traditional Wilson profession; but Steuart did not like the thought:

"Surely a private schoolmaster is worse than any form of slavery. I have been working for other people ever since I began to do anything at all and surely if nobody is willing to be a servant because they have had the advantages of a liberal education, then education is wrong somewhere."

Steuart sang in King's College Chapel choir as a lay-clerk from 1908 to 1910, but according to the King's Annual Report, "he found this uncongenial and Dr. Mann's musical tastes were too conservative for his liking." This view is corroborated in a letter to me from Harold Hight who was a contemporary at King's. "Daddy Mann was very much of the old type. It was a splendid type and he and others like him (e.g. Varley Roberts of Magdalen, Oxford) did much to keep up the level of music in this country when it had fallen pretty low. But Steuart was essentially forward-looking and even in those early days was singing Vaughan Williams songs and telling us that V.W. was the coming composer. I should never have expected Steuart and Daddy to get on together musically and yet I never heard any criticisms."

Like all the generations of Cambridge musicians who worked with Mann, Steuart had a great affection for him. He wrote from America in 1929:

"I see my old Daddy Mann has died at Cambridge. Fifty-three years in the same job and it was quite absurd to say that he wasn't doing it efficiently at the end. . . . He and I were always at loggerheads and lately, after twenty years, he wanted to make it up and when I went up there last summer we had a great crack and parted huge friends. I never quarrelled with him but he thought he had offended me—anyway I'm glad we buried whatever hatchet there might have been."

Steuart had music lessons with Dr. C. B. Rootham, organist of St. John's College, between September 1908 and June 1911. But, as both the King's Report and Harold Hight agree, the strongest influence on him in his undergraduate days was undoubtedly that of Edward J. Dent, who was then living in Cambridge. Dent, a brilliant scholar and musicologist, with a caustic (at times cruel) wit, was "always helpful and stimulating to young musicians."

Thanks to Dent's diaries and his early letters to his Manchester friend Lawrence Haward, which are preserved in King's Library, there is a pretty full record of the way in which Dent was able to help and stimulate Steuart at Cambridge. Their first meeting was on 10th October 1908 at the home of Charles Sayle, the assistant University Librarian. They struck up a friendship which lasted until Dent's death. The diaries are full of references to Steuart—having tea in his college rooms, playing Schubert duets, introducing him to Berlioz songs and going for walks in the flat Cambridgeshire countryside.

Steuart's first appearance on a Cambridge stage was in Aristophanes' *The Wasps*, for which Vaughan Williams had written the incidental music. *The Wasps* was performed in the original Greek at the New Theatre from 26th November to 1st December 1909 and the programme shows that "J. S. Wilson of King's" was in the Chorus and sang the solo serenade in Act I. On 2nd December, Dent records, there was a small dinner party in honour of the composer, for which Steuart provided "an amusing menu of Greek and musical jokes." "After dinner, several others came in. We were rather crowded. It was a delightfully cheerful party, with no dress, speeches or formality. As V.W. and I came away at 12 we met Hugh Dalton who walked home with me and stayed till about 2."

Steuart's sister Margaret wrote to Ruth Darwin (27th November 1909): "It was nice hearing that Mr. Vaughan Williams had singled out my Steuart as a promising person. That dear person is almost *too* successful in everyday life, but I don't think he is spoiled yet". She expressed the hope that Steuart would often visit The Orchard, the home of Sir Horace and Lady Darwin (Ruth's parents) ... "Your household is just the sort his soul loves." Steuart evidently did take advantage of the open invitation, and Ruth remembers how, a few days before the play opened, V. W., Dent, Clive Carey and Steuart met at The Orchard to correct the scores and the parts. A battle royal developed between V.W. and Charles Wood, the then Music Professor, who had trained the Chorus. Dent noted:

"I hear from Denis (Browne) and Steuart that V.W. has been very badly treated all round by Wood, Durnford* and Edwards* that they would have cut the Nocturne and the final dance for Philocleon, if the Chorus had not put pressure on them to keep it, also that Wood insisted very much on his own Tempi instead of V.W.'s."

However, he reported on 26th November "The play went well on the whole . . . The music is really great and I was quite moved by it."

In later life, Steuart recalled: "I first met Ralph at an early rehearsal of *The Wasps*. He was very much like what he always was, very bulky, with a great shaggy head of hair, wearing a loose tweed suit and smoking a pipe." Ralph was taken with the younger singer. "Much to my surprise," Steuart said, "he suggested I should sing at a lecture he was giving in Cambridge in a lecture room, twice the size of the Guildhall."

Vaughan Williams's song cycle *On Wenlock Edge*, a setting of some poems from A. E. Housman's *Shropshire Lad*, had been given its first performance in November 1909 with Gervase Elwes as the tenor soloist. Steuart was to succeed Elwes as one of the great interpreters of *On Wenlock Edge*, particularly in the tragic and disillusioned song "Is my team ploughing?" He sang it for the first time at the Oxford University Music Club in 1911 and at the Cambridge University Music Club's 500th concert on 7th December 1912. Dent heard this performance and wrote: "V.W. was there. S. sang them very movingly but it was a great nervous strain and I quite thought he would collapse." One is tempted to ask whether possibly Steuart had a hangover? He recalled that on the evening before at a Founders' Feast, he imbibed "freely rather than wisely" for about the first— and only—time in his life.

Vaughan Williams was so impressed with Steuart's promise that he decided to write a composition for him. This was the *Four Hymns* for tenor voice with viola obbligato which he dedicated to 'J.S.W.' Steuart was to have sung the Hymns at the 1914 Worcester Festival, but the Festival was cancelled because of the War.

Steuart and Dent were in complete agreement about the greatness

* Walter Durnford, Fellow of King's and H. J. Edwards of Peterhouse were joint stage managers.

of Vaughan Williams, as they were about Mozart, Purcell and the Elizabethans. But they had a sharp disagreement about the music of Elgar which Dent regarded as vulgar pseudo-Wagnerian stuff— "when Elgar is vulgar outright he is at his best; when he wishes to be noble he makes me uncomfortable," and he would refer to *The Dream of Gerontius* scathingly as "Gerry's nightmare".* Steuart on the other hand was a great devotee of Elgar. He had heard the *Coronation Ode* when, as a small boy in Rochdale, he was taken over as a great treat to a Hallé concert in Manchester and he first heard *The Dream of Gerontius* at the Three Choirs Festival in Worcester. In 1909, at Cambridge, he had sung it in Dr. Mann's mixed "Town and Gown" choir and later said:

"I fell completely in love with it and knew it bar by bar, so far as the chorus went. Armstrong Gibbs (my year at school and at Trinity) also sang and, as a more professional musician, he made me interested in the orchestral details. We lay in a punt all one afternoon after the performance and botanized over it endlessly."

No doubt Steuart ought to have spent the afternoon botanizing over his Thucydides!

Steuart's biggest musical experience at Cambridge and his first major singing triumph, was as Tamino in *The Magic Flute* in December 1911. This was the memorable production of an opera which *The Times* noted was "wholly unfamiliar to the present generation of opera-goers." Its critic praised the enterprise of the Cambridge musicians in staging this "interesting and remarkable revival" and thereby "advancing the cause of classical opera in England." *The Magic Flute* was produced by Clive Carey and conducted by Dr. Cyril Bradley Rootham, organist of St. John's College. Dent and A. F. Scholfield were joint stage managers, the lighting was the responsibility of Francis Toye; the scenery and costumes were designed by Mrs. Sidney Cockerell (wife of the Keeper of the Fitzwilliam Museum and mother of the inventor of the Hovercraft) and an army of Cambridge ladies made the costumes under the eagle eye of Mrs. Rootham. Clive Carey, as well as producing, took the part of

* It was ironic that at Professor Dent's funeral, when none of his musical friends was available for consultation, it was left to his valet to select the music. One of the items chosen was "The Angel's Farewell" from the *Dream.*

Papageno; Victoria Hopper was the Queen of Night; Mrs. Walter
Fletcher, Pamina; and H. G. Hiller, a King's choral scholar, was
Sarastro. Jan Hubrecht, a Dutch student then at Jesus, played the
part of Monostatos and Rupert Brooke took the part of one of his
slaves "to oblige Dent and Clive Carey" and thoroughly enjoyed the
experience.

The first performance 'went without a hitch'. The theatre was full
and the audience enthusiastic. But there was a crisis at the matinée.
"Mrs. Fletcher lost her voice completely and as we had no under-
study we were in a state of despair," Dent wrote. "I had to make an
apology and Miss Marchant (Papagena) sang her part for her in the
wings." When Dent appeared on the stage to make this announcement, a small child was heard to ask in a piping voice "Is that the
serpent, Mummy?" This was the origin of the nickname which Dent
retained all his life.

The evening performance went even better. "There was a huge
cue [sic] and a packed house. Receipts £171 for the matinée and
£210 for the evening. Mrs. F. still voiceless. Steuart sang marvellously. I never thought he could have done it so well," wrote Dent.

The Times said of Steuart: "Mr. J. S. Wilson (Tamino) has a good
tenor voice and its tone in the more impassioned moments such as
in the ceremony of initiations was of full volume." Arthur Bliss
recalls:

"He was a very good actor as well as a good singer and I can still
see him scuttling across the stage when the curtain goes up pur-
sued by this serpent with a face expressing real terror—it started
the whole opera off in the right way."

At Cambridge, Steuart had his first experience of the problems of
a music critic, and his first encounter with the threat of litigation. He
wrote a paragraph in the Cambridge Review (for which he was music
critic) about a piano recital by Harold Bauer, in which he said that
the pianist was badly served by the piano. The makers immediately
threatened the magazine with a writ for libel, and though the matter
was settled out of court with an apology and a contribution to charity
(Steuart said he hoped it was for "decayed piano tuners") it was an
unnerving experience. Steuart, however, told his father: "I am not
in the least anxious or worrying over the affair. X is well-known as a
first-class shark and is after some free advertisement."

Apart from this incident, his university life was singularly smooth and unruffled and it was for him an almost idyllic period. He was completely absorbed in music, revelling in the choral works and anthems which he sang in the Chapel, as well as in the beauty of the Chapel itself, and discovering the newer composers. He had a wide circle of friends, which went beyond King's, and his Cambridge contemporaries included many exciting personalities. Many of those who survived the War later became eminent in the Law, politics, medicine, the Arts and literature. Steuart's closest friends were the musicians Armstrong Gibbs and W. Denis Browne.

King's at that time was an exclusively male society and most of its dons were bachelors. Women hardly entered into the picture at all. The students of Newnham and Girton were kept in nunlike seclusion, chaperoned everywhere and resented by the men's colleges. Steuart to his credit, and thanks to Mona's influence, had progressive, if vague, views about women's emancipation, though he had little use for the militant suffragettes. His sister Margaret quoted her brothers Hugh and Steuart as saying that "the peaceful contented middle-aged married women of England are wiser than these screaming women who would have us *all* put politics first." (This sounds more like Hugh than Steuart!)

Steuart, in common with most Kingsmen of his generation, was too deeply involved in the intellectual friendship and companionship of his contemporaries, to become seriously interested in any individual young woman. He tended to romanticize about women, but he was—though this seems hard to credit—shy of them.

CHAPTER FOUR

APPRENTICESHIP

I T had been a wrench for Steuart to leave Winchester. It was even more of a wrench to leave Cambridge. He had stayed up an extra term to take part in *The Magic Flute* and at one stage he was hoping to remain for a complete year and read for his Mus. Bac. This plan did not come off and he launched out into the musical profession, without obtaining any academic qualifications for it. He wrote in 1929:

> "I do not claim to be an authority on anything, I have passed no examination in music, or in anything else since I took a Bombing Certificate in 1916."

He also had to think about his bread and butter, and in 1912 took on the job of tutoring the young son of the Earl of Lytton, at Crabbet Park, near Crawley in Sussex. He taught English, Latin and Greek, arithmetic and French, indeed every conceivable subject, to the young Anthony (whom he always referred to in his letters as 'the pup'.) It seems to have been a remarkably unexacting job, for Steuart was able to combine coaching with music and devote nearly all his time to furthering his career.

There is no record that he received any fees for tutoring. Possibly it was agreed that he should get his board and lodging and also be free to carry on his music. His father made him a reasonably generous allowance and Steuart was then (as he was throughout his life) extremely punctilious about keeping accounts. He wrote home (12th May 1912):

"Out of £50 I had to pay tailor for new dress suit and other garments £9. Moving furniture from Cambridge £5. 10. Singing lessons £9. Lodgings in London which I could not take £2 in compensation. £12 to Mrs. Patman for my rent for this term. £2 in Vails (tips) here and journey to Kendal and back £2. Total £41.10. I had £5 odd left when I asked Papa for more leaving £3.10. unaccounted for as outgoings in music, sundries, etc. (a new luggage basket at Worcester, razor at P'field and the like . . .) Next quarter there will be no tailor, no moving of furniture, no lodging and cheaper travelling to London. My season ticket saves £2 and I save about 9d. a week by a monthly cloak-room ticket for my bicycle. . . . I am not a fool about money at all; I do not like owing people money and never do let bills run over the quarter—a fact which will increase my credit if ever I want to use it. My extravagances are in books (music of course is necessary) and in travelling—both of which are I submit worth it."

Most of his money was spent on concerts and plays in London. One evening he wrote to his mother, "I went with Mona to the Russian Ballet and saw a very fine new ballet called *L'Oiseau de Feu*." Another time, he went to hear Caruso

"and profited a good deal by it. It is really a magnificent voice, and not one of the kind that make you hate its owner. It's quite genuine and a marvel of technical skill: it encouraged me a great deal to hear him, because he does nothing that I am physically incapable of doing, only he does it a thousand times better than I do it now. You see the obvious inference?"

He was not so enamoured of a concert in the Aeolian Hall, where Neville Lytton and Clive Carey danced a Gavotte and Minuet and where he heard "some ancient music for harpsichord, viol d'amore and viol da gamba—all very pleasant but a trifle long. There is a monotony about the tone of ancient instruments which is soothing for the first half-hour and then becomes boring to me."

It wasn't necessary to be in London to hear good music. Lord Lytton was an enthusiastic amateur and organized many week-end musical house-parties. The d'Aranyi sisters were regular guests. In November 1912, Steuart wrote to his mother:

"The Aranyis came and a viola player and on Sunday a cellist appeared, so we had a great day of quartets and a Bach double concerto for two vlns and piano which I played and got so excited over it. I could hardly sleep after it. Then we danced and ended up with charades and various rigolades till about midnight."

Jelly d'Aranyi, then 18, was talented and beautiful. Steuart had first heard her play the violin at Cambridge in the spring of 1911 and worshipped her from afar. He wrote her passionate but highly respectful letters, very much in the manner of an Elizabethan courtier addressing his lady love.*

"You can hate me, abuse me, trample on me if you like, but you can't stop me thinking about you and very occasionally writing to you. Or on the other hand you can be rather nice to me—if not very nice—and I shall come and feed out of your hand like a tame canary and spend a fortune on stamps to Budapesth. As a matter of fact you won't do either, you'll just say 'Well there's another of them, poor fools.'"

From Crabbet, he penned a letter in French, not altogether grammatical but deeply sincere:

"Chere Mademoiselle Jelly,
"Vous devez penser que 'le jeune homme' qui était presenté à vous par M. Lytton était complètement idiot parcequi'il n'avait au cune chose à dire. Si j'avais eu assez de courage je m'aurais présenté moi-même à vous plus tôt . . . Alors vous voyez c'était une manque de confidence en moi-même et vraiment une signe du terreur que les gens si distingués que vous infligent sur un tel timide comme moi, qui est toujours malaisé dans la compagnie . . . si vous me donnerez un jour il me donnera le plus grand plaisir de la vie de vous montrer que je ne suis pas complètement idiot. Je demande pardon maintenant autant pour mon impudence que pour cette lettre, dans une langue étrangère vraiment terrible. Mais je signerai
Votre J. S. Wilson."

A few months later, he pleaded:

"Do be nice to me because you make me so absurdly happy (unless

* Joseph Macleod refers to these letters in The d'Aranyi Sisters, Allen & Unwin, 1969.

you stab me with a hatpin) that I sing like one possessed and the world jumps round me . . . I shall be up on Friday again—could I come to tea, in great fear and trembling that you will use the hatpin on me? You did not miss very much by not seeing Neville dance. The concert was *very* long and I thought rather dull (don't tell him so) and also I was thinking of other things . . . Do please write and say whether you will be in for tea on Friday and whether you hate me for writing and asking myself and whether you will try the Bach and Schubert or whether the hatpin will be used instead . . . You will certainly think the 'jeune homme de Crabbet' is something strange. Really, tho' he says it himself, he is quite nice (sometimes very nice) and is in fact entirely and absolutely

Yours J. Steuart Wilson."

What Jelly on her side thought of these declarations by the "jeune homme de Crabbet" is not related; but it is strange to find Steuart so naïve and gauche, and admitting to being ill-at-ease in company. He was, after all, in his twenty-third year. It is also sad to find him depressed about his future. He wrote to Jelly (1st December 1912):

> "I sometimes get horribly frightened when I think that after 4, 5 or 6 years more work I may be an utter failure and then what the diable et enfer shall I do with myself—blow my head off, drown myself or what? or become a clerk in an office? Oh it makes me sweat with terror sometimes."

On 22nd December: "Wish me good luck on Dec. 26th. It is my first big concert at Birmingham in the Town Hall. I am not nervous naturally—I only hope I shall get through it alright." This was a performance of *The Messiah*, with the Birmingham Festival Choral Society. Steuart had "a very bad throat before the concert and cold during it," but the occasion seems to have passed off satisfactorily.

He worked off his emotions and his worries by taking long walks on the Sussex downs. "I had a noble walk yesterday," he reported, "I did my 19 miles in 5 hours' walking and 1 hours' rest and felt very contented. Got back here 7.30, bath and shave and a bottle of Trinity Audit Ale for dinner—all of which things comforted me not a little." When possible he slept out.

"Yesterday was literally the first fine day in June. I bathed in the afternoon up in the Forest and practised fairly hard down here and slept out on my new mattress for the first time last night. It was warm, though a little wind got up about midnight and I was woken up by the clammy touch of a frog inspecting my pillow."

In the winter of 1912 he went on a skiing holiday in the Engadine with Clive Carey and Denis Browne, and the following spring went walking in the Lakes, where he stayed with friends at Seatoller House in Borrowdale. One day he got hopelessly lost in a storm.

"I have never been so utterly soaked. I had been really wet to the skin since about 2 o'clock, and also I had been walking without stopping a moment for nearly 8 hours in a raging gale ... I reckon I did 21 miles going there and 27 coming back. The journey there took me about 5½ hours walk and coming back about 9½ hours."

Another remarkable walk took him across the Alps into Italy. "Very few people nowadays make their first entry into Italy on foot as I did," he wrote to his mother. "There have been others since Hannibal I believe but he is my prototype."

As well as walking, 'rigolades' and being love-lorn, Steuart was working extremely hard at singing during his period at Crabbet. From the beginning of 1912 until the middle of 1913, when he left the Lyttons, he had regular lessons in London with J. H. Ley, who had also been Clive Carey's teacher. Early in 1912 he consulted Dr. Peppin of Rugby about his future, and reported home:

"I got a long letter from Peppin this morning. He gives very forcibly the dangers—other than financial—of singing which I know all too well—but I am glad to have rubbed in. But then he writes as a musician who is gradually leaving music and coming back to nature as his mainspring. All that he says is hatefully true about the shallowness—intellectually and emotionally—of most musicians, and particularly singers, and that it is in a way beneath the dignity of a gentleman to live by giving emotional pleasure to others. Of course that is so if it were so—but there are grades and grades of singing and singers and one's state of mind must vary with one's surroundings and with one's occupation at the moment, e.g. to sing good music in Cathedral rather than feeble stuff in a third-rate provincial concert room. If you regard music as a high and noble art—as both he and I do really I believe—one would think that it was worthwhile putting one's best into it—the best for the highest as Watts used to say. There is a necessity I admit of keeping a good deal of intellectual ballast if one is to carry much emotional sail for fear of capsizing altogether. It is a difficult matter."

When he left Crabbet in the summer of 1913 he moved to 10 Edwardes Square in Earl's Court, where he lodged with his sister Mona. One of his first actions was to seek professional advice about his singing. "I am going some day soon to get an outside opinion on my voice and prospects generally from one William Shakespeare (not the defunct playwright of that name, but a well-known Counsel in this line) and will report further to you on the matter." Shakespeare, a well-known tenor:

"reported favourably, saying that my voice was of a good quality, I had good style, and that though it was not large it was larger than his was when he began. As to production he said that—as I well knew—there was much to be learnt. I disliked him personally a good deal and nothing would induce me to have lessons from him at any price. Both he and Ley are really exactly agreeing in their objects, but Shakespeare gradually builds up the voice, while Ley gets all he can to begin with in order to strengthen the muscles and then begins to refine on that. So rare a phenomenon as a singer who does not believe that all time is wasted that is not spent with his last and present master—is practically unknown. I comfort myself with Zur Mühlen's dictum that there are no good or bad teachers, only good and bad pupils."

He also went to consult his friend Ralph Vaughan Williams, who gave him "most sound advice". This was not to take any jobs for a year at least but to go on working steadily. "He was encouraging on the whole, saying that I had clearly turned a corner and must now be criticized on a higher standard," he wrote.

Steuart was glad of the advice, but did not pay over-much attention to it. His programme from the middle of 1913 onwards was an extremely heavy one, even though it was not financially very rewarding. His earnings totalled £49.15.6 that year. He sang at many public schools, at Petersfield, at private parties and, under Mona's influence, for many charitable and radical organizations.

One of these was at a concert for the Anti-sweating League in the Holborn Restaurant. He wrote to his father:

"I did not get any cash out of it, but I made them pay my accompanist very well instead. The Bp of Oxford was there and spoke very nicely to me afterwards—I behaved very pretty and (Mamma will be glad to hear this) wore a stand-up collar and a white waistcoat for the first time in my life. They were both hatefully uncomfortable and I felt very conscious of my inordinate respectability. I managed to call the Bp 'My Lord' but entirely broke down when introduced to Lord Henry Bentinck."

He also sang frequently at the Working Men's College and at Toynbee Hall and other missions. On 1st July 1914, he gave a recital at Number Ten Downing Street for Mrs. Asquith. Rupert Brooke was present and recalls that, in addition, Ruth Draper recited. Steuart was such a success that he was invited back a fortnight later, although he was suffering from a serious attack of tonsilitis.

Steuart's repertoire at this time was not particularly adventurous and was largely geared to the tastes of his audiences. As he himself wrote later, "Before 1914 a singer's concert life was largely ballad concerts and concert parties." There were some Elizabethan songs and folk songs, works by Coleridge Taylor and Somervell, Handel, and Bach, and, as often as he could, he included music by contemporary composers—Vaughan Williams, Rootham, Armstrong Gibbs and Denis Browne. In the summer of 1914, the Cambridge University Music Society, as ever enterprising, performed Berlioz' *Faust* at its May Week concert. The *Cambridge Review* said of Steuart's singing: "Mr. Steuart Wilson, of whom Cambridge may well be proud, was unfortunately suffering from an affection of the throat but took the part of Faust superbly in spite of this. His singing has improved much of late and his expression in the emotional parts was quite beyond praise."

Soon after this concert, Steuart set out with his brother Hugh on a caravanning holiday in the West Country. They had done this every summer since 1908 and Steuart had kept a faithful log of their adventures and their mileage. (1908: 6 days, 100 miles; 1909: 16 days, 102 miles; 1910: 32 days, 182 miles; 1911: 18 days, 83 miles; 1912: 10 days, 197 miles; 1913: 14 days, 89 miles.) They originally trekked with a pony and a cart which Hugh had picked up in the vegetable market at Basle. This was the cart which Rupert Brooke and Dudley Ward borrowed in 1910 for a tour of open-air meetings in Dorset to promote the cause of women's suffrage.

Rupert Brooke christened the horse 'Guy', but Steuart always referred to him as 'Monsieur le Horse', 'Nag' or 'Mosha'. For the 1912 tour, the Wilsons had decided that human power was more reliable than horse power. "Moshas," wrote Steuart, "were *varium et mutabile semper*, whether male or female, but however varied and mutable they were more trouble than they were worth . . . So it was resolved that our dumb friend should be abolished and that we should substitute ourselves as the motive power."

There is no record in the Log of the 1914 trek because other events intervened, but Steuart described in his autobiographical fragment how he became caught up in the First World War on 4th August 1914:

"We had come that day over the Dorset downs and a small gipsy boy said, 'I've 'eard as there is full War.' We came off the Downs into Beer from near Lyme early in the morning and walked on to Ottery St. Mary arriving about 9 o'clock. Sure enough the yeomanry were mobilizing amid great excitement and it was clear that the holiday was over.

"We packed up the cart, cleaned up the cooking utensils and made arrangements with the stables at a pub to leave everything until we sent for it. But at that point a Yeomanry sergeant, with a young officer, came up to question us—camping in 1914 was eccentric and unusual. 'Where had we come from?' We replied, 'Beer' (about 8 miles away). 'Never heard of it,' was the answer. 'What are you doing?'—'Just walking.' The sergeant added 'They've got maps.' By this time a considerable crowd had gathered, the spy game had begun. The young officer said, 'I can't regard your answers as satisfactory' and it looked as if the first job of the squadron would be a summary execution without a Court-martial. But the matter was allowed and no action taken. Almost at once the inn-keeper came along to say that he was sorry but after all he had no room in the stable to put up the little cart.

Visit to another pub, less suspicious character, who took the whole concern into one of his sheds and we left our names and all that and a gold half sovereign as an earnest-money. Train to Exeter, great jam of troops and travellers. Hugh went home to Worcester, I went to London."

CHAPTER FIVE

WORLD WAR ONE

STEUART joined the 6th Battalion, Kings Royal Rifle Corps on
8th August 1914. He cancelled all his music engagements
planned for the autumn, including the Three Choirs Festival,
the Norwich Festival, a performance of *Der Freischütz* with Adrian
Boult at Birkenhead and the Verdi *Requiem* at Oxford under Sir Hugh
Allen. He was appointed second lieutenant in the Special Reserve of
Officers from 15th August. He wrote home, explaining his reasons
for enlisting so promptly:

> 'If this business is really going to be serious (*a*) there will be no
> possibility of work in my own profession, (*b*) a strong and lusty
> man like me cannot stand aside, (*c*) joining Territorials would
> equally prevent me working and would not give me the chance of
> using my one valuable asset, i.e. colloquial French. So there it is,
> I've done it now.'

His battalion was posted to Sheerness, to take charge of the Med-
way defences in case of German invasion, which many believed to be
imminent. "What they fear here is a sudden German raid of des-
troyers, backed up by transports," Steuart wrote. His first job was
acting adjutant to the Major, plus various quartermaster duties.
He had to cope with an influx of about 1,000 recruits for Kitchener's
Army and fix all the details of documents, pay sheets, separation
allowances, billeting and so on. He met every trainload of recruits—
"No train is allowed to leave without my orders"—and was on duty
continuously from 6.30 a.m. to 10.45 p.m. At first he wrote home,
"It's great fun for me and I can only hope that all my very irregular
ways will be passed over. Anyway I have got this thing under way."

D

It was a heavy responsibility for a young man, who had only just joined up, and who had no previous experience of administration or of soldiering, apart from the O.T.C. at Winchester.

By September, we find Steuart complaining that none of the officers had received any pay and getting increasingly impatient to get out to France. He was critical of his immediate superior: "He would have driven me mad in no time—it takes him about a month to make up his mind on the smallest point and the waste of labour, overlapping of sentries, needless patrols and so on, is perfectly ghastly."

Despite his criticisms Steuart was recommended for promotion and gazetted as Captain on 22nd September. "Of course I am highly flattered and so on," he wrote, "but I fear it puts the stopper on any hope of getting out, for it is clear that I am thought more use as an organizer here than as a fighter over there."

This fear was shortlived. On 21st November, he wrote: "I have just got orders to take out a big draft, 250 men and 4 subalterns to the front. I take it therefore that I shall command them as a company out there, which will be a big job. I am splendidly fit. I have, after much cogitation, propounded a will—not that I have much to leave—but I think it ought to be done." To his mother, while waiting to disembark at Le Havre he wrote that he had had a "most awfully kind letter" from the C.O. at Sheerness, "telling me that I had done extraordinarily well and that no man could have done more and that though he was v. sorry I was going, that no one deserved to get 'out' more than I did."

Steuart was not 'out' for long. On Boxing Day, 26th December 1914, he was wounded at Givenchy in the Battle of Ypres-Armentières. A bullet penetrated his chest. The War Office sent a telegram to his father:

"Regret to inform you that Captain J. S. Wilson 2nd K.R.R.C. was wounded on 28 December degree not stated Secretary War Office."

Steuart described his condition in letters and postcards home:

"I am still in bed and am diagnosed as being v. lucky. The liver is jostled and the lung bruised. I shall rest here for at least 10 days . . . The bullet came in low down in my back right side and came out at the 2nd waistcoat button, i.e. plum in the chest . . . A *rapid* cure is impossible because the absorption takes so long. I'm v. well looked after as there are lots of civilian doctors such as Sir Antony Bowlby and Sir William Herringham out here as consultants who see me about every 2 days. They were here this p.m. and tapped me all over and were v. encouraging, said I should live to fight again very soon!"

To his half-sister Mona: "I'm all right here except the bed is a bit short. Peace perfect Peace with loved ones far away! I hear from Clive Carey," he added, "that R.V.W. has joined the R.A.M.C. He will be damned funny at it, but it is very sporting of him."

After about a fortnight at the clearing hospital Steuart was moved to Boulogne and thence to England, to the Royal Victoria Hospital at Netley, near Southampton. At Netley, because it was thought that he was not going to live, he was placed in a small north-facing room by himself. Netley, Steuart used to say, "had been meant for Madras, but the War Office of the day had got the plans mixed up and when it was finished near Southampton, it was found to be north-facing and totally sunless." Fortunately, there was a young house surgeon who was interested in lung cases and his care and attention almost certainly saved Steuart's life.

His recovery was slow. On 5th February 1915, he wrote:

"I don't see any signs of progress in myself and I don't think there will be any till I can get this lung cleared . . . I pass the day as usual, reading books and some music scores which Sweeting from Winchester sent me which are a great consolation, writing letters, going out in the morning and then, like the shepherd, whiles I sits and thinks and whiles I just sits."

His reading matter included Zola, *War and Peace*, Gibbon's *Decline and Fall* and the manuscript of Dent's new book on Opera.

Arnold Wilson, who was then out in Basrah, wrote a worried letter home: "I am sorry to see from a letter from Grace that Steuart is so dilapidated. I fear his singing days must be over?" This fear was shared by Steuart himself and by all his friends and admirers in the musical world.

In the last letter I have found from Netley, Steuart reports, on 7th April 1915: "An X ray showed a considerable increase of movement in the diaphragm on the right side, which cheered me up a lot. If I can get back my old strength in that region, I don't care whether I get back the full use of the lung or not."

He left hospital on 3rd May and a week later had his first singing lesson after being wounded. "Found voice improved considerably since August and no ill effects," he wrote in his Ledger. He continued the singing lessons for a couple of months, until an Army Medical Board passed him fit for service again. Steuart described his interview:

"The Board consisted of an old R.A.M.C. doctor as President and a young civilian doctor, I think. After examination, the President: 'Is there anything you wish to tell the Board?'—'Yes, Sir,' says I, 'I find that I can't consume as much alcohol as I used to'.

"As quick as a needle he was on to it: 'Is that on account of the price?' I was just as quick. 'No, Sir, I mean what other people stand you.' The young civilian said, 'I don't think we ought to put that sort of thing in the report.' 'Why not?' says the old Colonel, 'it's a very real disability.' And he slowly began to write: 'Cannot consume . . . etc.' I wonder if my file really did contain those magic words!"

As if their anxiety about Steuart were not enough tribulation, Canon and Mrs. Wilson suffered a catastrophic blow that same year when their second son, Hugh was killed in action on 14th September, at Hébuterne, Pas de Calais, shortly before his thirtieth birthday.

Meantime Steuart was back in Sheerness, performing much the same kind of duties as in the previous year. But the fear of imminent invasion seems to have receded; at any rate we find an extraordinarily non-military request in a letter home (26th October):

"Where can one best buy *bulbs* in large mixed quantities? We want at least 1,000 mixed, possibly 2,000 for spaces in front of and between our huts, an idea of mine blessed by the CO (it is not all my ideas that are.)"

A few months later, he reported:

"My bulbs are great and have materially softened the hard hearts of all who look at them. They are very late in appearing but I have had no misfires among those that are up."

During the autumn and winter of 1915–16 he managed to leave

Sheerness for long enough to sing at Winchester and Rugby and found to his satisfaction that his voice was "settling down well". After three lessons with his old teacher, J. H. Ley, he reported: "Voice in excellent condition, considerable improvement in mezza voce." But he was restless and looking forward to "getting out of this miserable place . . . I feel on the whole pleased with life, but it is very boring here and I feel acutely conscious of getting stale and losing interest in the whole thing". He expressed his dissatisfaction in a letter to his brother Arnold:

"Money is being wasted on incompetent officials from top to bottom and there is, to an impartial observer, no sort of system of administration. Not being a professional soldier I find it difficult to sit down under it and when I raise my voice against it I am (quite rightly) told that I am damned insubordinate."

He had applied for a transfer but had had no reply. "It makes me bloody wild as eight months of my job here would exhaust Job and his comforters."

The transfer duly came through and on 13th July 1916 Steuart rejoined his regiment in France.

His letters home reflect his acute anxiety about his mother who was in extremely poor health, having developed a cancer. "I do hope you are not having to endure a lot of pain," he wrote on 29th July, "I only wish it was my turn again, instead of yours."

It was to be his turn again, sooner than he expected. On 20th August 1916 he received his second and even more serious wound, at Delville Wood, during the battle of the Somme. Major Guy M. Atkinson, who was in command of the battalion, described the circumstances in a letter to Canon Wilson (6th September):

"On the night of the 19th and 20th the 2nd Batt. was ordered up into the front line, with special instructions to push forward and occupy ground considerably in advance of the line we were then holding. This would at anytime have been a difficult operation, but it was made doubly so by the fact that High Wood, which touched our right flank, was held by the Enemy who seemed disinclined to withdraw.

"As I considered your son a very capable officer, I ordered his Company to lead an advance and occupy the forward position.

This was carried out most successfully, in spite of an extremely dark night and unknown ground and by day-light our line had pushed 200 or 300 yards forward, had connected up with the unit on the left and had made dispositions for safeguarding our right flank. In fact your son had carried out in a most capable manner the instructions I had had from the Brigade Commander. At about 7.30 a.m. the Germans commenced an energetic counter-attack and until the time your son was wounded at about 10 a.m. he very gallantly held on to the advanced line and ... the Battalion was entirely indebted to him that we were able to repel their first attacks. As a matter of fact I was hit too about midday and went down to the Clearing Station in the same ambulance as your son. I am afraid at the time he looked terribly ill, but I was very glad to hear from Col. Brownlow that he has been successfully operated on and is in good hands. I most sincerely hope that he will pull through and that you will have him at home before very long."

Sir William Herringham, the consultant, wrote to Mona Wilson:

"As regards the actual wound, he was hit by a piece of shell which entered at the right side of the back passed through the right lobe of the liver, smashed the right kidney and came out through the front wall of the abdomen ... The kidney was removed as it was too much destroyed to leave.

"He seems to have done very well for so severe a wound, and Surgeon Capt. Lockwood has no misgivings about his future recovery."

Despite the doctor's optimism, many people had already written off Steuart's chances of survival. The story is told that when the stretcher party first picked him up, one of the bearers said, "He's a gonner." Steuart sat bolt upright and said, "I bloody well ain't."

As they were taking him away, a shell burst and one bearer was killed and two others wounded. Steuart "fell with a considerable bang on the ground and broke a couple of ribs." He was given an injection of morphia, which immediately brought out an irritating rash all over his body. From the field hospital, he wrote: "I could see our quarter-master Robinson riding over on his white horse and I believe that I could also see that he was carrying the named cross to

put on my grave. He and I had often discussed how we should spend
the next War. We had decided on becoming R.T.O.s. He was from
Bristol and wanted Clifton Down station, and I had decided to be
level-crossing keeper at Kingsferndene, just outside Petersfield."

The events of the next 10 months are recorded laconically, in the
Ledger:

"Op. Aug. 16.1916. To No. 2 Red X Rouen Sep 3 To Lady Ridley
10 Carlton House Terrace Oct. 5. Dis Hosp. Nov 6 Readmitted
Jan 1 1917 second op. Dis Jan 21 Bad septic throat. To Rees
several times; influenza. Did not attempt to sing for two months,
rather husky through lack of practice, but seemed all right after a
little practice. Two or three lessons during May. Voice all right no
signs of weakening.
June 28 1917 Married."

There is hardly any reference in his letters home to his engagement to Ann Bowles, who was the daughter of a naval officer, then
stationed at Sheerness, where they first met. In one letter from Lady
Ridley's hospital, he wrote (9th January 1917): "Ann comes daily to
comfort her 'lonely soldier' which is very delightful for me. I have to
endure a good many jests from the young and foolish V.A.D.s who
nurse here, but I can generally rout them with some remark to
which they cannot easily find a rejoinder."

Steuart sought her father's permission in May, and they were
married on 28th June, at St. Margaret's, Westminster. Canon
Wilson officiated, and the witnesses were Ann's father Captain F. A.
Bowles and Steuart's brother-in-law Frank Padwick. Steuart was
then 27 and Ann was 19.

By then, Steuart had been found fit 'for Home Service only' by a
Medical Board and had joined the Intelligence division of the War
Office. It might have been thought that after his continuous service
in the Army and his severe wounds, he had done his bit. But no, the
Army still wanted him and at that stage of the War it was so desperately short of manpower that even the half able-bodied had to be
retained. It might also have been thought that Steuart might have
received some official recognition for his valour. He did, but from
the Italian, not the British Government. In May 1917, the King of
Italy conferred upon him the Order of the Crown of Italy (Cavalier).

Steuart joined M.I.3 branch of the War Office, and was attached

to section 'C', which was concerned with Germany. His immediate
superior in this section was Major E. E. Wynne, and the branch was
headed by Colonel E. W. Cox. General MacDonagh was head of
Military Intelligence. His colleagues were an assorted lot.

"British Museum, Egyptian antiquities, bookseller, fur merchant,
engineering student from Swiss Cottage, recently joined young
member of the Foreign Office staff. The B.M. man was responsible for the German order of battle, the engineering student for
identifications, the bookseller and the fur mechant dealt with
press and letters; every point was noted and indexed and change
of German order of battle noted to other fronts, a long absence
of any identifications being specially noted as a possible evidence
of movement to another theatre, not a routine period of rest.
In addition to this our military attaché in Holland kept close
watch on train movements through Belgium towards the Western
Front which could provide very early notice of reinforcements on
a large scale involving heavy rail traffic. (This early notice was
unheeded by G.H.Q. at a crucial moment—Cambrai, November
1917)."

He did not like the Whitehall atmosphere. To his father (26th April
1917):

"I find it *very* uncongenial though it is perhaps interesting to some.
I find soldiers so very 'donnish' in their attitude of mind. They
love dotting i's and crossing t's, and seem seldom to think of the
matter, but are very punctilious as to the manner. In fact they are
as remote from men of action as a great many dons are from men
of learning!"

He records that he spent his days as an assistant "learning the
general arrangements and doing whatever odd jobs turned up—and
they *were* odd!"

One of the oddest jobs involved an expedition to the Map room of
the British Museum.

"The D.M.I. wanted, or thought he might possibly need in the
future, some geographical information about the possible re-
institution of a Polish Republic at the end of the War. The issue
needed was how the country could be partitioned without separat-

ing its agricultural interests, e.g. cattle must not be separated by frontiers from their pastures, nor pigs from their clover. I had an introduction to the keeper of the Map room and general directions as to the information needed. I was welcomed with the news that I could not at present see the best detailed maps and handbooks because they were being used by 'a gentleman from the Admiralty', and there he was at the desk in the Map room at the B.M. on precisely the same task, just in case the Director of Naval Intelligence might be asked for his views on Poland's future!"

Until he joined Intelligence, Steuart had been fighting the War very much as a cog in the military machine, without much knowledge of what was going on anywhere on the Front outside his own particular section, whether it was Sheerness or France. At no point in his letters do we find any reference to the wider issues of the War, or to the bitter wrangles between Lloyd George and the generals which usually occupy so much space in war memoirs. Nor do we find any trace of bitterness or anger at the folly and futility of it all, and at the unnecessary slaughter that killed off Hugh Wilson, Rupert Brooke, Denis Browne and so many of his Cambridge friends and contemporaries.

In M.I.3, however, he began to take a more active interest in the wider issues and in the details of the campaigns. He experienced the frustration of the Intelligence men when their careful reports were ignored by the brass-hats at G.H.Q.

"It was apparent to me very soon, even as a most junior and inexperienced officer that the real battle was between G.H.Q. and London," he wrote. "The word 'fact' was itself a word which had different meanings in G.H.Q. and the War Office." Brigadier-General John Charteris was then Field-Marshal Haig's right hand man at G.H.Q.; "his influence was paramount" and he refused to accept the deductions made by Intelligence.

Steuart wrote: "It became a commonplace in the section of M.I.3. where I was working that our enemy was the incurable optimism, based on incorrect, even falsified information." Charteris, however, had the ear of the C. in C. and "Haig combined his personal loyalty to his subordinates with his apparent distrust of Military Intelligence, based on intellectual inferences and deductions. The results were so appallingly disastrous that only an intervention from the Secretary of State for War could end the quarrel that had developed.'

Towards Christmas 1917, Steuart decided he had had enough of the in-fighting at the War Office. "Living in London, a hard office job, a relentless grind, all combined to reduce my vitality to a very low point and I felt I must get out." But to what? He could not face another winter at Sheerness, he was not fit enough for foreign service and he was not unfit enough to be invalided out—"nor could I have easily tolerated that". He thought of working in a Prisoner of War camp, but before this scheme had matured, Colonel Cox asked him to accompany him to France as his personal assistant at G.H.Q. at Montreuil-sur-Mer. Although he was a 'Home Service only' man, nobody questioned the propriety of his returning to France. Steuart accepted eagerly. He had a great admiration for Cox's intellect, vigour and energy—the only trouble was that Cox did not really require an assistant. So again, Steuart found himself doing odd tasks —and one of these was even odder than the foray into the British Museum:

> "Cox decided that the G.H.Q. Intelligence summary (which in past times had been known to Battalion Intelligence Officers as 'Bollocky Bill's Comic Cuts') should carry a brief resumé of the Russian Revolution and the past history of Russian politics. My 'library' for such an essay was absolutely nil, my personal past interest in it extremely limited and in early 1918 even words like 'Bolshevist' were new and in restricted circulation. I had to remember that the officers for whom I was writing probably knew less, and there lay my only comfort! I don't remember how it was done. I only remember that I got from somewhere a long spiel about the Cossacks and their importance in Russian history. Where the rest of it came from, other than my own fictional brain, I cannot imagine."

Another remarkable achievement was his lecture on the general state of the War all over the world, delivered to the 47th division as a stand-in for Cox, who had been taken ill.

"I ordered the staff car, put the maps inside and drove off myself to the point. There I was met by the G.S.O. 1. I had not had time to telephone anybody to say that Cox was not coming and had to produce myself as a captain intelligence corps in place of a full-blooded B.G.G.S.

"The G.S.O. 1 was suitably unimpressed and made the sort of face 'I suppose you will have to go through with it now you are here.' The place of assembly was an aeroplane hangar of considerable size and as I thought pretty poor accoustically. However, I got the maps up, put the lecture notes on a music stand I had brought with me, put the stand behind me and delivered my lecture without looking at it, just with reference to the maps. Just before I began I gathered that the G.O.C. was Gorringe, generally known as 'the Blood Orange' from his complexion and habit, and realized that he had been the General who had got into some difficulties in the early part of the Mesopotamian campaign, and it would be unwise to use the prologue of that campaign that I had written. So we started by saying, 'after the successful campaign of Gen. Gorringe' and then went on from there hoping that that would be a good overture. I was subsequently introduced to the General who thought it absolutely wonderful that I could give somebody's lecture by heart. I pretended that of course I had been able to read Gen. Cox's notes in the car coming down. I did not give away the show, but I told the General who was very complimentary."

Steuart came back 'fairly well satisfied' with himself and he was asked to repeat the lecture many times—the most alarming being at Fifth Army H.Q. under Field-Marshal Birdwood, where none of his audience was under the rank of full Colonel. He prepared his lecture with the help of wall maps illustrating Europe and Germany and was intrigued to find a stream of high-ranking brass-hats coming in to look at them and saying: "So that's where Bavaria is," or something like that.

Steuart left France at the end of July for a well-earned leave, returning to Steep to attend his first daughter's christening by Canon Wilson. On his way to the church, he was intercepted by a telegraph boy bearing the news that Cox had been drowned while bathing near Montreuil. He at once interrupted his leave, went back to France to collect Cox's personal belongings and returned to the War Office to report to General MacDonagh. MacDonagh invited him to become his personal aide, but the next day there was a reshuffle at the War Office and MacDonagh was made Adjutant-General. Steuart heard no more from him. So he reported back to the War Office, where they discovered that he ought not to have gone out to France at all, because he was still a 'Home Service only' man. Even then, the Army did not let him go. He was posted on 2nd September to a course for senior officers at Aldershot. This was handy because he could get home by bicycle for week-ends.

Ten weeks later, on 11th November 1918, Armistice was declared, and the war was over. Steuart was demobilized on 22nd January 1919:

"Now, January 22 1919, I had paraded for the last time at the Crystal Palace, marched through Halls, corridors and transepts and came out once more a civilian. All this was quick work. The Senior Officers School finished its course on December 14. I had kept my War Office pass, so I went in by the usual staff side door— the front door was only for Generals!—went back to see my old friends in M.I.3, left my Sam Browne hanging up on the door and visited the 'Demob Section' and inquired, as for a friend, 'What is the quickest way to get demobbed?' The answer came pat: 'One man business, fit for Home Service only, married with at least one child. I thanked him properly and reflected 'That's ME' I went back—I'm sorry, this officer proceeded—to Steep, filled in the proper forms and in a month it was all over."

Captain J. S. Wilson had served his King and Country for four and a half years, the full span of the war. He had, in the process, acquired self-confidence and authority and the ability to handle and lead men; but he had lost a kidney, the best part of one lung and suffered permanent damage to his health. He had also lost his favourite brother, his best friend and many of his school and university contemporaries.

PART TWO
SINGER

CHAPTER SIX

THE ENGLISH SINGERS

STEUART WILSON had at various times thought about a permanent Army career, about taking up medicine and about joining the Indian civil service. He had even toyed with the idea of becoming a farmer—no doubt remembering his great-great-grandfather Jonathan of Westward. He wrote:

"During my time at G.H.Q. I had attended lectures by the Army education instructors and I decided that I would consider farming—no previous experience necessary I was assured. So with note-book and pencil, I sat at a desk before an enthusiastic young Scot and bought a standard work on agriculture which I read in bed, also a gardening class—practical work this—on spare ground in the old citadel of Montreuil-sur-Mer, a beautifully preserved Vauban fort, taught by whatever was then the equivalent of a W.A.H.C. (War agriculture horticulture committee). That remained a dream-venture. I never had the courage to put my hand to the plough."

The one thing he was determined he would not do was to follow in the footsteps of his father and become a schoolmaster or a clergyman.

But there can be no doubt that, all the time, he was set on taking up music and that nothing could have deflected him from this course. He himself put it laconically, some years later, in a publicity blurb for his Decca records: "At the end of the War I could not think of any other occupation except music and therefore I am still a musician."

Music had entered his soul and, ever since his Cambridge days, nothing else had really mattered to him. His *credo* was movingly expressed in a letter to a friend:

"What a curious pursuit Art is—it does swallow up everything else. I wouldn't advise anybody to take art seriously unless he was prepared to give up everything to it. It is like Religion—it is my Religion I think—for demanding everything you've got and giving you everything you want. The lovely thing about music is that you must share it with others and that it isn't music at all until you do. I'm frightfully ambitious and I want to make everybody see and feel music as I feel it—so that it may make them in their turn think that there is nothing else in the world so important."

The first thing was to establish that his voice had not been irretrievably damaged as a result of his lung wound. He consulted various teachers and medical specialists, who gave him a clean bill of health. People who had heard him sing both before and after the war, however, agreed that his voice did not have quite the same carrying-power after the wound. Sir Arthur Bliss told me in 1968 that the voice had not changed very much: "It seemed really as good as ever, perhaps a little strained in *Gerontius* —but in Lieder it was excellent and he didn't have to force it. It had a timbre unlike many tenor voices which was essentially masculine." He added, that when Steuart got tired he was sometimes inclined to sing a little flat, as he had never done before the war.

The second thing was to re-establish himself in the musical world. "I had to get back to practise and to pick up what threads had got lost in August 1914, so I wrote round and announced that I was still alive." One of the contacts which was to prove most valuable to him and provide him with a launching-pad was his friend Cuthbert Kelly. Kelly had been organizing a series of wartime Saturday afternoon concerts in St. Martin-in-the-Fields and in March 1917 was looking for a singer to replace the tenor, Harold Wilde, who had been called up.

Steuart, who was at that time working in the War Office and was able to get away on Saturday afternoons, stepped in and continued with the quartet until he was posted back to France. As soon as he was demobilized he re-joined them. This was the origin of The English Singers.*

Cuthbert Kelly was a remarkable man and musician. He was a civil servant who used to spend all his spare time doing social work in Bethnal Green; he started the Oxford House Choral Society which, in 1912, gave a Queen's Hall performance of the *Dream of Gerontius*, with himself as conductor and Gervase Elwes as soloist. The Kelly wartime concerts in St. Martin's kept the flame of music alive in wartime London, in the same way that twenty years later Dame Myra Hess thrilled a different generation of war workers with her National Gallery concerts.

The concerts began again in December 1919. The original four were: Flora Mann, soprano; Lillian Berger, contralto; Steuart Wilson, tenor; and Cuthbert Kelly, bass. A programme at St. Martin's on 13th December, shows that the quartet sang the Palestrina *Missa Brevis*, and motets by Morley and John Redford, a Parry anthem "There rolls the deep", and a concluding Bach chorale "God is our Hope and Strength." A string quartet played Schubert's A minor, not straight through, but with a movement alternating with a group of songs. A note on this programme states: "It is hoped that many people besides the members of this congregation may find in these performances of music recreation of a kind that is needed in these restless days."

It was on Steuart's suggestion that the quartet was enlarged to a sextet (S.S.A.T.Bar.B.) so that it could increase its repertoire and include English madrigals in the programme. It was on his suggestion, too, that Clive Carey was invited to join the group. The second soprano was Winifred Whelen; Kelly acted as musical leader and Steuart, 'as the junior in age', was given the job of organizing and managing them, and finding the necessary music.

He had originally been introduced to madrigals in his Cambridge days by Edward J. Dent. With a small group of like-minded musicians, he had sung madrigals, glees, part-songs and catches at afternoon parties given by 'the eccentric and amiable' E. J. Nixon, his elderly classical tutor. Steuart also had a long-standing acquaintance with Dr. Edmund Fellowes, who was then a Minor Canon of St. George's Chapel, Windsor.

* Steuart told the story of The English Singers in an article in *Recorded Sound* (October 1965) and most of what follows has been taken from his account there.

E

Fellowes can justifiably be regarded as the man who revived the English madrigal and his editions are still the standard ones. In his memoirs, he has told how Steuart came to consult him about a concert at which the sextet proposed to sing part-songs. Dr. Fellowes gladly placed all his manuscripts at the Singers' disposal, as well as the volumes that had been published. Steuart copied them out for the group.

The English Singers also owed a lot to Edward J. Dent, who advised them on programmes in general and on "new and interesting Italian material, especially the *Intermedi* of the puppet plays *Commedia del Arte* of the sixteenth and seventeenth centuries".

"The plan was thus roughly drawn, but none of us had the least idea what the building would ultimately become," Steuart wrote. One immediate problem was the difficulty of rehearsals. Cuthbert Kelly was free only in the evenings, Clive Carey had many professional engagements, and Steuart was commuting from Petersfield. "In these difficult and unpropitious circumstances I booked the Aeolian Hall for February 28th 1920."

The Sextet gave its first concert to a crowded and enthusiastic audience. They had no name and were simply billed as individual singers, giving a concert of "canzonets, madrigals and other English music by Morley, Weelkes, Wilbye, Bateson, Gibbons and Purcell". Fellowes reported: "It was the first occasion upon which in modern times madrigals were properly interpreted on a concert platform, and it was the first appearance in public of The English Singers, though it was not till later in the year that they took that title. The audience was entranced. Here was something quite new to an English audience and they rose to it." Many of the songs had not been heard for over 300 years.

Steuart, who conceived the title, has told the story of how the English Singers got their name:

"In March, we received an invitation from Mrs. Hammersley, a well-known and generous patron of music, to sing at her house where M. Fleury, the famous French flautist, was to play a work of Vaughan Williams. Fleury was most enthusiastic, but asked, had we a name—how could he get in touch or engage or recommend us? Innocently enough, it had not occurred to any of us that it would be essential. The decision had to be taken promptly. A week later the original quartet were booked for a special concert at the National Gallery to mark the opening of an Italian Room to celebrate the National Art Collections Fund. I suggested the title 'The English Singers'—it was agreed, without enthusiasm, but merely as a necessity. And so we were born."

Two further concerts were arranged at the Aeolian Hall that autumn, and during 1920 the Group had altogether eighteen engagements. They received enthusiastic notices. Dr. Percy Buck, whose lectures on madrigals at the Royal Institution were illustrated by the Sextet, wrote: "The madrigal singing of the English Singers is not only the best I have ever heard—it is truly better than any I ever expected to hear in my life." And Dr. Fellowes himself wrote: "It may be doubted whether madrigals have been sung with such finish and such telling effect as that produced by the English Singers since the period in which the madrigal composers lived."

A legend which originated with Steuart and which in after years he took great delight in exploding, was that the Group's habit of singing seated round a table derived from the practice of Elizabethan days. This, in his story, is what happened:

"We had decided not to attempt to sing without music. In the first place it was not yet the fashion on the concert platform, except for song recitals with piano; never in oratorio and often not in orchestral concerts. What should we do with our music if we had to hold it? Should we use music stands or should we sit like a string sextet? We decided to have music stands to hold the music, but to stand behind them in a semi-circle. Soon this became increasingly cumbersome and the climax was reached when I attempted to go by bus to a concert in Red Lion Square carrying a bag of music and six music stands which soon became involved with every other passenger, causing much loss of 'face' to me and to several others loss of hats and paper bags. I decided it would be easier to sit, as in fact we rehearsed, round a table and without waiting for chapter and verse, I announced that it was the Elizabethan custom and from henceforward it was so. Our lives were easier, and Morley's 'Plain and Easy' justified us."

Red Lion Square or not, the practice became a part of the English Singers tradition—the modern word would perhaps be 'gimmick'—and has been followed ever since by madrigal groups, no doubt in the full confidence that they are pursuing the best Elizabethan custom. Steuart was amused at an advertisement which appeared during the Singers' very successful tour of America in 1930: "The English Singers give their programs seated around a table as in the Elizabethan days when the mistress of the house, according to custom was wont to serve out the part-books and call upon her guests to join with the family in singing madrigals."

Fame and acclaim met the English Singers everywhere, but financial rewards were slow in following. It was not until 1921, when they had a total of thirty engagements, that they began to break even. They were in demand everywhere and made their first recording with H.M.V. ("six noses crowded into a single horn") in December. Their repertoire was extended, and we find them performing not only madrigals and motets, but in the Beethoven *Mass* at Oxford, the Bach *Mass in B Minor* at Portsmouth, Handel's *Messiah* at Petersfield and *Acis and Galatea* at the Excelsior Kinema in Bethnal Green. They also continued the St. Martin's concerts, but their programme was extended far beyond the hymns and carols of wartime days.

In January 1922, the Singers were invited to visit Prague and Vienna, where Adrian Boult was to conduct Elgar's Second Symphony and a new work of Arthur Bliss, *Mêlée Fantasque*, with the Prague and Vienna symphony orchestras. They all travelled out together, Steuart making himself responsible for the arrangements. "On one occasion," Sir Arthur Bliss, who was one of the party, told me, "Steuart's organization was put to the test. We were going to Vienna and we had to change at, I think, Frankfurt and we all got into one train which was going to Vienna. There was another train standing at a parallel platform and suddenly Steuart exclaimed 'By Jove, the music—it must be in the other train'. He darted across and into the train which began to move off. We thought 'Where on earth is he going? and what shall we do? We've lost our tenor and we've lost our music.' But he found his way back. I shall never forget the sight of him sprinting across the platform." Re-united with their tenor-manager, and their music, the English Singers continued on what was to prove a triumphal tour, so triumphal that it was extended to more towns in Czechoslovakia and Austria, and later to Berlin.

Sir Arthur recalls the wild, almost delirious scenes of enthusiasm—the sort of reception that is now accorded to pop-singers. At the end of a very long concert in Prague, the audience rushed the platform and would not disperse until they had been given an encore. The Singers came back and sang "On the plains", this time without their music and standing up. In one city, crowds came to the station to see the party off and the Singers sang a final number as the train steamed away.

Their repertoire on this Czech tour included madrigals by Weelkes, Gibbons, Morley, Byrd, Wilbye, and Tomkins, Purcell duets ("Let us wander" and "Sound the Trumpet"), a group of Italian street songs and English folksongs arranged by Vaughan Williams ("The turtle dove," "A farmer's son," "The dark-eyed sailor" and "Springtime of the year"). The folksongs in particular, Steuart wrote, completely bowled the audience over and "they had to be repeated until we ourselves became exhausted." He reported:

"The concerts created great enthusiasm. It was a lucky moment. Those who were already familiar with music in general were astonished at the complexity of the rhythms and the occasional harmonic audacity; those who came primarily out of curiosity were astounded that a vocal ensemble should have a delicacy equal to chamber music."

In Prague, incidentally, he found it a great advantage to bear the name of *Wilson*, which the Czechs associated with the American President and the creation of their nation.

Steuart, according to Bliss, was very much the dominant figure in the Group, although all had strong and attractive personalities, which was one of the reasons for their instantaneous success. Another was the fact that they worked in perfect harmony, not only as musicians but as people. Steuart's zest and gaiety contributed a great deal to this harmony.

It was a particularly bold venture to take English Elizabethan music into Germany, which was still suffering from the aftermath of war and inflation, and where anti-Allied feeling was running high. Moreover, the Germans held the general view that the English were complete Philistines in the art of music. The English Singers soon dispelled this idea. Professor Dent, who accompanied the Group on their travels, wrote in the *Illustrated London News* (6th May 1922) that the success in Prague was "gratifying but not astonishing" as it was natural that the Bohemians should be predisposed in favour of

English folk music. But Berlin was a different proposition. Dent wrote:

"The English Singers started against considerable difficulties. It seems perfectly obvious to any Englishman that the German is a figure of fun; less obvious perhaps that the Englishman is equally a figure of fun to the German mind. Many people were tempted to laughter when six typically English figures walked on to the platform and seated themselves comfortably and informally at a table.

There was a complete absence of the usual professional platform manners. The moment they began to sing, the audience was hushed. What conquered the German audience at once was the faultless technique of their singing. There was no incompetent amateurism about that. The faultlessness of the technique not only won the audience's respect; it made it perfectly easy for them to enter into the spirit of music that was quite unfamiliar to them. Even to the learned there was much in those English madrigals that was strange and new. But they gradually accustomed themselves to the idiom, and as they grew to understand the old English music better and better, they began to see that the informality of its presentation gave it an added charm. . . .

This English triumph in Germany is of importance, not so much because the English Singers have convinced the Germans that there is a really English art of music, as because of the particular kind of music which has brought about this conversion. The fine accomplishment of the English Singers is the result of learning and of research. The German critics who said it was traditional in England were not quite right. The English Singers' style is a protest against bad traditions. That sensitive and supple interpretation by which they bring out the hidden loveliness of our old English composers has not been handed down from singer to singer. It has been deliberately reconstructed by the scientific erudition of Dr. E. H. Fellowes. He and the English Singers have shown Germany, if they have not yet convinced England, that such beauty as this comes not from inspiration, but from scholarship."

Professor Dent's views have been quoted extensively, because he was not only an acknowledged authority on English music of the sixteenth and seventeenth centuries, but an enthusiastic, if critical, student of Germany. He was not given to hyperbole and his praise for the English Singers is all the more telling. It was on this Berlin trip, incidentally, that Dent was told by a German professor that one of his English translations was inaccurate. Dent's caustic remark: "You have the advantage of me, Herr Professor. You *learned* English —I only picked it up."

The Singers re-visited Berlin in the spring of 1922 and again in 1923. Steuart noted: "The Berlin concerts coincided with the political crisis when the French occupied the Ruhr. In the choice of an opening number for our first programme I risked a good deal by proposing the Byrd Psalm, 'Turn our captivity, O Lord'. It might have created a mild disturbance, but the phrase 'They that sow in tears shall reap in joy' was heard in a deep abstracted silence that was more emotional than any applause." On all their visits they had ecstatic reviews in the German papers.

As well as their foreign visits, the Singers undertook extensive programmes in England and in 1923 had a tally of thirty-two engagements in the provinces and in London. A major occasion was Byrd's tercentenary concert in the Aeolian Hall on 4th July.

In October they toured Holland, where they had a reception which almost outdid that given them by the Czechs. This was the last European tour in which Steuart took part. Both he and Clive Carey had decided to go to France to study with Jean de Reszke, a decision which meant they could no longer work full time with the group.

Steuart's place was eventually taken by Norman Notley and that of Clive Carey by Norman Stone. Steuart recommended Nellie Carson, whom he had 'discovered' at a Lancashire competition festival, as second soprano. Although no longer a member of the group, he continued to take a keen interest in its progress and in 1930, when in America, his stay in New York coincided with that of the English Singers. He wrote to Flora Mann and Lillian Berger:

"When I heard *O Magnum* again, my mind went back a good many years to that cold St. Martin's gallery when we first met in the War in 1917 at Christmas and out of that meeting came so much for all of us. Well you deserve your fortune. I'm listening to you tonight with a critical ear on 'balance' . . . I like being critical of you all, because there can be no doubt that I am right on the main point, namely that I'm still *moved* by the thing."

In 1966, looking back over his long career, Steuart wrote: "Getting the English Singers under way was quite a task and that might be my only claim to distinction in the musical world." This was a typical piece of self-depreciation. Many would regard Steuart Wilson's singing of the Evangelist, his Samson or his Gerontius, his Schubert translations, his teaching and his ability to lead and inspire, as equally 'claims to distinction'. Nevertheless, it is true to say that the launching of the English Singers nearly fifty years ago marked the beginning of the upsurge of interest in Elizabethan music and brought to a wide music-loving public the pleasure and enjoyment in madrigals which had hitherto been limited to somewhat esoteric circles.

CHAPTER SEVEN

ON THE LADDER

THE early 1920s were an exciting period for any aspiring young musician. As Ursula Vaughan Williams wrote in her biography *R.V.W.*: "Musical life was vigorous and absorbing, set against a background of treaties, trade agreements, reparations, alliances, depressions and political crises." There was also the background of the 'Bright young things', the Charleston, the flappers with their short skirts and shingled hair, Oxford bags, the game of Beaver, cocktails and cigarettes—all of which incurred the disapproval of the older generation. But this was not Steuart's world. He was far too busy to enter into the hectic 'fun-making' of the period, and he would not in any case have enjoyed it.

In England, the older leaders of musical life, Parry and Stanford, were being succeeded by a new generation, and Arthur Bliss, Arnold Bax and William Walton were making their names. Vaughan Williams and Holst were at the height of their powers.* The Carnegie Trust was helping young composers in various ways and the BBC, established in 1922, provided a platform for young performers. The fears expressed by Sir Edward Elgar and shared by many that "broadcasting is killing all the concert rooms" was to prove unfounded. Far from killing live music, the BBC, from its early Savoy Hill days to the present time, brought music to far wider audiences than could be contained in "all the concert rooms" of the country.

The same thing was happening in Europe. Fauré, Puccini and

* Vaughan Williams's Pastoral Symphony, Mass in G minor, *Shepherds of the Delectable Mountains, Old King Cole, Hugh the Drover, Flos Campi* and *Sancta Civitas* all belong to the first half of the decade. Holst's *The Perfect Fool* and *At the Boar's Head* were composed between 1920 and 1924.

Busoni were still alive, but in their last years. Ravel, however, was still composing and so was Stravinsky, and new names like Kodály, Bartók and Honegger were appearing in 'highbrow' London journals, if not on popular concert platforms.

The star of music may have been in the ascendant, but all the same, there wasn't much money to be made in it. It was far harder for a musician to climb the ladder in those days than it is today, when state patronage of the arts is an accepted feature of everyday life. Steuart was determined to establish himself as a singer in his own right. He told Cuthbert Kelly why he could no longer work full-time with the English Singers:

> "I must frankly look after myself more than I have done in the past . . . I've got to make myself known as an important soloist."

He admitted that he started with certain advantages.

> "The prospects weren't bad. I had got a start among the younger ones. I realize that I owed a lot to my friendship with Ralph Vaughan Williams, to my long acquaintance with Sir Hugh Allen (then Director of the Royal College of Music and behind the throne in all musical policy) and other people who gave me a chance when others might not have got it and would have deserved it more, and justified themselves more abundantly."

It was owing to tragic mischance that Steuart first came to the very front rank as a tenor. The great singer Gervase Elwes was killed in a cruel accident while on tour in the United States, in January 1921. "As his completely undistinguished substitute, a good many chances came my way," Steuart wrote and, in a broadcast talk* shortly before his own death in 1966, he said:

> "I remembered and still remember him and his kindness to me personally as a very young beginner in his own field, and I have always been acutely conscious that his early death meant a chance

---

* In this same broadcast, Steuart told how the accident happened. "He was with his wife in a railway train coming to Boston and stopping as usual at Back Bay, the residential quarter. They got out of the Pullman on to the low platform, almost at rail level and Gervase noticed at once that the Pullman porter had handed out the heavy coat—it was winter time—not his, but belonging to another passenger. He tried, as the train was slowly moving, to throw it on to the steps of the carriage, but the weight of the heavy coat overbalanced him and he was caught by the wheels and killed. So, trying to prevent an inconvenience to a total stranger, this man lost his life and the musical profession lost an unique figure."

for me personally which I was not then, if ever I should become,
worthy to inherit."

Elwes had been the leading interpreter of Elgar's *Dream of Gerontius*
and of the Evangelist in Bach's *Passions*. In both these roles Steuart
was to follow in Elwes' footsteps.

"The struggle was hard," Steuart wrote. "The Ledger shows
these figures: 1919: £150; 1920: £240; 1921: £550; 1922: £640—
not such a bad graph. But it meant hard sledding almost without a
break."

The 'Ledger' is the key to Steuart's professional career. It records
every engagement and the work performed (whether for a fee or for
expenses) with a note on the opposite page of the conductor, the
other soloists and/or accompanists. (See Appendix B.) Originally intended for satisfying the eagle eye of the Income Tax Inspector, it
today serves as a complete history, not only of Steuart Wilson's own
career, but of the development of music in England over twenty-
eight years. The very first entry is of a concert at Winchester in 1909
and the last is of a Vaughan Williams recital in Chelsea on 16th
December 1937.

The Ledger shows what an amazing variety of engagements
Steuart undertook and what a growing range of music he performed.
He was, as might be expected, in great demand by London hostesses
to sing at soirées and receptions. (This was perhaps one of his least
favourite commitments. I have found a letter to his friend Valentine
Oppé—undated— in which he says: "No you won't find me at Lady
X's tonight. I can't stand their incessant 'foreign patronage' and this
Chelsea second-rate foreigner ramp. I'd go anywhere else but I'll
go to Lady X only when they bring forward some native talent to
make a fuss about.") He sang a lot for charitable purposes and,
usually without a fee, for public schools—Rugby, Harrow, Charterhouse, Sherborne (boys and girls) as well as for his beloved Winchester. He performed at numerous local clubs and societies, and had
engagements at both Oxford and Cambridge. He did a certain
amount of private teaching too, as well as his one day a week at the
Royal College of Music. All this in addition to the English Singers—
in 1922, he records, he had at least ninety engagements 'of varying
importance'.

One of his earliest public appearances in London was at the

Aeolian Hall on 19th October 1920 where he sang the Vaughan Williams *Four Hymns*, which had been dedicated to him, conducted by the composer. The first ever performance of the *Hymns* was given in Cardiff that summer, with the London Symphony Orchestra and Julius Harrison conducting. There was nearly a crisis. The L.S.O. had been playing in a mining village up the valley the night before and Steuart remembered: "We all drove in early morning to find the instrument van had not arrived by train, and didn't in fact arrive until half an hour before the concert! . . . I had just a chance for the orchestra to look at the parts, but scarcely even a run-through."

At that time, Steuart's main accompanists were C. Thornton Lofthouse, Anthony Bernard, Claud Biggs and Reginald Paul. He always 'rang the changes' and later, the names of Gerald Moore, Phyllis Arnott, Jean Hamilton and Mollie Hull appear in his Ledger.

For all his devotion to the Elizabethans and to Bach and Handel, Steuart was always ready to experiment and innovate. He was most anxious that the music of the new generation of composers should be heard, and usually managed to include in his recitals songs by the less, as well as by the more famous.

One of his earliest ventures into modern music arose through his friendship from Cambridge days with Arthur Bliss who was up at Pembroke, studying for Mus. Bac. when Steuart was at King's. Bliss often accompanied him in some of his early concerts and used to go down to Petersfield to rehearse. They gave a joint recital of Schubert Lieder at the Wigmore Hall where, Sir Arthur told me, he baulked at the 'Erlkönig,' as beyond his powers as a pianist. In 1920, Steuart sang the Bliss *Rhapsody* for tenor and soprano, at the Wigmore Hall with Dorothy Helmridge, and a small chamber orchestra. Also at this concert was performed Bach's 'Schlage Doch', in which Steuart played the bells.

One of the most ambitious ventures in which he co-operated with Bliss was the performance at the Aldwych Theatre in February 1921 of *The Tempest*, for which Bliss had written the incidental music. From Sir Arthur's account, it must have been a hilarious occasion. Henry Ainley was Prospero and Ariel was a musical comedy star "a rather heavy girl who had to be swung up and down on ropes . . . One of the Tree Girls was in it and her mother used to sit in the front row of the stalls saying 'my dear, it's just too wonderful'. It wasn't wonderful at all, it was really rather awful." Steuart was joined by Ivan Firth, a bass baritone, and during the storm they had to make themselves heard shouting "We sink, we sink" above the noise of the drums ("I had as many drums as possible!" said Bliss). To complete the chaos, vast quantities of rice (presumably representing rain and hail) were flung down on to the stage and into the pit.

In June 1921, Steuart performed with Myra Hess a concerto for tenor and piano, which Bliss had specially written for them. It was later re-arranged for two pianos and, again, for three hands so that Phyllis Sellick and Cyril Smith could play it. That same month, Steuart took part, with Bliss conducting, in a production of Holst's chamber opera *Savitri* at the Lyric, Hammersmith. This is the moving one-act opera which Holst composed in 1910, based on the Indian story of the woodman, his wife and Death. Dorothy Silk and Clive Carey were the other soloists. Steuart worked with and for Gustav Holst, both professionally and personally. He often joined in the performance of Bach cantatas at St. Paul's Girls' School where Holst was director of music.

It is easy to understand Steuart's friendship with Arthur Bliss and with older musicians like Vaughan Williams and Holst. It is perhaps less easy to appreciate the reasons for his long and intimate association with the composer, Rutland Boughton, which began in 1919 and lasted until the latter's death in 1960. Boughton seems to have exercised a magnetic spell over Steuart, as he did over so many even more unlikely characters—Shaw, Elgar, Beecham, Dent, John Galsworthy, Henry Wood and Vaughan Williams—and he managed to secure business backing for his productions from surprising sources.

A dedicated Socialist—he was a member of the Communist Party from the mid-1920s until the Hungarian uprising of 1956—Boughton impressed everyone with his unbounded enthusiasm and almost childlike simplicity and unworldliness.

He had actually launched a series of festivals at Glastonbury before the War, with the ambitious aim of establishing there a kind of 'Arthurian Bayreuth'. The Festivals were interrupted by the War but were revived in the summer of 1919 when Steuart was summoned to Glastonbury by Edward Dent, to take part at very short notice in the masque *Cupid and Death*, which Dent had arranged and was conducting. Steuart arrived just in time for the dress rehearsal. Many years later he recalled in a broadcast talk about *The Immortal Hour*, Boughton's music drama:

"I was at first too preoccupied with failing to learn *Cupid and Death* in time for the first performance (in which I had to be prompted with a more than Italian liberality). But very quickly the spell was working . . . I was then, and am to a large extent still, immune to Celtic mysticism. So it was not escapism, nor the call of eternal youth that held me—What had anybody got to escape from who had come out alive from 1914–18, and why should I, at the age of 30, be desiring eternal youth—I was just stepping into it, so I thought. It was the music alone . . ."

In the New Year of 1921, Steuart took the part of Herod in Boughton's *Bethlehem*—"the tearing raging part of Herod needs a big tenor" Boughton had written—and went on tour with the production to Bath, Burnham and Bristol. *Bethlehem* is a music drama, adapted from a fourteenth-century nativity play, with additional carols. Steuart said it was "a surefire hit, no one could resist Christmas carols anyway or the music of the shepherds and the three Kings, the complete simplicity of the Lullaby."

The following year, he played Admetus in *Alkestis*—Clive Carey. Frederick Woodhouse and Astra Desmond were among the cast, The libretto was an adaptation of Gilbert Murray's translation of the Euripides drama. Steuart noted "Dent, Clive Carey and myself represented the sort of highbrow Cambridge gang who talked and argued—we had all read *Alkestis* in the original Greek."

Boughton's big success, however, was *The Immortal Hour*, which was brought to London in 1922. It had a spectacular run, and was revived in 1926 and 1932. People were haunted, almost hypnotized by the music and the strange Celtic drama by Fiona Macleod and vied with one another about who could see it most often. The success of the London run relieved Boughton of financial worry and he went ahead with bold plans for the future of Glastonbury. But his schemes came to an untimely end, precipitated by political and domestic complications. These also produced a cooling-off in his relations with Steuart.

Without consulting any of his associates and much to their fury, Boughton planned to mount a modern working-class version of *Bethlehem* with Christ born in a miner's home and Herod as the cigar-smoking capitalist tycoon. I do not think Steuart minded much about Boughton's Communism, as he was at that time uninterested in politics, but he was decidedly upset about Rutland's marital affairs. Boughton had, since 1910, been 'sharing' his life with Christina Walshe, a member of the Musical Fellowship at Birmingham where he was then teaching. In 1923 he fell in love with one of the Glastonbury singers, Kathleen Davis, then a pupil at the Royal College of Music and a new alliance was formed.

Steuart was concerned about the damaging effect this was having on the Festival and its performers. It seems strange to find him "reading the riot act" to Rutland Boughton when he was so soon to get into deep waters himself. In March 1923 he wrote to Astra Desmond:

> "I saw R.B. after all this evening, met him by chance and talked to him here. His case is roughly that Chris refused marital relations with him, that as soon as he first saw Kathleen he recognized an affinity, that Chris threw them together and precipitated this crisis and that the facts were not within his power to control.
>
> I pointed out that people's motives in this sort of thing can't be explained or argued about profitably. It is between them and their consciences. My argument is that he has shown himself to be a person who can't be trusted in personal relations and that therefore the Festival at Glastonbury can't go on as it was. He can't see that ... It is quite useless to discuss the thing with him, as he takes the line that an impulse of this kind is uncontrollable; if so, it must lead *him* wherever it will, but it need not lead me with him to give any kind of sanction to that idea."

Steuart also wrote to Sir Hugh Allen at the Royal College of Music and planned to talk things over with him and with Kathleen's father. His intervention did not have any effect. Boughton lived happily with Kathleen whom he was later able to marry. He and Steuart were not reconciled until the 1930s.

If Glastonbury was identified with the name of Rutland Boughton, Cambridge music in the 1920s was strongly associated with that of the composer Dr. C. B. Rootham. Steuart always had a high opinion of Rootham's choral compositions and performed in many of these; he included many Rootham songs in his repertoire and often sang under his baton. In February 1922 he took the main part in Root-ham's opera *The Two Sisters*. This was the gloomy story, put in modern idiom, of a jilted young woman who drowns her sister because she has stolen her boy-friend. A wandering harper (Steuart) strings his harp with her hair and at the wedding reception at the Castle, the harp sings out "There stands my sister who drowned me." The production was by Dennis Arundell (his first operatic production) and the chorus and orchestra were largely amateurs drawn from the University and from local residents.

The Two Sisters did not get a good reception from the press and was never performed again in public. There was little but praise for Steuart's own performance. The *Daily Telegraph* said that he sang "with surprising conviction" and J. B. Priestley wrote in the *Cambridge Review*:

> "Mr. Steuart Wilson sings the difficult music allotted to him with great skill, though on Tuesday night he was not always sure of his cues. His make-up on the first night was unhappy. Instead of suggesting a ragged old harper, he simply looked like a respectable gentleman wearing false whiskers and a new silk suit."

The opera was not without its comic incidents. The bass who had to sing the word 'Stupidly' could not reach low enough, so he sang 'Stu' and the 'pidly', an octave lower was filled in from the wings by a choral scholar of St. John's (Owen Fulljames) who ever after was nicknamed Pidly.

Steuart himself was clearly not happy about the production, whether because of his costume or his cues, for we find him writing to Clive Carey a few years later: "I never go near Cambridge now. I think *The Two Sisters* finished me off there."

CHAPTER EIGHT

PETERSFIELD DAYS

D URING the early 1920s Steuart carried out all his engagements from his base in Hampshire. He had settled—perhaps not the right word for one of his profession—in the village of Steep, on the outskirts of Petersfield, in 1918.

He had always had a deep attachment to Petersfield and appreciated "the endless variety of beauty which that corner of Hampshire affords." When he was at Winchester, he used often to bicycle over to visit his Padwick relations, and to walk over Stoner Hill. He used to say, in later life, that he would like to be made a Life Peer, so that he could take the title of Lord Steep!

It was in the Steep house (Hither Northfield) that his first three children were born—one died in infancy. Steuart described the house as 'small'—it was in fact amply large enough to house him, his growing family and his grand piano, which "took up most of the living-room." The most distinctive feature was the all-black ceiling in the bedroom, put in because he said it helped him get to sleep. There was a fairly big garden and "luckily the house stood alone, for not only my neighbours but the whole tiny village suffered" from his practising. 'Suffered' is a typical Steuart word—many people connected with the school remember how they used to enjoy the sounds that poured out across the road, when Steuart was doing his home-work, preparing for a concert.

In September 1921, he was appointed music director of Bedales School. Mr. J. H. Badley, the Chief, accepted his stipulation that he should be free to undertake professional engagements outside and he was paid a salary of £33 6s. 8d. a term. As his house was just opposite the School, the arrangement was mutually convenient and as the train service—in the old days of steam—was at least as good as in the 1960s, he could fulfil his commitments in London and in the school.

After playing for morning prayers at 8.30, he would cycle to the station, often with a suitcase on the carrier, arrive in London in time for a morning rehearsal or to teach at the Royal College of Music. He would return to Petersfield by a train which arrived about 6.30 p.m., collect his bicycle and be back in time for the choir practice which began at 6.35. "I seldom arrived exactly on time, but I had the perfect colleague, the senior assistant master, Basil Gimson, who delighted in taking the practices for me and was as methodical as anyone could have wished."

The habit of cycling to the station died hard with him, though he soon found that a rucksack was easier to manage than a suitcase. He used to carry dress clothes and a boiled shirt in his rucksack—one wonders in what condition they emerged when he reached the concert platform! He once heard it reported from a Leeds festival that he had been seen walking back to London.

On one occasion he dumped his rucksack in the hall of the house where he was staying and found, when he went to change, that it had disappeared. It had been picked up by his host's Boy Scout son who had taken it off to a Scout rally.

Ronald Biggs, who succeeded Steuart as Music Director, has written:

"Music, in Mr. Badley's concept of education, had an important place and in the early days it owed much to the care and enthusiasm of Mrs. Badley. It is evident from what Mr. Badley wrote in 1900 that Whole School Singing was the root from which other forms of music sprang, for ten years inspired by the infectious enthusiasm of O. B. Powell."

Soon after the 1914–18 War, Mrs. Badley retired and Steuart took over the music. Biggs wrote:

"His dynamic personality was a breath of very strong fresh air. He was uncompromising, made some sweeping changes, pleased some people and offended others, bequeathed to me some problems, but things began to hum."

Ronald has described his first meeting with Steuart, during the Petersfield Festival of 1923. "He was looking like nothing on earth, cycling through the village, wearing a large pink hat and a scarlet scarf." Ronald met his future wife, Cécile, at the Wilsons' house.

Rolf Gardiner, nephew of the composer Balfour Gardiner, was a pupil at Bedales when Steuart was teaching there. He has told me:

"In 1919 I went to Bedales and it was there in the spring or summer that I first met Steuart Wilson. He was married to his first wife Ann, who, pushing a pram with her first-born, herself looked almost like a child—she had a pretty young figure and wore her hair bobbed like a page. Having settled at Steep, they were in close touch with Bedalian life. It was at a School evening service that I first heard Steuart sing the Dutch Easter carol 'This joyful Eastertide, away with sin and sorrow'. I was thrilled to the marrow ... Steuart was leanly handsome, with a tendency to gauntness and impressive in a rather eagle-like way. His quick, vibrant masculine manner of speaking sounded usually slightly gruff. But his expression was always penetrating and smiling, and his crusty humour was delightful, sardonic and amusing ... At Bedales I asked Steuart to test my voice. But my vocal chords had already been roughened by too much forcing at the time my voice had begun to break and he rightly gave me no encouragement as a vocalist, although I have continued to enjoy taking part in choral music all my life."

Steuart's main job was taking choir practices, in which the whole school joined. He wrote:

"Music is an excellent recreation but with a mixed chorus, nothing can be done without discipline and order, which was not in those days an essential element in the Bedales tradition."

Brought up in the Wykehamist and classical tradition, he was completely out of sympathy with the 'free and easy' ways of Bedales and found it almost beyond his powers to conduct the 'whole school singing' on which Mr. Badley placed such store.

He wrote to Iris Lemare, a former Bedales pupil who became a lifelong friend:

"I wish you were still here, as we are having quite a proper stir up of singing. Last Sunday we managed a Bach Chorale with strings 'Jesu joy of man's desiring' as a voluntary, two psalms unaccompanied, not even a piano, only a chord to start them with and quite a difficult Bach hymn chorale with strings only ... They didn't do too badly, though they sing most stinkingly flat as a rule. The whole school singing periods are rather a nightmare still. The little kids in front are simply a blamed nuisance and don't try to do anything. I whack their heads and pull their ears when they get too noisy, but as for *teaching* them, that's out of the question."

[He added]: "I've become so much the schoolmaster at Bedales, shouting and roaring up and down the new Hall, that I never see anyone except when I'm in the throes of trying to teach them something.'

He had many rows with the members of the staff—rehearsals for those he was to encounter throughout his musical career. In one letter he wrote: "I've had more than my fair share of worry this term ... In a certain section of the school and staff I'm the most unpopular man in the world! And it's only by refusing to be in the least annoyed in public by what is said that I can keep any sort of hold on the situation. Damn them all!"

One of the clashes occurred over the teaching of stringed instruments. At that time, music at Dunhurst, the Bedales preparatory school, was in the hands of the great Arnold Dolmetsch and his family. They taught the children to play violins as if they were viols, holding them between their knees, with frets on the finger boards and the bow held horizontally with the palm upwards. When the children came on to the main school, Steuart insisted that they should play in the modern way, with their fiddles under the chin, without frets and bowing in the modern way. There was considerable acrimony and more than once Steuart exploded: "That nonsense had its last chance in the seventeenth century and lost ... Why don't you go back to the seventeenth century where you belong?"

Bedales continued for some years to be a target for his sarcasm. He wrote to Iris Lemare who was doing a course of Dalcroze in Switzerland: "After Bedales and Dalcroze you ought to have your head as full of cranks as a beehive of bees." Yet, in spite of his concern at the lack of discipline and his initial doubts about co-education, Steuart enjoyed his period as a music master and he certainly, to use Ronald Biggs's phrase, 'made things hum'. (It is only fair to say that later he grew to appreciate the qualities of Bedales and Bedalians.) He retired from the school in July 1923 to concentrate on his professional career.

As well as his 'part-time' work for Bedales, Steuart took part in many local musical activities. We find him producng Gilbert and Sullivan opera at Steep and playing Malvolio to Geoffrey Crump's Sir Toby Belch in an open air performance of *Twelfth Night* at Bedales. He acted and sang in the Shakespeare productions (with Purcell incidental music) in the garden of Fair Oak, the home of Colonel Douglas Carnegie at Rogate in Sussex. Steuart was Amiens in *As You Like It* and Philostrate in *Midsummer Night's Dream*. Dennis Arundell was Puck in *The Dream*, and Steuart's wife Ann appeared as an attendant on Hippolyta. Both performances were given in aid of the Rogate girl guides. Whenever possible, he took part in the musical activities organized by the formidable Susan Lushington at her home near Alton. Steuart also took the straight part of a young scientist in a one-act play by Geoffrey Crump *Safety First*, performed in the Petersfield Drill Hall in 1921. "He was a good actor, but he wouldn't learn his lines," was Crump's verdict.

Steuart was closely associated with the Petersfield Music Festival, whether as singer, choir conductor, adjudicator or member of the committee. He and Adrian Boult were the driving-force behind the Festival in the 1920s, raising it from the level of a purely local competition to the pinnacle of national fame. "Mr. Steuart Wilson, now a citizen of Petersfield, became the prime instigator in many daring schemes," reported the *Petersfield Courier*. Steuart, indeed, became largely responsible for planning future programmes, suggesting soloists, looking after publicity and money-raising; it was mainly thanks to his influence that the festival became more ambitious in its projects and added a whole range of new works to its repertoire. He also trained and conducted local choirs and in 1920, somewhat pluralistically, he conducted Steep, Petersfield I and Petersfield II. His Steep choir, which consisted chiefly of Bedales staff and families, was awarded top marks all round by Gustav Holst, the adjudicator.

The Festival during the 1920s attracted such a galaxy of talent as Plunket Greene, Myra Hess, Harold Samuel, Dorothy Silk, John Coates, Arthur Cranmer and many others who had come, as

Steuart put it "because they were personal friends of those who directed the music and because they enjoyed the atmosphere of music, friendliness and high ambitions which they found here." Malcolm Sargent was a frequent visitor, as conductor, judge and solo pianist.

Steuart had very definite ideas about how such a music festival should be run, ideas which we find re-echoed later when he came to wider national platforms. In an article in the local paper, he wrote:

"We would never consent to recommend to the choirs music which we felt was unworthy simply because it was easy for them to learn. The only path worth treading in music is a stony one and a steep one. We don't for a moment claim that we have never chosen music which turned out to be not worthy or that we have never underestimated the difficulty of some of the things we have recommended. But we do claim that we have been guided and consciously guided by these principles, that we will not choose music which we think to be inferior, because it will be easy for the choirs who are to perform it."

The festival had its 21st birthday in April 1926 and Steuart was responsible for the celebration arrangements. That year the main work was Vaughan Williams's *Sea Symphony* and the choice was an example of Steuart's policy. The *Sea Symphony*, he wrote, had been said to be too difficult for any but a Leeds choir. "But we have got our teeth into it and it will show us what real virile English music is."

Donald Tovey presented the banners and at a birthday party in the Drill Hall "scenes of great enthusiasm followed when Mr. Steuart Wilson entered the hall bearing a small birthday cake with its twenty-one lighted candles which, as he remarked in a genial speech, represented twenty-one years of good work for the Festival by many . . . who had made that festival possible in the past and made it now a beacon light to which these twenty-one candles were nothing," the local paper reported.

Steuart continued to serve on the music committee, along with Adrian Boult, Ronald Biggs and Kathleen Merritt, and appeared regularly on Festival platforms. A performance of Haydn's *Creation* in 1933, in his and A. H. Fox Strangways' translation, was his last appearance as a soloist at the festival. He resigned from the committee in March 1934.

The Petersfield festival was important, because it gave Steuart insight and experience in coaching and conducting amateur choirs, assessing their needs and capabilities, and provided a firm foundation for his later work as administrator and adjudicator.

On the whole, his life in Petersfield during the years immediately after the War was happy; the domestic tensions of subsequent years had not yet begun to build up. But it was a punishing programme and he was already having ulcer trouble. "It's a dog's life" he wrote to Geoffrey Keynes in 1922.

It is no wonder that, whenever he could get away, he would snatch a few days to stay with the Gleadowes at Calamansac, on the Helford river in Cornwall—sailing all day and singing madrigals all evening. Dick Gleadow, who had been his best friend at Winchester, was a fine musician and artist (much later he designed the Stalingrad sword).

They made a hilarious pair, and Cecil, Dick's widow, recalls that she "ached with laughing the whole time." One night a farmer heard glorious singing coming from the disused Norman church of St. Anthony in Meneage. "It's the angels," he said to his wife. He collected his gun and together they went to the church, where they found two enormous and not unangelic-looking young men—Steuart and Dick—sitting in the choir stalls, singing at the tops of their voices. The story of the angelic giants is still told in Meneage.

CHAPTER NINE

LESSONS WITH DE RESZKE

F OR some time Steuart had been turning over the idea of going
to the south of France, to have lessons with the great Polish
tenor Jean de Reszke. Ralph Vaughan Williams, Sir Hugh
Allen and others had advised him that a complete change and break
from his overloaded programme were absolutely essential if he was
to preserve his health, let alone become a good singer. Vaughan
Williams wrote to Sir Alexander Kaye Butterworth, father of the
composer George Butterworth, who was killed in action in 1916,
suggesting that Steuart might be helped from the Trust established
in his son's memory. (The date is illegible but it was probably in
December 1922):

"We both feel that where help is most needed is with musicians
between 25 and 35, when the real fire is beginning to show itself
and a timely help may be of great advantage. Steuart Wilson—
he is badly in need of rest and a quiet time in which to study his
art (say 3 months or so) and get his voice into *real* order (which it
is not at present). He is much overworked and finds it necessary
to take all the engagements he can—with the result that he has not
time to get over certain defects of production which I am afraid
will spoil his voice if he is not careful. He is, as I daresay you know,
a fine musician and a splendid singer and if he could get over
certain vocal difficulties ought, in my opinion, to be able to take
the place left empty by the death of Elwes and which no one has
yet filled. He is about 31 and is married with two children. He
was, as I daresay you know, badly wounded twice."

An offer of help was duly made, but Steuart wrote to Sir Alexander Butterworth (3rd May 1922) declining it:

"My dear Sir,

I need hardly tell you how surprised I was at your letter and I think I should make a very complete answer—in case there should be any misunderstanding as to my financial position.

I am married—with two children—and with a private secured income of about £80 a year net, and a pension for wounds amounting with bonus to £217 a year. I am thus secured the necessaries of life on a modest scale. My earnings from music last year were £550 after making reasonable deductions for expenses and on a fair average I should this year make £600 at least. I cannot therefore allow that I am really 'necessitous', considering how many people have to live on considerably less. Perhaps the people who may have advised you did not know of these facts so exactly.

I should also say that I cannot at this moment get free to enable myself to profit by any grant to go off and study, so that I should have to postpone that for at least a year until I can see my way clearly to getting free of various jobs in this country—school work, engagements, etc.

I cannot help feeling that there are other people who would profit more immediately by such assistance, though no one could be more grateful than I am for the kind thoughts that prompted you. I did know George, though not at all well, and, like every other musician who met him, I have the greatest faith in what he wrote as being genuine. That is why I felt I must put the true facts of my case before you so that you may reconsider your letter. Though I must again assure you how very much I am moved by your letter. If I were really free I would go at once to work, but I cannot leave at present.

Yours sincerely,
Steuart Wilson"

However, the situation changed, once the decision to study with De Reszke had been taken. Steuart found that, after all, his finances were insufficient, especially as the price of lessons had been raised. He wrote (29th October 1923) to Sir Alexander Butterworth:

"In May 1922 you wrote to me offering me a sum of money from the Trust Fund in memory of your son George. I felt obliged at the time to decline the offer, as my then circumstances did not seem to me to warrant my accepting money that others might need more.

In April of this present year I decided to take the risk of breaking off my work in England completely and taking 6 months course of lessons with Jean de Reszke here in Nice, I arranged for my lessons, 2 a week at 100fr. each, and as I am married I decided to let my house in England and take one here to which I could bring my family. I had some savings from the year before and this year, and I expected with the rent for my house in England and my other sources, to be able to manage easily. But since that arrangement was entered into the price of lessons has risen considerably, and as a concession to those who arranged beforehand ours are only raised to 200fr. a lesson. So that my budget has to find 200fr. a week in excess of the estimate.

Now I don't wish to give an impression that this is an unsurmountable difficulty. It isn't at all. But I thought I might justifiably write to you again to say that, though I had felt bound to refuse a previous offer of help, yet if it had come at this moment instead of 18 months ago I should have felt justified in accepting it. I have no doubt that the income of the trust is already allocated, and I don't desire, as I said, to give any false impression that I am in a real difficulty. I'm not going to give up the purpose for which I came and it only means that I shall have to sell out some shares in War Loan which I had meant to keep as a reserve for some more serious crisis.

Might I ask you two things? One is not to regard the increase of price of lessons as a breach of faith on M. de Reszke's part. The history is somewhat complicated to tell, but I don't think it is a breach of faith. Secondly, to excuse my writing to you in this very candid way what must appear to be almost a begging letter."

Sir Alexander sought the advice of Mr. William Harman, the secretary of the Leeds Triennial Festival, who replied: "If I were in your place, it would be a special pleasure to me to give help to such a man. He will be, I hope and believe, a really great artist. I have heard him several times sing the Narrator's part in the *St. Matthew Passion* at the York Palm Sunday Service, and I believe he will one day be a worthy successor to Gervase Elwes."

As a result, the Trust sent him a cheque for £25. Steuart wrote to Sir Alexander: "It just makes the difference to me between a feeling of real struggle and the feeling of 'room to move' which is essential to study. It now only remains for me to show that your confidence has not been misplaced."

Another source of help was his old friend and benefactor E. J. Dent, who organized a whip-round on his behalf. Steuart wrote to his mother (30th November 1923):

> "I forgot whether I told you that Dent had got up a fund to help me here among his friends and mine and has sent me already £100. The Trustees of George Butterworth's fund for musicians sent me £25 so I have been most wonderfully succoured. The result is that I have not touched my current a/c balance at the bank yet, which will be £150 by the beginning of the New Year, and only used the £150 deposit balance which paid our rent and our exes out here. So you see that financially I am much sounder than I expected to be. Our living exes are well under 2,000fr. a month at present exchange £25 and my lessons another 2,000 fr. And I still have 4000fr. in the bank here. The children are rather becolded, otherwise all goes well.
>
> Ever your loving son
J.S.W."

Steuart spent two periods studying with de Reszke, from October 1923 to April 1924, and from October 1924 to February 1925, returning in between to give concerts in England and to undertake a tour in Holland.

When he first went to Nice, he was desperately in need of a change. He wrote to Clive Carey in June 1923:

> "I'm *immensely* looking forward to six months' work in peace and quiet. I honestly feel at the end of my tether now. And I believe I'm not too late to learn how to sing. All you said in the past to me wasn't wasted, although I didn't want to believe it then, but I didn't forget it."

Steuart was greatly encouraged by his initial reception and wrote to his father (3rd November 1923):

"I am just getting into my old habits of steady work at singing uninterrupted by any distractions and I find it very pleasant to be back again at purely technical study. My first two lessons with the old man have been quite successful and have already opened my eyes wide to the number of things I have yet to learn. I go in twice a week, which takes about 40–80 minutes according as I go on bicycle or by tram with the chance of missing the connection, the mornings from 9.30 onwards I give up to work with intervals of writing, doing about ½ hour of singing then 10 minutes writing and so on, learning things by heart, practising particular tricks and so on and certain mechanical things to get agility."

A month later, he wrote home:

"I am very pleased with the progress I have made and I am glad that 'the Master' is pleased too; he told me I was 'le plus intelligent de tous les élèves' and he regards me as a 'travailleur formidable' between lessons. It is a great blessing to me to have nothing else to think of."

The Master—"we learn to call him 'Cher Maître'"—had his own very special methods of teaching, which he preferred to call 'ideas' rather than methods. Some of his pupils were driven to tears and were alternately translated from the heights of self-congratulation to the depths of despair.

Steuart came to know and accept the Master's moods, to brave the storms of his disapproval (and that of Koko the green parrot who sat on de Reszke's shoulder and screeched when the singer was bad) and to refrain from undue elation when he received the rare word of praise.

He wrote to Clive Carey—this was on his second visit to Nice in November 1924:

"I have had 4 lessons with the Master, who is in great form and very pleased at getting your letter. The hunt for 'the place' is more insistent than ever. The game now is to keep the lower ribs out all the time and heave from the kidney; no more holding on to the diaphragm from in front as you might say. He is quite candid about it being a change of view from the former one. No more écraser-ing and above all no chest! I'm on Otello and doing rather well on it so far. There's no doubt the new place is a great help, when you get it and keep it you can do anything. No more change of register and I sing a creditable B flat always and a C at a pinch and as for falsetto I tried (alone!) the famous Rubini air from Bellini's Puritani which goes up to F and got it!"

By the beginning of 1925 de Reszke (whose 75th birthday fell on 14th January) was in failing health. He had for some time been suffering from chronic bronchial catarrh, and had never recovered from the death of his only son Jean in the War—a cruel blow which had caused the complete breakdown of his wife. He could no longer take the same interest in his pupils and grew more unpredictable. Steuart evidently felt the change, for he wrote in February "I've had my nose well to the grindstone, but somehow or other I seem to be stuck now and to be making absolutely no progress."

It was planned to give a special performance of Mozart's *Don Giovanni* in Cannes in the spring of 1925 with a cast consisting of the Master's pupils. The opera had had several successful performances in Nice, and on 8th December 1924, Steuart had appeared in the chorus of villagers, at the Théâtre des Variétés. De Reszke caught a chill at the dress rehearsal at Cannes. All lessons were cancelled and the performance went on without him.

The chill developed into pneumonia, and Jean de Reszke died on Good Friday, 3rd April 1925. Steuart who had returned to England at the end of February for a series of concerts (including his own Schubert recital in the Wigmore Hall) immediately rushed back to Nice, as soon as he heard of the Master's illness. He wrote to his mother:

"You will have heard that poor old Jean de R is dead. I knew he was desperately ill when I was in London, and as soon as I came back I went up to enquire, but quite clearly he had very little hope then. He died on Friday afternoon and was buried with the usual appalling pomp on Monday. What with one thing and another I have done nothing since I came back except tear about.

We took it in turns to "wake him" between Friday and Monday morning and that seemed to fill up much of one's times. I wrote this little poem for a wreath for him, which gave so much satisfaction that I had it printed, to send to his pupils etc. and then this letter for his English pupils, so I have had divers businesses to do . . ."

TO OUR MASTER
With a wreath of Laurel and Rosemary
Here is the wreath that Walther won,
The greatest Master-Singer he,
Whose skill and love combined in one
To show us perfect mastery

Here's laurel for a Siegfried's brow
The hero valiant for truth
And tribute to a Vasco dead
Who showed new worlds to questing youth

Here's rosemary for a Romeo's love,
Remembered through long nights and dark
For Lohengrin has seen the dove
That calls him back to Monsalvat

Here is our love and honour for our friend
And Master; may he never fail
In heart, and strive until the end
To seek and find our Holy Grail.

S.W.

Steuart gave Clive Carey a graphic account of the funeral:

"He was 'waked' by relays of us all Friday, Sat., and Sunday in his room where he lay and downstairs in the Salon on Sunday when he was coffined, with tall candles all round. Crowds of people and flowers—tears and all that. The funeral at Nôtre Dame here was a masterpiece of ill-organized pomp. We all came down from the Villa in fiacres or rather closed barouches, they had to transfer all the wreaths and things from one vehicle to another as the gigantic hearse wouldn't go under the railway bridge. Nôtre Dame was packed so tight that we could hardly get in, pushing and swearing crowd of women, no reserved seats, most of us stood in the aisle. Singing which must have made him turn in his grave! A baritone who sang with great fervour a semitone sharp and a quite incredible tenor. Rows of unusually grubby priests and filthy little enfants de chœur: when it was all over we walked him up to the railway station, round at the back into a truck to go to Paris. I quite lost my self-control on discovering that the shed we were going to was labelled 'Arrivée de Viande' and got funeral giggles. Poor Minia is absolutely spent with being 'hostess' to all the crowds who've been up at the Villa. They all go to Paris today to lay him in the vault with the son, and in about 3 weeks a Mass to which everyone in Paris will go. Madame hardly realizes anything and has so much piqûre that she spends the whole day more or less asleep. What she will do, Lord knows. She can't decide and no one can decide for her apparently. The whole affair has been so unmanaged and nobody in charge that it's a wonder the poor old dear ever got buried at all.

I'm told the scenes at the funeral in Paris were incredible. They tore across from station to cemetery, so fast that they got to the cemetery, half hour before time and before you could say Bo, 6 stalwart diggers spat on their hands and heaved the coffin into the vault, and when all the company turned up it was all over!"

Steuart wrote a moving (anonymous) article in *The Times*, describing what Jean de Reszke had meant to him:

"He wished to equip his pupils with his own ever-increasing range of colour and subtlety of tone, so that gradually technique began to mean to them no longer the power of accomplishing their own desires in interpretation, but rather the opening up of new worlds as yet undreamt of. Indeed what made his teaching baffling to so many was the constant disappearance of the horizon the nearer one approached to it . . . His pupils learned from him no easy standard, but one of unattainable perfection, ever sought but never found. The Best for the Highest. Other constellations may rise in the heavens, but they must steer by the memory of a star that has set."

CHAPTER TEN

OURS IS A NICE LIFE

Quite apart from his singing lessons, Steuart enjoyed his two spells at Nice and was happy with his family. He wrote to Jean Farquharson: "It's rather odd to think that since we married, which is six years ago, we've only once had as long as this together."

On the first visit, they rented a villa at Villefranche-sur-Mer, a few miles from Nice. Steuart, whose knowledge of France was largely confined to the mud and flat fields of the north, was entranced by the Riviera. This was long before the developers had moved in and ravaged the coastline. "The villa", he wrote to Jean Farquharson,

"is really a very decent house with plumb south view, over Villefranche harbour and Cap Ferrat, standing on a steep hillside so that you climb up the back garden by steps and out on to the hill and then you can climb 1000 ft. straight up, limestone with rosemary, thyme and odds and ends of stinking stuff in the crevices, pine woods and so on, every now and then a precipitous bit of old quarry, the highest point near and immediately behind is about 1400 and from there you can look North right up to the Alps, with the hills gradually getting higher until they fade into the clouds. Nice is a grubby rather unpleasant town, but suitable to invalids because it's on the flat and not like this place all on the hill. Olives of course everywhere, palms and cactuses of all kinds, rather repellent the latter. Oranges, wonderful scarlet persimmons, lemons and so on, but few flowers to give any colour."

To his mother, rather more prosaically:
"The villa is all right, good rooms and reasonable comfort—the
beds excellent."

The Wilsons were installed at the Villa Margot towards the end of
October 1923.

As soon as he arrived, a 'bombshell' burst. Lord Curzon, then
Foreign Secretary, wired the British Consul at Nice, telling him to
find Steuart and inform him that the Prime Minister (then Stanley
Baldwin) wished the English Singers to appear at Chequers on
Sunday, to sing to the Dominion Prime Ministers. Steuart talked
it over with Clive Carey, who was also in Nice and they consulted
de Reszke who "very sagely said that we couldn't follow up the
advertisement it would give us and after all, was it really an important artistic event?" Steuart wired a refusal, but the next day,
the Consul sent another appeal. Steuart wrote home:

"P.M.'s secretary telegraphs P.M. would be very disappointed if
you don't come, can you reconsider. I wired back to the Consul
'impossible change decision for all the Ministers and even the
O.B.E.' And I am satisfied I did well."

The household at the Villa consisted of Steuart and Ann, their
two children Margaret and Frances and two domestic helps from
Petersfield—Nellie Shirley and Alice Petter. (It seems strange in
1969 to think of a penurious artist travelling with two domestic
servants to look after his house and two children!) Both Nellie
Shirley (now Mrs. Aldroyd) and Miss Petter have described to me
the gay and carefree life of those days. When Steuart was not working, he would often hire a car and take the whole party for a drive
in the country, or entertain them all to dinner at a little restaurant
overlooking the harbour.

In the afternoons, he either walked or played golf on the links at
Cagnes. "Very bad golf," he confessed "but a most stunning view of
the hills and a superb sea and sky, and little olive groves and
orangeries," adding "I never realized the appeal in Goethe's 'Kennst
du das Land wo die Zitronen Blühn' until I saw an orange tree
actually in fruit. I'm not sure that this holiday hasn't permanently
demoralized me. I've eaten the Lotos in fact." They joined a local
book club, had *The Times*, the *Manchester Guardian Weekly*, *Punch* and

G

the *New Statesman* sent out from England. "I felt I shouldn't like to miss all the things that must happen before May or only see them through French eyes." Both he and Ann worked hard learning Italian.

His letters home are full of news about the children. They "are growing quickly and are very well, learning no French of course, but one couldn't expect that. The hills they have to climb are making them stalwart in the leg." Frances's birthday, on 28th December, was a red-lettter day. He described the occasion:

"As a great treat we went into Nice and I hired a little tiny donkey landau with just room for the two kids and they could drive and hold the reins and so on. The unfortunate Frances—the 'treatee'—simply loathed it and had to be removed in tears. She is the most obstinate little devil I know at 4 yrs. old defies Satan himself to play at cherrypit."

The party at Villa Margot was completed by Joan Elwes, who was also studying with de Reszke. Clive Carey was there for part of the time. Steuart wrote:

"Clive Carey—my colleague in the English Singers—is out here and dieting strangely and has taught Joan Elwes—our stable companion here—his methods. It's a wierd or is it weird mixture of avoidances of starch and acids and makes you wonder whether an egg is acid or starch or entirely taboo and whether you may treat farinaceous foods as a 'mcat cquivalent'. Ralph Vaughan Williams told me that when he was a private in the R.A.M.C. his sergeant always referred to 'ferocious diet'—such a nice expression for such mild things as 'rice pudding'."

The Wilsons kept open house and provided a port of call for the many English people who came to Nice. Edward J. Dent was a regular visitor. He used to stay at Nice with his elderly uncle, and to judge from his account of the daily routine, he was no doubt glad to escape to the Wilsons' more congenial establishment:

"Though we dress for dinner, we eat it almost in silence except for a few grumbles about the cooking, a few remarks on the weather and the state of the flowers on the table, a few observations on the health of the Duke of Connaught—at last comes my coffee. My uncle won't retire like a lady. He sits there in silence, obviously bored, while I drink it, sitting bolt upright and without smoke. He hates smoke and he can't digest coffee, so that he has a curious hostility to both, only comparable to my hostility to the Church".

In February 1924, Dent reported to his friend J. B. Trend on a visit to the Villa Margot:

"In the afternoon I went to see Steuart at Villefranche. They have got a pleasant house and seem very happy. Steuart looks 10 years younger and his speaking voice is very vigorous and healthy. Ann is expecting a baby in about a month's time or less. Steuart was rather worried lest he should become the father of a Frenchman but he has found out about the necessary formalities and I hope it will go smoothly. She seems very well and the two little girls are very lively, though they don't think Villefranche is their idea of the seaside. We all agree in hating Nice and the Riviera generally. Music at Nice is quite appalling and Steuart says the Opera is abominable."

The baby to which Dent referred was born on 24th February somewhat earlier than expected. Steuart wrote to his father: "I'm sure you'll be as pleased as we are to welcome a new Jonathan into the world. You see we are determined to have a Jonathan to hand on the torch, such as it may be when I have done with it." And to Jean Farquharson, he expressed his joy and his fears for the new baby's health (2nd March 1924):

"The heavens opened last Friday and brought us a son; a few days before he was expected, we had run the nurse rather fine in any case, so we had rather a scramble. He is a 'piccolino' but appears to enjoy life and waxes reasonably. I can't tell you what a relief it is to us and in a way what an anxiety still. We had, perhaps you know, an infant boy born 3 years ago, who died within 3 days having shown no signs of being anything unusually wrong except that he was jaundiced and we were told it was quite common for babies especially boys to be jaundiced. It was a real bad knock to us both.

We've called our piccolino, Jonathan, a sonorous polysyllable, which belonged aforetime to his great-great-grandfather and before that time had never been out of the family as a name; but the taste of the early 19th cent. when my father was born who should have been called Jonathan in his turn, forbade it. The eldest sons had alternated Edward and Jonathan from the time when they first emerge into the light.

Conceive us happy—me in particular, I have gained what I hoped, and not lost what I had feared.

Ann had been desperately ill the summer before last so the whole of this babe's arrival has been anxious and to crown it all, this wee mite was yellow with jaundice too. However, he has cast it nearly all off and is now eight days old and I don't think he'll look back but for two days we daren't almost tell anybody, after the last calamity. In fact I hardly like to feel too pleased about it now in case the heavens open again and take him back."

Jonathan was a delicate baby and the anxieties continued. Steuart reported to his mother during their second stay in Nice:

"We have installed a weighing machine which will weigh us all, hired it for 6 months for £2 which is not expensive and we can all keep an eye on ourselves. But we haven't had time to observe Jno partly because the machine hasn't been here a week yet and partly because he was not really properly weighed last time."

The machine evidently worked, because a postcard to his mother a few days later announced: "Jonathan gained 8 oz. this week and now totals approx 9 lbs. ¼ oz. The nights are much better in fact good and all marches prosperously."

The Wilsons returned to England in April 1924. Steuart had a major operation for an ulcer in May—of which more later—followed by a busy series of engagements. He managed to find some-one to take his place in the English Singers, which enabled him, with a clear conscience, to return to Nice for further study. At first he feared that for financial reasons he would have to go alone, but thanks to the generosity of his father it was possible for the whole family to travel out to Nice. Writing to Canon Wilson, Steuart said:

"I haven't half expressed my gratitude. It's true that all this is part of the sequel of the War, but I am compensated by my pension for the injuries and if I had not been ambitious I might have lived a quieter life. But I had to get my feet on the ladder: they are there now and I shall not have the same struggle again."

They went out by boat—on the Rotterdam Lloyd *Patria* from Southampton to Marseilles—and had a comfortable journey. This time the Wilsons stayed in Nice itself. Alice and Nellie did not accompany them but their friend from Bedales days Rosamund Carr came out to stay with them. They lodged in two adjoining apartments in the Chemin de Fabron.

The routine during this second period at Nice was much as it had been on their first visit—lessons, practising, writing, walking, occasional drives and games of golf. "We've had an uneventful winter—except that all the children have been ill which has made plenty of events for Ann," he wrote home in February 1925.

While he was at Nice, he went up to Vence to see Jacques Raverat, the painter and his wife Gwen, née Darwin, an artist in her own right. Jacques had been a friend of Hugh Wilson's at Cambridge. He was badly paralysed and unable to move or do anything without help. Steuart and Ann offered to take the two children, who were much the same age as their own little girls, or to help in any way they could.

In spite of de Reszke's death in April 1925 the Wilsons decided to stay on in Nice until the end of May and travel home by a Dutch boat from Marseilles to Southampton. This was to prove a fateful decision. When they reached Marseilles there was trouble with the propellor and they were delayed nearly a week. A new baby was on the way and they had planned to arrive home in plenty of time for it to be born in England. What with the delayed departure and bad weather on the way, the baby, a boy, was born on 4th June in the English Channel. He too was jaundiced and caused his parents acute anxiety. Steuart wrote on 13th June:

"For 3 or 4 days it looked as if he might not live, but we are out of anxiety now, though he is still a little yellower than a Christian ought to be. Being born on a Dutch boat at sea he is a Dutchman by nationality. Everyone was frightfully good to us, the Captain drank our health in Champagne (with me), the steward gave us a cake, the baker lent his scales to weigh him and everyone offered compliments. One old dear—a Dutch retired

Admiral—sent the Purser round with an English £ note 'for the boy's money-box'. Aren't they nice!"

When they arrived at Southampton, Ann and the baby, whom they called Richard, were rushed to a nursing home, before undertaking the journey to the Wilson (senior) house at Worcester. Steuart reported ten days later that although the jaundice had not quite cleared up, the baby should get absolutely all right:

"This being Sunday, I've been 'in charge' since lunch time and like a model bourgeois father have pushed a push chair round several rather hot streets with two other children dawdling behind, a typical Sunday procession! I'm getting well versed in how children's clothes do up—a complete and awful mystery to me so far. I take the two elders to school each morning and Margaret's trousers fell off on the way through the Cathedral. I had a great struggle, but made it possible for us to continue our journey, at any rate in decency if not in order."

In the autumn of 1925 Steuart and his family moved to 23 Chepstow Villas, Notting Hill Gate, in London, leaving Steep after nearly seven years. Steuart's parents gave up their Worcester house and came to live in the house at Steep which Steuart had vacated. Steuart continued to live in Chepstow Villas until 1957; moving from number 23 to number 19 soon after the Second World War.

CHAPTER ELEVEN

CRESCENDO

T HERE was general agreement that Steuart had benefited enormously from his time in Nice, both in his health and his technique. In 1924, soon after returning from his first spell with de Reszke, he sang in the Three Choirs Festival—it was Hereford's year—and was greatly encouraged by the reactions of the cognoscenti. He sang in the *B Minor Mass* in the Cathedral and gave *On Wenlock Edge* at the town concert. He wrote to Clive Carey:

"Everybody who spoke to me personally such as Adrian, Napier, the Aspidistra*, Silk, Tom Tillett, etc. (even Sir Ivor Atkins) were unanimous that I was much better. One paper, the *Manchester Guardian*, said I sang too loud 'yet very beautifully and with a far more polished vocalization than we had previously heard from him ... *Times* and *Telegraph* and *Morning Post* all nice— 'admirably sung and so on'. But Sheldon in the *B'ham Post* still saying my voice is rough and ugly and shows no beauty of tone like Tudor Davies."

Iris Lemare noted that summer: "There is no conception how his voice has changed. It has become far fuller, at least more rounded and concentrated and truer and a little nasal. I can't help missing the old, rugged spread-out voice, but technically there is no denying the enormous improvement."

Up till then Steuart had been known mainly as one of The English Singers, as a singer of folksongs and ballads and a performer at local

* Astra Desmond, now Lady Neame, the contralto, who was one of Steuart's closest friends and musical associates in performances of Bach and Elgar.

Festivals. It was only after he returned from France that he built up a national reputation as a soloist. By 1924–5 he was very near the top of the ladder and he steadily rose in popularity and esteem, reaching his peak—most observers agree—in the late 1920s and early 1930s.

In the spring of 1925 he was billed to give two solo recitals in London. For the first, and probably the only time in his career, he confessed to nerves. "I've begun to think seriously about my two recitals in London in March," he wrote to Clive Carey in February. "They frighten me to death. I mean, at present, to do a Schubert in English, one to advertise our book of translations of which you will get a copy, and one of Vaughan Williams, with string 4tet, doing *Wenlock Edge*."

The book of translations was the English version of Schubert songs* on which he and A. H. Fox Strangways had been working for some years. They made an ideal combination. Fox Strangways was music critic and editor of *Music and Letters*, a German scholar and teacher, twenty years older than Steuart, who, as a practical performer knew from personal experience about the 'singability' of words and had a magic touch with language.

The book includes the song-cycles *Schoene Müllerin* and *Winterreise* and a number of the better and less well-known songs, such as *Erlkönig*, *Lachen und Weinen* and the *Doppelgänger*. The translators admitted to being 'entirely defeated' by *Heidenröslein* and *Der König in Thule*. Their book received much praise. The *Times Literary Supplement*, which devoted nearly six columns to it, said: "Mr Fox Strangways and Mr Steuart Wilson have given a courageous lead and it must be followed up. Their volume is admirably adapted to the singer's needs. . . . We count on the book to give new impetus to the study of Schubert in this country."

There was less unanimity in the critics' reviews of Steuart's recital in the Wigmore Hall on 9th March. *The Times* commented: "Mr Wilson's diction is the best part of his singing. There was no need to read the words in the programme to know what the songs were about." But the *Musical Times* critic thought differently. "Mr. Wilson has still to work on his diction if he would make the telling verbal effect of Elwes in the past and of our ever-admired John Coates. At present, he scarcely does justice to his own translation and the book of words was always necessary."

* *Schubert songs translated*, Oxford University Press, 1925.

Steuart himself wrote to Clive Carey:

"I was frankly disappointed with what I did at my Schubert recital. It ought to have been better than it was. I know I was trying too hard to 'get it across', but all the same it was miles better than it used to be. At Cambridge the week before I had sung jolly well in the Mozart *Requiem* and extremely well as the Narrator in the Mat Pass for the Bach Choir. So it was aggravating just to miss in the recital."

A friend who accompanied him to the concert recalls that on the way to the Hall Steuart was 'very worked up' and said that, although he had never in his life felt physically afraid, or suffered from platform 'nerves', he was conscious of the importance of the occasion and of the need to do well.

The Vaughan Williams recital at the Aeolian Hall a fortnight later was a complete success and even Steuart admitted: "I thought I did well and I got a good press on the whole. I'm content I think— couldn't have expected more and I don't deserve more. I don't think I've detracted from my reputation anyway."

The programme included the *Four Hymns, On Wenlock Edge* (with the Snow quartet and Anthony Bernard), *Merciless Beauty* (a setting of three Chaucer rondels), and a selection of new settings of Shakespeare and Walt Whitman poems. A typical note appeared in *The Times*:

"It was a remarkable feat, both physically and intellectually. He was in good voice and at the top of his powers and there was a sign or two towards the end that he had used both to the utmost; it is to be hoped that he does not mean to keep on at this high pressure and so bring our pleasure and his to an end prematurely."

Far from heeding this excellent advice, Steuart went on piling on the pressure and plunged into a vortex of activities. That autumn he went to Venice, at very short notice, for a conference of the International Society for Contemporary Music, where he sang Vaughan Williams's *Merciless Beauty* and Gruenberg's *Daniel Jazz*.*

* Steuart thereafter often included the *Daniel Jazz* in his repertoire. In 1926, when he sang it for the BBC, Julian Herbage recalls that the announcer and the eight instrumentalists were all in dinner jackets (then *de rigueur* in Savoy Hill) but Steuart turned up in an "offwhite high-necked sweater, singing the solo part with incredible intensity and also athletically conducting the ensemble."

The Jazz, a setting of Vachell Lindsay's rollicking verse, was not altogether his normal line of country, but he sang it with verve and won great praise. Professor Dent, a prominent figure in the Society—they used to call it Dent's Zoo—wrote to J. B. Trend:

"Steuart made a really big success—even the Italians admired his singing. Malipiero was particularly impressed with him. The *Daniel Jazz* is a wretched work I think. I don't so much mind its vulgarity—it is its abominably bad workmanship that I can't stand. However Steuart put it across marvellously."

The Venice Festival ended up with a midnight party at the Lido, described by Dent as "something between Wembley and a Turkish bath . . . waiters dressed up as orientals offering the ladies the sort of necklaces I bought for Steuart's children and females posturing in mauve lights—mauve tights too I dare say".

Back in England, Steuart went to Leeds to perform with the British National Opera Company in Holst's *At The Boar's Head* and Bach's *Coffee Cantata*. Then followed a round of Festivals, music clubs, *Messiahs*, public schools, very much as before but even more so! And so the days wore on. Steuart himself wrote disparagingly: "My professional career was not in the least interesting. I just made a living with a few trimmings, but not 'affluence' still less opulence. My main round was with the Choral Societies of the Midlands and North—what we called the 'Oratorio Post', though I never became the legendary 'best bloody Messiah in the trade' and some concert clubs, with a fairly regular 'Passion crawl' round Easter—a highly exhausting time."

It would be exhausting for the reader, too, to take him through the pages of Steuart's Ledger, but I have picked at random one month in 1928, to show the variety, both in geography and in character, of his engagements. (The name of the conductor and/or accompanist is given in brackets):

March 3 Royal Choral Society, *Gerontius* (Elgar)
      4 Wellington College, recital lecture + folksongs (Jean Hamilton)
      5 Harley House, Mrs. E. G. Kemp, song recital (Jean Hamilton)
      7 Newbury Festival (Goldsbrough)

 9 Cambridge C.U.M.S. *Mass in B mi* (Rootham)
10 Guildford Symphony Concert (Blower)
11 Oxford Bach Choir, *St. John Passion* (W. H. Harris)
13 Worcester Festival choral, *Gerontius* (Atkins)
14 Battersea Town Hall, charity concert (Phyllis Arnott)
15 B. L. Richmond*, song recital (Jean Hamilton)
17 Southwark Cathedral, *St. Matthew Passion* (E. T. Cook)
20 Birmingham, *Magelone Lieder* (Jean Hamilton)
21 Leeds Philharmonic, *Gerontius* (Bairstow)
23 Bradford Festival Choral, *Gerontius* (Sargent)
24 Liverpool Welsh Choral, Beethoven *Mass in D* (Stiles
   Allen)
27 Derby, *B Mi Mass* (Stiles Allen)
29 Norwich, Schubert *Mass in B flat* (Bates)
30 Harrow School, judged singing competition
31 Bristol Philharmonic, *Apostles* (Baxter)

His total earnings in this month were just over £260.

From this list, we can pick out some of the highlights leaving
Steuart as an interpreter of the Evangelist in the St. Matthew
Passion to a later chapter. He sang *The Dream of Gerontius* on no
fewer than four occasions during the month. He had become a great
interpreter of the role and often sang it under Elgar's baton, both in
the Albert Hall and at the Three Choirs Festival. Of the performance
on 3rd March 1927, *The Times* wrote: "Mr Steuart Wilson sang the
part of Gerontius and his well-controlled reading of it recalled that of
Gervase Elwes, more particularly in his power of giving the words
their right declamatory value without excess ... He preserved
throughout it the atmosphere of wonder and awe conveyed by the
orchestral prelude ... In short he viewed poem and music together
as a whole."

It was his first performance with Elgar and, from all accounts, the
composer's beat was not the easiest in the world to follow. "The thing
I remember most was the kind of feeling that you caught up from
his mysterious way of conducting", Steuart recalled many years
later in a broadcast tribute. "Technically he (Elgar) was a bad
conductor, but emotionally he managed to make everybody give the
best performance of their lives."

---

* Bruce Richmond, then Editor of the *Times Literary Supplement*.

Steuart also recalled in this talk how Elgar had come to his house in Notting Hill Gate—"a part of London he had scarcely heard of" for a run-through with piano.

"When we got to the end of the Sanctus Fortis he looked rather pleased with himself and said, 'That's a good tune you know, Verdi would have been glad to write that.' I thought that was a very good one in the eye for the people who talk about a kind of sanctimonious *Gerontius*".

In the same broadcast, Steuart delighted listeners with his account of the memorial concert in 1934 after Elgar's death, where two orchestras had been engaged.

"He had always wanted to fill the Albert Hall. Looking at that appalling array of trombones and horns the whole Orchestra seemed nothing but brass and I can remember Adrian Boult saying 'Shall we keep them down?' and I said 'No, let them go, the old man would have loved them.' And how they went too! Four harps, you remember, he had great difficulty to get one while he was on earth but in Heaven he got all four harps."

An important event was the revival of Brahms' *Magelone Lieder*. Steuart, who had translated these very difficult and romantic poems by the German poet Tieck, first sang the cycle in May 1927, with Jean Hamilton as his accompanist. He had met Jean at a concert in Oxford the year before, where the first performance of Vaughan Williams's *Sancta Civitas* was given, and had been impressed by her playing. Steuart asked her: "I have always wanted to perform the *Magelone Lieder*—do you know them, would you be interested in playing for me?" She was thrilled at the prospect and they had lessons with Sir George Henschel, the great singer who had been a personal friend of Brahms and had made music with him and Clara Schumann. Jean Hamilton told me: "Henschel was then nearing 80, but was as lively and dynamic as ever—a small man, very handsome, with a curly beard and large dark flashing eyes. He was as excited as we were and the lessons were a most happy experience."

When a concert was planned, Jean Hamilton asked Steuart "Do you mind if I play by heart?" He was aghast at the prospect and

said, "But you'll show me up, I don't really know it by heart." But
he bravely took the risk and agreed.

The concert, in the Aeolian Hall on 6th May (Brahms' birthday)
went very well. Jean Hamilton remembers: "Afterwards Henschel
came to the artists room, flung his arms round me, gave me a
smacking salutation and said, 'A kiss from Brahms by proxy!'"
Henschel, according to his daughter Georgie, "thought a great deal
of Steuart's interpretation and also approved very much of his
translations of Lieder."

Although Jean Hamilton was usually Steuart's pianist in the
Magelone Lieder, there was at least one occasion when Gerald Moore
accompanied him, for Gerald remembers:

"An historic concert for me was Steuart Wilson's recital at the
Holywell Rooms, Oxford, of Brahms' Romances from Tieck's
Magelone. There are only fourteen songs in this cycle but they are
songs so long, so full of enormous technical problems for singer
and pianist alike that during fifty years of concert work I have
only performed the cycle some half-dozen times. Steuart's task on
this occasion was made much more taxing—on voice and concentration alike in that he acted as his own narrator. (Every time I
have performed or heard this work with other singers, Dietrich
Fischer-Dieskau for example, there has always been an actor or
speaker to recite between the songs, knitting the story together).
This performance with S.W. was my first performance of the work
—this splendid and glittering work—and the memory of Steuart
Wilson's singing of it will always be with me . . ."

Gerald Moore also collaborated with Steuart in a series of Decca
gramophone records*of folk-songs and Schubert's *Maid of the Mill*. He
recalls: "We recorded in that small hall in the King's Road, Chelsea,
known as the Chenil Galleries . . . His gusto, his characterization and
his intense conviction in everything he sang impressed not only me
but also the recording manager and recording staff."

Another new venture was the performance of Zoltan Kodály's
Psalmus Hungaricus. Steuart did not sing in the very first English
performance, which was at Cambridge (when Kodály stayed at
Girton Gate, my parents' home) but he was the soloist in the first

* Some of these records were re-issued as LP by Decca in 1968 "Steuart Wilson,
song recital 1929–30)."

London performance at the Queen's Hall in 1927 and again at the Three Choirs in September 1928. Kodály wrote to Dr. Herbert Sumsion, organist of Gloucester, who was conducting: "I am very touched you are preparing my work with such conscientious care . . . After such preparation and with Steuart Wilson as soloist I am sure to have a performance very wonderful."

Nearer the time, Kodály wrote again about the details:

"You are too good to occupy you even with our lodgment in London. Some hotels were us recomanded but I prefer the Gore and will write him. I think the 27th we are in London. You ask me if I wish to have Mr. Steuart Wilson to both rehearsals; naturally if he can and will even I would make a short piano rehearsal with him before the Orchestral. I hope he will not mistake this: I hear the best possible always from his mastery. With such singers is worth only to rehearsal. With many thanks for your carefulness."

The *Psalmus Hungaricus* was one of the most exciting pieces of new foreign music that had come to England for a long time, and it was received with tremendous enthusiasm by the critics. The *Morning Post* reported: "All the situations are conceived and expressed in the most dramatic fashion, especially where the soloist is concerned. Not improbably the music allotted to him is the finest of all, especially the tense passage in the middle. Mr. Steuart Wilson sang the whole of it magnificently, throwing the whole of himself into every phrase. It is a pleasure to hear so fine a musician tackle an exacting part like this."

Steuart gave concert recitals in Holland for the English Association in 1926 and 1929, singing in all the major Dutch towns. His programme included ballads and folksongs from England, Scotland and Ireland, as well as contemporary music. Mollie Hull, wife of the organist of Hereford Cathedral, P. C. Hull, was his accompanist on both visits, and at one hotel the receptionist asked "Are you married?" "Yes" replied Steuart, "but not to each other." It was in Holland that he met Anneke Schilthuis, who was to become a lifelong friend.

Let no one imagine from the account of his overloaded programme and from the solemnity of the works performed, that there was no fun in life for Steuart during this time. Whatever he was doing he made *fun* and infected others with his spontaneous gaiety. Not many people remember the details of incidents, or anecdotes which depend so much on the telling, but the general impression of zest and humour remains. A few stories survive, some of them told against himself by Steuart. Thus, the time after dashing off a train to sing the Evangelist in the *St. Matthew Passion* he arrived breathless at the concert hall and started off "Now Jesus . . . I mean Peter." And once when he was singing in the *Messiah* he discovered to his horror that he was wearing two right shoes—he "just did not know how to stand up for the pain."

On one very cold evening in Glasgow Cathedral, at a *B Minor Mass*, he sat with a hot water bottle on his lap completely enveloped in an enormous fur-lined coat which had (apocryphally) belonged to Burne-Jones.

Both Roy Henderson and Norman Allin have told me how Steuart enlivened the long and tedious railway journeys which it was their misfortune to endure, with amusing stories and how they mutually commiserated with one another on the trials of a professional singer's life.

Roy Henderson said that they made a joint tally of the slightest mistake they made during a performance—half a beat, wrong words etc. "We must have performed together well over 60 times, if not 100. The result was one all."

On the concert platform and in the artists' room, before and after performances, Steuart was always entertaining and lavish in his encouragement to his fellow soloists, especially if they were suffering from 'butterflies'. Astra Desmond has told me that he would make some quip or tell a funny story which would make it hard for the singers to keep from laughing, even in the most solemn moments. One of his favourite 'irreverent' anecdotes was about the two Conservative gentlemen who saw a poster advertising "B Minor Mass" in the Forest of Dean, during a mining strike. "What is it all about?" asked one. The other replied, "Oh, something to do with those b— miners".

CHAPTER TWELVE

OPERA

"Y OU know I'm not really an opera singer—I'm an oratorio josser." This is what Steuart told Alfred Reynolds, one day after a performance of Mozart's *Così fan Tutte* at the Royal Court Theatre in London, where Reynolds was deputy conductor to Adrian Boult. Steuart always regarded oratorio as his bread and butter, but he did not let it interfere with his appearance in opera, which was his first love. Ever since he played Tamino in the Cambridge *Magic Flute* he had cherished ambitions to become a great opera singer, and at Nice in 1924–5 he had studied the roles of Otello, Parsifal and Tristan under de Reszke. From Nice he wrote to Clive Carey:

"I feel strongly inclined to try and get a job at Vienna in the Volksoper or somewhere and get away from England . . . There is no opera in England that I would care to go in for, so it would mean living abroad most of one's life. I think that I personally shouldn't mind that a bit."

Luckily for English music, that resolve was never put to test. Steuart's main appearances in opera were with the group known as the Bristol Opera Company, which was launched in 1924, thanks to the generosity of P. Napier Miles, the wealthy landowner who had been a patron of Rutland Boughton and the Glastonbury festivals. Miles, known locally as 'Squire Miles', was himself a composer.

The Bristol season opened rather inauspiciously and amateurishly in October 1924, with a week's presentation of opera in English in the very unsuitable surroundings of the Victoria Rooms, Clifton.

The works included Purcell's *Dido and Aeneas*, Falla's *Puppet Show of Master Pedro*, Vaughan Williams's *Shepherds of the Delectable Mountains* and three operas by Napier Miles, *Markheim, Fireflies* and *Music Comes*. Steuart sent a full report to Clive Carey, which shows the struggles faced by even such a competent professional cast—it included Astra Desmond, W. Johnstone Douglas, Arthur Cranmer and Muriel Tannahill, with Adrian Boult and Malcolm Sargent sharing the conducting:

"I thought the whole show would collapse, as the builders were working absolutely up to the time of the 1st performance, the lighting was finished at 6 p.m. on Monday, the whole proscenium fell in on Friday and you couldn't get near the hall for trenches and debris and muck."

Some productions were more successful than others. Thus:

"Dido was excellently staged and sung. Aspidistra had a bad throat, the stage was dirty and the curtains shook clouds of paint dust in the air. J.D. (Johnstone Douglas) as Aeneas was good, soft singing in particular. The whole production was *most* effective. *Music Comes*, same as before, except that Napier one night got control of the lighting and it was played in *complete* obscurity, reminded me of the Marlowe Society 'Incompetent amateurs mumbling nonsense in the dark'. The *Puppet Show* was the 'clou' of the whole week. The music is quite first-rate, brilliantly clever, only wants a fine band of first-class players."

Napier Miles's opera *Fireflies* seems to have been particularly exacting. At any rate, Steuart wrote that "Adrian wrote to me beforehand that it was impossibly difficult and he couldn't face it! I had a fiendish job to learn it, every bar in a different time signature, very fast and scherzando with far too many words."

In the end he decided to dispense with the orchestra and have a piano. "If we had had orchestra there would have been a complete and irretrievable fiasco and/or buggering up." Steuart also reported that Boult had conducted the last day's performance with no rehearsals at all:

"He was quite extraordinarily good and got in some ways better performances than Malcolm did. He's not nearly so full of beans and vitality but he keeps things in hand so much better and the

H

climaxes get bigger in consequence and the whole thing steadier and more in proportion."

Of his own performance he wrote:

"I was pleased. I was right on top of the orchestra in *Markheim* and acted a good deal less stiffly. In *Fireflies*, I had my work cut out to keep the thing together and pull up the loose ends, but even so, I sang it decently and hopped lightly about the stage. What pleased me most was that I kept *absolutely* fresh and in command of my voice."

The Bristol Opera season was repeated in the autumn of 1926 in the lovely eighteenth-century Theatre Royal, on a more ambitious scale and with a more ambitious programme. It ran for three weeks and additional works in the repertoire included *Così fan Tutte*, Vaughan Williams's ballet *Old King Cole*, Stanford's *Travelling Companion*, a ballet by Clive Carey *All Fool's Day* and the first performance of Ethel Smyth's *Entente Cordiale* which she herself conducted. Many of the original performers took part, but there were some new names, among them Sumner Austin, Dorothy d'Orsay and Audrey Mildmay.

Così fan Tutte was the mainstay of the season and received enthusiastic notices. A. H. Fox Strangways in the *Observer* expressed himself delighted by the whole performance, the wit of the translation and the zest of the performers—he noted that "no clothes seemed to fit Ferrando". Such was the success of the Bristol performance that Johnstone Douglas decided, boldly, to bring *Così* to London. Thanks to the generosity of Sir Barry Jackson, the opera opened at the Kingsway Theatre on 23rd March 1927, and was transferred to the Royal Court Theatre on 18th April. It ran until 14th May, with fifty-six performances in all, establishing, as Ernest Newman pointed out, "the longest continuous run it had ever had." The cast was:

Ferrando	Steuart Wilson
Guglielmo	W. Johnstone Douglas
Don Alfonso	Arthur Cranmer
Fiordiligi	Louise Trenton
Dorabella	Dorothy d'Orsay
Despina	Vivienne Chatterton

Johnstone-Douglas produced and Adrian Boult and Alfred Reynolds shared the conducting.

Così was then a sadly neglected opera. It had not been performed in England since 1910 when Beecham revived it at His Majesty's Theatre; to most British audiences a Mozart opera meant *Figaro* or *The Magic Flute*. *Così* had been a failure when it was first performed in Vienna in 1790 and had not been widely presented on the Continent until Richard Strauss produced it at Munich at the turn of this century.

Music in England thus owes a great debt to Johnstone Douglas, Napier Miles, Steuart Wilson, Adrian Boult and the others who were responsible for reviving *Così* at Bristol, and later bringing it to London. The Beecham production had been given in Italian. The Bristol company played in English, using a translation of Da Ponte's libretto by the Rev. Marmaduke Browne.

The 1927 season was rapturously received by Londoners and by the critics.

"On recent nights the entire house has been sold out," wrote the *Observer* (3.4.27). "Last Friday night at the Kingsway, the Government was present (in the person of the Prime Minister) the Peerage was represented and the public attended to the extent of completely filling the stalls, pit, circles and gallery."

Mr. Johnstone Douglas's scrapbook of press cuttings contains a massive array of notices, nearly all wildly enthusiastic, not only from the more sedate national papers and the musical journals, but from the popular papers, the provincial weeklies and the glossy monthlies. Reviews appeared in such unexpected quarters as *Vogue*, the *Licensed Victualler*, the *Tatler*, the *Field*, the *Civil and Military Gazette* of Lahore, and *Horse and Hound*, whose music critic reported: "Everything about it is jolly—it breathes the spirit of real fun." *Punch* burst into rhyme on the occasion of the fiftieth performance:

> "Here's to an Opera's fiftieth night
> Here's to its welcome longevity
> Here's to the company merry and bright
> Linked in beneficent levity
> Let the prig snort, here's to the sport
> Furnished by Love and Mozart at the Court."

The more serious and sophisticated critics were full of praise for the excellence of the ensemble work and the balance of the performance. Ernest Newman wrote: "The performance is good, the production is charming . . . the principals sing well and act intelligently as individuals besides making an excellent team." There was high praise for Steuart's performance, both as a singer and an actor. Many people suggested that the Bristol group could form the nucleus for a permanent Mozartian opera house in London.

The only sour note was struck by W. J. Turner in the *New Statesman*, seeing it during its second London run. He said that the majority of the large audience present seemed to enjoy the performance whole-heartedly, and "When I left at the end of the Second Act, not being able to stand another five minutes of it, I left alone." The singing of the principals was "extremely crude and insensitive" and the orchestra playing under Boult was "of the same rigid mechanical character." He was particularly scathing about Ferrando:

"The tenor was, as tenors usually are, not a tower of strength, but a source of weakness. It is extremely rare to hear a good English tenor . . . but even an English tenor might be more flexible and expressive and less brittle and sticklike than this Ferrando."

Mr. Turner was alone, not only in leaving the theatre before the end, but in his judgement.

The 1927 season broke even—just—but it had given its sponsors some anxious moments. Steuart wrote to Clive Carey (11th July 1927):

"We are rather broke, as usual, as owing to the jobs I had to cancel while *Così* was on I lost about £150. *Così* brought in £55 a piece odd, after paying all guarantees back in full. Not bad as a result, but little enough for eight weeks' work."

Financially and musically, however, the first season was successful enough for Johnstone-Douglas to venture a second season at the Royal Court. This opened on 29th May 1928 with *Così*, for one week. Then for a fortnight, there was a Triple Bill, with the two Bristol successes, *The Shepherds* and *The Puppet Show*, and Schubert's early opera, *The Faithful Sentinel*, translated by Steuart. From 26th June to

7th July, the company presented Cimarosa's *Secret Marriage* and the
season wound up with a final week of *Così*. Boult was again the
conductor-in-chief.

The *Faithful Sentinel (Der Vierjahrige Posten)* was composed when
Schubert was only 16 and seems to have been too naïve for some of
the critics. Much to Steuart's dismay, it received some very bad
reviews—*The Times* said it was "an empty little piece which dragged
through the best part of an hour". But the *Observer* wrote that the
three principals, Steuart Wilson, Dorothy Silk and Astra Desmond
"gave us in a small theatre musical singing such as we only dream of
in a large one," and the *Daily Herald* noted "Steuart Wilson, as the
deserter sweetheart is in wonderful voice."

That year, London audiences proved fickle and apart from turning up in large numbers for *Così*, they did not give the Bristol company the support it deserved. The second season was a financial
flop. The idea that the company could form the nucleus of a permanent small opera house in London was to prove a pipe-dream.
No more shows were planned, either in London 'or in Bristol. The
company disbanded and dispersed, and never performed together
again.

For Steuart, the collapse of the plans which he and Johnstone-
Douglas had built up was a serious blow, both financially and
professionally. Ann told Iris Lemare: "*Così* having gone phut, we
are broke to the wide and can do nothing but sit tight and hope for
the best. Bloody, ain't it!"

It was Steuart's last appearance on the London operatic stage for
some years, although he continued to take part in various operatic
enterprises in the provinces, such as the production of *Il Seraglio* at
the home of Lord Glentanar in Aberfoyle, *Acis and Galatea* at Winchester and Alton, and Bach's *Coffee Cantata*.* He never appeared on
the stage at Glyndebourne, but it is amusing to find him turning up
at John Christie's house one Sunday in June 1928 (in between the
runs at the Royal Court) for a concert performance of Act III of *The
Meistersinger*. Steuart sang Walther, to John Christie's Beckmesser,
before an invited audience of friends, house guests, tenants and

---

* In fact the last record of a London opera performance was in Dennis Arundell's
production of *Tantivy Towers* by A. P. Herbert and Thomas Dunhill at the Lyric,
Hammersmith in June 1935. Steuart was Hugh Heather, the fox-hunting gentleman, with Maggie Teyte as Lady Ann Gallop and Frank Phillips as Captain
Bareback.

employees. He adored singing the Preislied—what tenor doesn't?—and included it in his repertoire as often as possible.

But the failure of *Così* put an end to his dreams of becoming an opera josser. For all his musicianship, it is extremely doubtful whether he could have made a success as a tenor in grand opera, in the Gigli style. He might have, before the War, but his reduced lung power would have placed him under great strain in filling Covent Garden, La Scala or the Vienna Opera. He certainly didn't have the figure of the traditional Siegfried, being thin, almost gaunt, at this time.

There was some divergence of opinion about his acting ability. Johnstone-Douglas told me many years later,

"As a producer I was always keen to have him in the cast. Though not a great actor, he was always most co-operative with a delightful sense of humour."

But Arthur Bliss thought Steuart was "a very fine actor."

Any doubts about the dramatic content of Steuart's singing were dispelled by his performances in the stage productions of Handel oratorios, for which the Cambridge University Musical Society became justly famous in the early 1930s. He took the parts of Samson in 1932 and Jephtha in 1934. Both performances could be classed as part-opera and part-oratorio. The Cambridge Guildhall was not equipped as a theatre and the performers had little room to manœuvre on the stage. Writing of *Samson, The Times* critic (29th February 1932) said that Mrs. Camille Prior (the doyenne of Cambridge productions) had applied "the classical methods of Greek drama, rightly and successfully . . . to the Handelian music-drama of the eighteenth century." The costumes and scenery, designed by Gwen Raverat, reproducing the Minoan civilization from Cretan vases, were exceptionally striking.

Steuart, bewigged and bearded, with his eyes blacked out and in a loose white tunic, was led on in chains by a small child (Sophie Raverat, Gwen's younger daughter). His singing of "Total Eclipse" was most moving and dramatic and, said *The Times*, gained in poignancy from being acted, rather than sung as a tenor's 'exhibition piece'.

There was an unforgettable incident at the dress rehearsal. Dr. Rootham, who was conducting, called out rather crossly: "Steuart,

I wish you'd watch my beat." To which Steuart replied: "Rootham
—don't you know I'm blind!"

Margaret Field-Hyde was the other professional in both productions, playing Dalila in Samson and Iphis, Jephtha's daughter. Both
won much praise from the reviewers. Of Steuart's performance
in Jephtha, Percy Young, writing in *The Gownsman*, said he was
"mightily impressive . . . 'Deeper and deeper still' is one of the great
moments of the work. Here Mr. Wilson appeared as a fine dignified
actor and his final 'I can no more' was accomplished with the
supreme dignity of compressed despair."

CHAPTER THIRTEEN

AMBASSADOR OF MUSIC

B Y the late 1920s, Steuart had acquired an international as
well as a national reputation. He visited the United States for
the first time in the autumn of 1929. His visit was arranged by
the Music Teachers Association and he had been approached by a
Miss Glenn of Kansas City at a teachers' conference in Lausanne
that summer, to ask if he would sing at some school concerts. He
agreed with alacrity and suggested a fee of £50 a week plus travelling
expenses. His agent John Tillett was shocked—"You ought to have
asked for £50 a concert," he said.

Steuart wrote about his American experiences in his autobiographical fragment:

"The conditions appeared arduous; but the party was a young
pianist, Dalies Franz, and myself only. The programme could
remain constant, being shortened or lengthened as the local
demand was known. The Touring arrangements were made by an
agent who had managed Chatanqua circuits. That name conveyed nothing to me, but it was a sort of educational Y.W.C.A.
combined with a circus and a theatre or variety show, descending
like a travelling fair upon large centres for some weeks, small
places for a one-night stand. We had to collect a certain share of
the whole fee which was paid in instalments, finance our own
travel and remit balances due to the year. I was the more experienced and was accountant in chief. Our programme was
extremely, severely in fact, classical. My opening numbers were
Bach, Handel, Schubert and Dalies Franz played Mozart,

Beethoven and Chopin. As a *bonne bouche* he would throw off Liszt or Godovsky arrangements and I sang the Mountain Songs arranged by Howard Brockway and the great favourite was Moussorgsky's 'Song of the Flea'.

Our tour was well arranged geographically, so that with a minimum of travelling we could get in five concerts a week and one week we managed to pile in nine. Three in one day with a long motor ride between number one at 9.30 a.m. and number two at 3.30 p.m. about 100 miles away, number three a train journey from 5–6.30 and then thirty miles in a taxi to a Training College. So long as you keep the same programme this is no strain at all."

Steuart was not particularly knowledgeable about world finance, but nobody could avoid the subject in the winter of 1929—when the great Recession was sweeping the States. He wrote:

"It was, for the U.S.A. the year of disaster. I had landed in New York on the very day the Stock Market collapsed and brokers and speculators were throwing themselves into the street. It was a common wisecrack that if you rented a room in a hotel, the reception clerk would say 'Is it for sleeping or leaping?'"

His own tour, however, lay entirely in the Middle West, which was not affected to the same extent as the Eastern seaboard. He enjoyed the small-town atmosphere which reminded him of Rochdale at the turn of the century.

But the Middle West was a cultural desert, and he deplored the scarcity of bookshops and the absence of theatres and concerts, except in the larger towns. He went to a few football games but found the technique and strategy beyond comprehension. The weekends were mostly "deadly dull with no escape in any direction." Steuart made a pretty close study of Prohibition and how people got round it. He himself was teetotal at this time—having been forbidden because of his health to touch alcohol.

"It was Prohibition time and all the effort was to stop alcohol traffic. The law could not, however, do more than prevent alcohol, in any proportion that could have any effect, being transported from any one to any other place. Hence the 'bootleggers' who bribed their way into business; or another strictly legal form of bootlegging was to transfer wine at such a low temperature that the percentage of alcohol was deliberately kept low. Keep in a nice warm place and it would revive and become wine—drinkable in a moment of desperation. Or again, you got someone with enough elementary chemical knowledge to home-brew what was known as 'bath-tub' gin. If the prescription went at all wrong or the chemical ingredients were impure, the result could be either intensely disagreeable or mildly or severely emetic or, in rather rare cases, fatal. The Volstead Act may have stopped some people drinking, but it seemed to me to ensure that those who did drink did so at far greater risk. There were numerous stories: my favourite of an obvious Prohibition agent hailing a taxi on Broadway: 'Take us somewhere where we can get a drink.' Up Broadway they went, after an hour the agent says 'Here, how much further are you taking us?' Answer from the taxi driver 'To Canada'."

The whole trip was exhausting, with long-distance travelling in cruelly cold weather and blizzards. Steuart wrote "All the same, it is very comfortable travel, Pullmans are good and one can sleep in them." No such luck on one journey to Indianapolis from Kansas city, where he had sung in *The Messiah* with a Swedish choir and "a foully bad orchestra—only their hearts in the right place, nothing else." *En route*, he wrote:

"In this Pullman there is a baby who wakes up and yells every now and then—it isn't a sleeper but a 'chair' car or Parlour Car— and a fat man who goes to sleep and snores and the man behind him shouts 'Wake up' and the man in front leans over him and suddenly makes a noise like a dog and everyone shouts with laughter and the man looks a fool and the baby yells and the cycle begins all over again."

He took to America as much as America took to him. American audiences quickly succumbed to his charm and were thrilled by what they called his 'brogue'. Steuart ended one of his letters:

'Well I must be off now to sing to 1,800 children and see them smile at each other when they hear my 'English accent'. That's what makes me a success . . . Quite definitely I have fallen among people who are sympathetic to my view of music, and that is a great thing. I have managed to make them think that what I do is what they ought to like, and they do like it. So far so good."

Steuart paid a second visit to the States the following winter, first of all with the group known as the "New English Singers" (Dorothy Silk, Nellie Carson, Joyce Sutton, Steuart Wilson, Norman Notley and Cuthbert Kelly.) "This tour," he wrote to a friend, "has been harder work than the others. To begin with I've been keeping the accounts and writing the reports to the manager and generally doing the business side . . . I find I can do it quite easily and balance up every night without being more than a few cents out any time." He then branched out on his own, giving recitals in New York and other Eastern cities, where the audiences were more sophisticated than in the Middle West.

"The New York recital went off very well as far as a 'succés d'estime' was concerned and very well as far as Press notices— but there was a fearful snowstorm and I got no audience at all, hardly visible in the gloom. However it's the Press that counts as usual, and I'm quite pleased with the result."

In the winter of 1932/3 he again went to America, but found the general atmosphere increasingly unfavourable for concert-giving:

"You've no idea how depressing this visit is. Everyone seems without hope and all they can do is to abuse either their Govt. (or ours) or else say it can't be worse so it must be better soon. Meanwhile the whole entertainment business is entirely shot to pieces, plays can't run, even films can't play to more than half empty houses and as for music! Why there's no one can fill a hall in these days. Everywhere the streets are full of men walking up and down if the weather is sunny, standing huddled in a doorway or under an awning if it's cold or wet. Just passing the time—no hope of a job of any sort."

He travelled out on this third visit with Gustav Holst, on the *Bremen*. Holst was conducting in Boston and New York. Steuart wrote:

"I heard the *Planets*; it was beautifully played but rather stylist and a bit finicky, quite unlike the English performances. He said he had lots of mistakes at the first show which I didn't hear, bars miscounted and so on. They aren't accustomed to getting a work ready in a short time. The strings are wonderful, the brass good, the woodwind, particularly reeds, rather colourless."

Steuart found the going hard. "It's a dreadful year and no one can get any good jobs," he wrote from New York. But life had its compensations. He spent a fortnight in Cambridge, Mass. with friends where he had "a marvellously good time but very little work indeed. However, the depression hasn't affected the nymphs!" He also went to concerts where he heard "some modern music— Prokofiev and a young Russian called Shostakovitch.

The N.Y. Press thinks the end of the world has come. They are intensely conservative here and only welcome new music if it is American and thoroughly nice! Stokowski rams new Russian music down their throats but they don't like it. I heard his famous orchestra and it really is everything they say about it—it is marvellous and so acutely musical and utterly free from show-manship in any form at all."

Steuart gave recitals in Boston, Philadelphia and Nova Scotia and, before coming home, had a trip to Toronto,

"stopping off at Niagara to do a little rubber-necking on the way. I've never seen the falls. They aren't much to look at in Winter but better than not seeing them at all. They light them up at night in the modern manner—unless the depression has killed that too— Too Swiss!"

Steuart arrived back in England—also riddled with depression and unemployment—in February 1933. He immediately set about organizing the arrangements for a tour of Australia. He wrote from America:

"The latest plan is that I go to Australia at the end of May for concerts there, returning in October. The guarantee is quite good and it looks like being quite a successful trip. I've planned to stop off and see Sister Margaret in the Solomon Islands *en route*. I shall probably buy an island and settle down with three black wives".

He left England in June and returned in mid-November. It was a hectic, but rewarding visit. He adjudicated at festivals and school competitions in Perth, Brisbane, Queensland and Melbourne and also gave a number of recitals.

As in America, Steuart regarded it as his role to "make them think that what I do is what they ought to like". I have found on yellowing paper, headed Savoy Hotel, Perth, West Australia, a hand-written draft—whether it was for a broadcast or a lecture I don't know, but it throws an illuminating light on Steuart's thinking in his 44th year. It amounts to a personal credo.

"Music is my sole reason of existence in this world, I have no other claim to be a useful citizen of the world, still less of any town in which I chance to live, so it behoves me sometimes to sit down and think what it is that I mean to do with my life—though God knows too much that I have failed over and over again. But I must imagine that there are some people listening who wonder what is this Music he speaks of, is it just the singing at concerts, or the teaching of pupils, or what is vaguely called appreciation? Or perhaps some who are listening are themselves fond of Music, but cannot believe that a man can find life in it. I know I am a bold, even a foolish man to speak to you about this but here I am ... I have a confession to make; that I have always been more moved by music than I care to admit, that it has always been present with me and that I have loved it too well sometimes, loving not only the spirit of music which should have made me go on and work harder at the other tasks of life, but I have been content sometimes to give myself up too much to the daydreams of music, as we all are. But in the practical life of a musician who must earn his living by transmitting his day dreams into hard work, this has been of necessity altered, but not without an attempt on my part to preserve the dream in my mind. The use of music in the human life is to keep sweet what might otherwise go sour, to keep our belief in the reality that lies behind the visible substance of things and to remind ourselves that there is a permanent way of escape open from the world that closes in upon us. . . .

One can be a clergyman and believe in a Creed and set up to it without blushing, because it has the sanction of ages, because it is the property of a community, and the faith for which your forefathers suffered. How can music be compared to this? It cannot in honest truth. We cannot say honestly 'I believe in Beethoven, in Michaelangelo and Milton' and expect that it will convince the world. Yet when Constantine said of the symbol of the Cross 'In hoc signo vinces' 'in this sign thou shalt conquer' he was giving it as a motto to everyone who leads a life devoted to one special purpose. Music is the stuff of which the cloth of beauty is woven, it is a tissue which is imperishable, the secret of weaving it is not lost nor secret. It is open to every human heart to learn and to appreciate, but not without work. Do you remember the words of Wordsworth I quoted just now 'it binds together by passion and knowledge the vast empire of human souls'. These words are thrilling to me, passion and knowledge. The exactness of accuracy of knowledge, meticulous, exacting, perhaps even pernickety, all caught up in the radiant glow of passion and transformed to something greater than we can believe—something greater than we could create for ourselves.

Music is so bound up in my mind with Poetry and Beauty, in all forms that I cannot detach it, but may I in conclusion read to you a fragment again from Shelley.

> I pant for the Music which is divine
>   My heart in its thirst is a dying flower
> Pour forth the sound like enchanted wine
>   Loosen the notes in a silver shower
> Like a heartless plain for the gentle rain
>   I gasp I faint till they wake again."

What struck him most about Australia was the vast musical potential and the thirst for music which was not being slaked. On his return to England he wrote an article in *The Times*: "The famous advice said to have been given by one distinguished performer to another 'Sing them muck' has too long ruled the policy of music-makers. This advice . . . has been faithfully followed." But, he said in a broadcast talk:

"There *is* a musical Australia, containing a sufficiently large population to be worth more consideration than the musical legislators have yet given it." The very first question put to a visiting musician was: "Tell us about modern music in England, we never get anything new out here." He found that the contemporary

music of Vaughan Williams and Holst, which he included in his
programme, aroused more interest even than the Elizabethans and
folksongs.

As an example of the attitude of 'playing down' to the audiences
which he so much deprecated, he quoted the case of the organist in
Queensland who played a Bach prelude and fugue—

> "Result was considerable applause. He then turned to the
> audience saying: 'Now I'll play you something you'll like' and
> burst into an arrangement of some shop-ballad: result some very
> perfunctory applause. Many a moral may be taken from that
> story, but the moral on which I should lay most stress is the
> extreme folly of a musician thinking his audience is as stupid as
> himself."

In Melbourne, his great friend the organist William McKie was
playing to steadily increasing audiences at the Town Hall, attracting
as many as 1,200 for his all-Bach programmes, 'the peak-load being
reached with the Passacaglia'. Steuart was impressed with the
efforts of the Australian Broadcasting Commission. The experience
of the A.B.C.'s general manager, he wrote in *The Times*,

> "has included schoolmastering, soldiering, managing theatres and
> circuses and governing a gaol and if in the course of this ex-
> perience Major Condor has not become an expert in music, at
> least he has not acquired a trace of the self-satisfaction that glows
> like a stage sunset over Portland Place . . . Australia is not a gold
> mine any longer and the Commission does not pretend to bound-
> less wealth. But it offers just what is denied to our young per-
> formers in England, the opportunity of performance in public;
> and more than that, the opportunity of being an ambassador of
> the good name of English music."

The good name of English music could have had no better ambassador than Steuart Wilson. It was a role he was to play again,
more than twenty years later, not as a singer, but as a teacher and
lecturer.

CHAPTER FOURTEEN

STRESSES AND STRAINS

EVERYBODY knew that Steuart Wilson had been seriously
wounded in the War; but what was not so generally known
and what few among his audiences can have realized, was his
constant battle against physical pain and suffering caused by his
duodenal ulcer. Only his own family and those in his circle of
closest friends knew about his struggle—Astra Desmond has described it as "a triumph of mind over matter." The constant mug of
milk at his side was the only visible token of his condition.

Steuart himself took an enormous interest in his inside, and in the
techniques of the various specialists and surgeons—no doubt remembering that at one time he had wanted to become a doctor. His illness
was the central theme of the autobiographical fragment which he
was in the middle of writing when he died in 1966. Called "Me and
my Ulcer", it contained graphic details of his haemorrhages and of
the different treatments he underwent.

In "Me and my Ulcer" Steuart posed the crucial problem:

"The perpetual question was whether you should cancel your
date when you felt pretty grimly ulcerous, or was it only when you
had such a bad cold or throat you couldn't get out a single
tolerable sound? Was it better to disappoint by *not* singing, or to
disappoint by singing badly? Does one wait till the last moment, or
does one realize at the first feeling of that touch of hard leather at
the back of the throat that the battle is already lost? Only those
who have faced this decision know how impossible it is to decide
wisely."

V. WINCHESTER COLLEGE FOOTBALL XV — *1907*
(STEUART WITH FOOTBALL)

VI. THREE GENERATIONS — 1925
(STEUART WITH HIS FATHER, MOTHER, WIFE AND CHILDREN)

VII. THE ENGLISH SINGERS, 1920
CUTHBERT KELLY, CLIVE CAREY, STEUART WILSON
FLORA MANN, LILLIAN BERGER, WINIFRED WHELEN

VIII. AT THE GLASTONBURY FESTIVAL — 1924

IX. IL SERAGLIO — 1927

These doubts assailed him after a particularly cruel attack in Edinburgh in 1928:

"I had a disastrous day, New Year's Day *Messiah* in Edinburgh, 11 a.m., no rehearsal and an evening concert of Scots music to follow. I was put up by some kind but servantless friends and on that morning I made up my bed as some token of good will and as I did, the unmistakable signs of haemorrhage occurred again. It was 10 o'clock and I couldn't find the courage to tell my hosts. I crawled up to the Hall; I expect I sang pretty badly. I had difficulty in getting a glass of milk—not a common request at that time in that place—the evening concert had to be gone through and some faint attempt at joviality, but I was clearly a 'bleeding failure'."

The Edinburgh Hogmanay attack was one of the worst, but as long ago as 1921 he wondered whether he "could hold out on the concert platform without being sick". Possibly, he wrote, the trouble had started even before then, for he remembered feeling extremely ill in Paris in 1908, when he was watching Nijinsky dancing in *Les Sylphides*. He recalled his

"rapt emotion when the curtain went up that I had suddenly entered another world. And to this day that particular Chopin prelude will still recall that special enchantment. I had never seen ballet before in any form, so I remembered it well, including the struggles to conceal and suppress my rising bursts of uneasy sensation, not yet worthy to be called pain".

He had had similar experiences when out walking and camping, and when he went for long times without food. During the War he had frequent attacks of what he termed the 'belly-ache'.

The first major attack occurred in London May 1924. He was then staying with his friend Fox Strangways, in Lansdowne Crescent, on the eve of a Bach Choir concert.

"I went to bed at the usual hour, feeling nothing unusual. I woke up some time during the night and got out of bed to get a drink of water from the tooth-glass but I found myself, mysteriously, flat on the floor, for how long I don't know. I got back into bed and slept again, but awoke with a thirst. So I went down the passage to the small handbasin carrying the water bottle to get a drink; once more I was surprised to find myself flat and the water bottle broken. I returned to bed, puzzled but not feeling anything unusual ... In the morning I could see from my face that something had happened, for I was dead-white, even to the gums of my teeth, and with a concert that evening I felt insecure ... The kind old Foxy came with me by taxi to the Harley Street area where my masseur practised and I saw him and reported what had happened and asked if he had, by accident, broken my neck—but he saw nothing wrong. I thought that while I was there I would go to see my throat specialist, the late Geoffrey Caste, then assistant to Sir Milsom Rees. I had scarcely gone up half the stairs to his room before he said 'What's happened to you? Go back to bed and I'll send a doctor to you.' So back to Lansdowne Crescent and telephone to cancel Concert and alert home; arrangements made for coming down to Steep, local GP informed and the general machine of invalidism set in motion."

Steuart decided to consult Sir William Arbuthnot Lane, the famous surgeon. He entered one of Lane's nursing homes in Manchester Street and was operated upon on 30th May 1924. He took with him, as reading matter, works by Romain Rolland and Zola, *Clarissa Harlowe* and a score of Schubert symphonies and wrote to a friend, shortly before the anaesthetic took over: "I go under the axe in a few minutes ... I shan't be visible for a week. Nightingales and hemlock. Keats at once and in a few minutes the drowsy numbness will be coming over me."

He was very miserable. He read *The Times* in bed but found it hurt too much to open it, and one very hot day, he saw a full page advertisement for beer, which made him "weep without shame". He was allowed two tablespoonfuls of water. "However, one day it was all over—I was discharged and my kind Sister provided a luxurious private ambulance in which I sailed down to Steep in a scarlet dressing-gown and was actually seen in Guildford High Street looking like a Cardinal in procession."

Despite the savage nature of his handling, Steuart remained an ardent advocate of Lane's methods.

"Arbuthnot Lane," he wrote, "had the fiercest critics among his own profession, but I had learned to respect his sanity of view, which was often suspect, and to admire with good reason his generosity. He would take no fee and wrote a report to the Medical Board which gave me an increase of 100 per cent in my wound pension. He also introduced me to 'Curtis's Abdominal Belt' a remarkable piece of engineering, a steel pad, shaped to the belly, fitted with a hoop and truss pads at the base of the spine. It was painful to begin with, but before long it was forgotten. Except when playing tennis at the net, I missed a smart return, was hit plumb amidships and the ball bounced back into court, I claimed that singers' diaphragms could always do that sort of thing—and I was believed."

Arbuthnot Lane did not mince words about Steuart's health. "I dare say Ann told you that Lane takes a very alarmist view of the future," Steuart wrote to his father "but I know him well enough to be aware that he must be taken with a very strong pinch of salt." Later: "Both Arbuthnot Lane and Nathan Mutch (his son-in-law) are very kind in their visits. Mutch warns me that in future I shall have to 'make my life centre round my duodenum'." Mutch also told him that his condition was due 50 per cent to war injuries and 50 per cent to refusing to admit them as a handicap.

Arbuthnot Lane advised Steuart that "an itinerant life as a singer with irregular meals, long travelling, etc., would ruin your health" and ended up with this homily: "Some men have money, some have health, you'll have neither." And to Steuart's parents he wrote: "I think if your son can get a permanent post where he will be fed regularly and well looked after, he will do very well. The irregular life he has led up to the present must cease. Even a man in robust health could not stand it for long."

Steuart, like Oscar Wilde, did not 'mind his doctor's orders'. "I couldn't very well get out of singing—into what? . . . I had to go through with it," he wrote.

The result was that in the summer of 1926 we find him again feeling faint and sick, and diagnosing the old familiar symptoms. This time, he was placed under the care of Dr. Mutch and sent to the Sister Agnes Hospital, near Belgrave Square, where he was subjected to medical rather than surgical care. He returned home a month later with a new diet sheet and more warnings.

"The diet sheet was nicknamed by my friends 'The Path' and I

kept to it fairly conscientiously. I soon realized that my fore-
boding to my Medical Board in 1915 would ring true like an
empty glass—no wine, no spirits—I couldn't afford them anyway, but it was an agony to stay for some musical occasion at the
houses of the hospitable rich and have to refuse vintage port and
Napoleon's own brandy. Once, after a concert in Leeds, the
conductor Keith Douglas laid on a beer party and I went for hot
milk. A good laugh at that, so when they said 'Same again all
round' I took my glass and so on, out of bravado for four or five
rounds, and I wasn't going to contract out.

At one house I showed my 'Path' on the demand of my hostess.
It started off, unfortunately with 'No tough meat'. 'Well that's a
thing you won't get here' and not much sympathy after that! Lane
was a great believer in 'roughage' for the digestion and bulk,
rather than concentrated, food. He told a story of the visitor at the
Zoo, who noticed an elephant eating the besom while the keeper
wasn't watching and then breaking off the stick and chewing that.
He warned the keeper what was happening. 'Don't you worry' says
the keeper. 'He knows what's good for him. He's constipated,
that's all."

In spite of surgery, treatment and dieting, Steuart had a recurrence and, after battling through a herculean programme during
1928, he gave up all work in the autumn and went into retreat at his
London home for three months.

He sent out a very impersonal round robin to his friends and
colleagues on 22nd October 1928 cancelling all his engagements
until Christmas.

"I know that you will be sympathetic and I venture to suggest
that the best way of showing this would be neither to telephone
nor to write, asking for news, because there will be no news, and
our household is not equipped for dealing with much extra work.
I shall withdraw into a strict seclusion for a limited period without
visitors and I hope that no one will be anxious on my account or
think that we are placed in any difficulty."

The rule of privacy was very strictly observed, and the enforced
rest turned out to be a blessing in disguise. It was in this period that
Steuart made his deep and penetrating study of the Evangelist's part
in the *St. Matthew Passion* (See appendix D).

In addition to his physical suffering, Steuart was probably under-going considerable emotional stress at this time. I do not know at what point, or why, his marriage to Ann began to go wrong. He never talked about it to me—indeed he was always too absorbed in the immediate task of the day (whether it was mending an electric kettle, preparing a stew for supper or writing a broadcast or lecture), to hark back into the past, particularly the unhappy past.

Jean Hamilton told me that when she went to see Steuart in the autumn of 1928, to discuss the *St. Matthew Passion*, he was being "devotedly tended by his wife and surrounded by his children." Others have suggested that there was some cooling-off even by then and a letter which Steuart wrote to a friend about that time reflects the mounting tension: "Human affairs are always in a muddle and if we straighten out one, we are only preparing another, so it seems to me. At any rate that seems to be my fate."

One friend noticed that Steuart was becoming somewhat over-powered by constant flattery and adulation and thought that Ann was perhaps feeling rather out of it. Steuart was enormously attrac-tive to women, who swarmed round him like bees round a honey-pot.

It isn't really hard to see why things went wrong. The answer lies in the Ledger, in that remorseless treadmill, day after day, night after night, on the concert platform, or the festival round. Steuart had all too little time to spend with his wife and family. Not only was he earning the daily bread, but he was utterly absorbed in music, to the exclusion of all else. I was told that at Steep, when Ann was in the middle of changing a nappy or some other chore, Steuart would suddenly ring up from somewhere and say "Please find such and such a score, or parts, from a certain drawer", and expect her to drop everything she was doing for the search.

Ann was herself musical and had a charming singing voice, but Steuart never encouraged her to develop it professionally. This, too, may have been a bone of contention. The daughter of a naval officer, she had a conventional background and may have been irked by the Bohemianism and irregularity of a musician's life, and felt a lack of security. She was several years younger than Steuart, who cannot have been altogether easy to live with in those days.

Steuart had been deeply saddened by the death of his mother in 1926 and was worried about his father, who came to Steep, to live on his own—when Steuart and Ann moved to 23 Chepstow Villas.

Canon Wilson lived there until his death in 1931. The old man was becoming increasingly deaf, though he took a lively interest in things and was devoted to his grandchildren. He was becoming increasingly preoccupied with death and Steuart remembers, one day in Steep post office, his father asked him in a loud voice: "Steuart, do you believe in life after death?" Steuart replied that in fact he did not, but did not think it a suitable topic for discussion in the post office. "Why not?" said the Canon.

Canon Wilson was convinced he was going to die and wanted the words included in his obituary "Canon Wilson died somewhat suddenly." In fact he died peacefully in his sleep at the age of 95 and was buried in Steep churchyard. By his express wish, only his children attended the funeral.

It was not until after his death, that the final break-up took place between Steuart and Ann. Steuart did the 'gentlemanly' thing, very much on the lines of A. P. Herbert's *Holy Deadlock*, and 'committed adultery' in a London hotel with an unnamed lady. Whoever she was, she had a sense of humour, for she was said to have noticed a hole in one of his socks and remarked "I don't look after you very well, do I?" The decree nisi was granted on 12th May 1932 and made absolute on 21st November.

The Wilsons had seemed to the outside world a well-matched couple and all but their closest friends were taken by surprise. In those days, when divorce was a scandal and had ruined many political and professional careers, the tongues wagged and the gossip mounted. Even today, nearly forty years later, I have found many people in Petersfield unwilling to talk about it and tending to take sides.

Steuart was bitterly hurt and for some time full of self-reproach. Ann married Adrian Boult in 1933, and it meant, for Steuart, the loss of a close friend, as well as of a wife. His mood was reflected in a letter he wrote to my sister Katharine to congratulate her on her engagement to George Thomson:

"I am delighted to hear the news. I'm not cynical about other people's happiness and I hope I never shall be . . . My very best love and good wishes to you. You have been a very kind friend to me and I value that a lot—at a time when it was most grateful to feel that I hadn't lost all my friends."

As time went on, he became more philosophical. He wrote to his friend Anneke in February 1934 that he thought he had had "to bear rather more than his fair share of blame ... But let that all pass." And in November of that year:

"Yes, Anneke, I *am* happy. I have failed to get one kind of happiness and perhaps I should have never attempted it if I had known myself better at the time, but I can't let the rest of my life be a failure because of that and I am determined it should not become a failure. I think I can always find something useful to do and some people to be useful to, and even if I have failed in the most obvious ways I may yet succeed in some smaller and less obvious ways ... I don't see many people because I'm away a lot. Some of my friends look a little down their noses but on the whole, people don't shun me. If they do I don't blame them for acting in accordance with what they believe to be their principles ..."

The divorce had some effect on him professionally. Being very conscientious, he thought it necessary to advise the authorities of Worcester Cathedral, where he was booked for the Three Choirs Festival. He wrote about this in his autobiography:

"It is—or at any rate, it was—difficult to keep one's private life and one's public appearances completely separate. When in 1931 I had made my first marriage a failure and divorce seemed the only solution, I had to take certain professional decisions in advance. I felt that I ought to warn the Dean of Worcester, for it would be the Three Choirs Festival in that Cathedral in 1932. I knew the Worcester ecclesiastical point of view; my father was no longer alive but I remembered previous scandals—an eminent singer, whose personal affairs had not yet reached such publicity as comes to the ears of Deans and Chapters, was engaged, together with the eminent musician with whom she was living 'in sin'. But when they each achieved divorce and got married, they were immediately barred as ecclesiastically and morally unfit. Similarly when I was unable to be engaged at Worcester, my place was taken by a singer whose private life was open to considerable moral speculation, but there, once again, so long as it is kept out of the public eye it is nobody's business to complain.

"The Church authorities differed in their views. The Minster of York continued to tolerate, even to welcome my presence and William Temple as Archbishop thanked me in person."

But the other cathedrals of the Three Choirs "felt obliged to maintain a common front" and Steuart was barred from all the Festivals. He did not re-appear until, at Worcester in 1957, he read the narrative of Honegger's *King David*—an appearance, he told Christopher Ede which would have made his grandfather (the Dean) turn in his grave.

Another cathedral to bar Steuart was St. Albans, where he had an engagement to sing in the spring of 1936. Steuart wrote a letter to Bishop Furse:

"Dear Lord Bishop,

Mr. Cuthbert Osmond, deputed by the Dean of St. Albans, has just been to see me to convey your personal veto against my singing in the Abbey in April. That you can thus proclaim that one particular lapse from morality can *never* be atoned, at least not before the Church seems to me to be hard, but not so hard to bear as the knowledge that my name has been for weeks prominently displayed as about to sing in the Abbey, and no protest from anyone was raised until I imagine some 'common informer' would drag to light the now five-year-old misfortune. Is there any other crime that would be so treated either by men or by the Church—I am sorry to draw this distinction? Had I been in prison many a hand would have been held out and it would be thought to be counted a Christian duty and pleasure to help me to my feet again and to say nothing of my past. But it appears to be in the matter of divorce a Christian duty to rake up the past as often as possible, in order that it may continue to injure me."

"Your Lordship's obedient servant,
Steuart Wilson"

The Rt. Rev. The Lord Bishop of St. Albans.

A postcard from the Bishop's secretary . . . "Your letter has been received and will have his attention," was the end of the correspondence.

It is small wonder that Steuart felt increasingly bitter about the Church Establishment.

CHAPTER FIFTEEN

EVANGELIST

IT is now time to consider Steuart in what might be regarded as the centre-piece of his professional career—his singing of the Evangelist in the Bach *Passions*. He had long been interested in the singing of the Recitative and as early as February 1913, he wrote to his mother:

"All that recitative which is mere narrative ought to be sung just as if one was reading it at the same pace and with the accents on the words that demand them. Every time I have heard it I have been annoyed with the false accents given and the lack of rhythm in it generally. One finds that the most stressed word is generally something like 'He turned to them SAYING or Jesus answered and SAID, with huge emphasis on the perfectly ordinary cadences like Clara Butt singing the *Messiah*".

He did not actually sing the part until Easter 1920 when the *St. Matthew Passion* was performed in Worcester Cathedral, although he was already making a name for himself as an interpreter of Bach in the *B Minor Mass* and the *Magnificat*. He sang the Passion in York Minster for Dr. Bairstow the following year—this was to become a regular annual event.

In 1924 he wrote to Iris Lemare: "You know I'm singing the Narrator in the Matth *Passion* for the Bach Choir in the East End? I've long wanted to do it and only twice had the chance, outside one small show." This performance was given in the People's Palace, with Vaughan Williams conducting, in February 1925.

In another letter to Iris Lemare, about the same time, he wrote:

"You're right about the Narrator being the big thing in the
Passion. It sounds so easy when it's done well, but to get it to
sound like good reading and yet to be music is v. difficult—hellish
in fact! Also it's got to be quite dispassionate except in a few
places and then you've got to be quite sure that very simple
dramatic means are used to gain your end. I've been through it
all 100 times at least, but I never feel as though I know how to do
it."

He sang it fairly often from then on, but as already mentioned it
was not until the autumn of 1928 when he was stricken with a
recurrence of his ulcer and confined to bed at home, that he was able
seriously to study the part in depth. He wrote in his autobiographical
fragment:

"During the three months in bed, October, November and
December, I made a detailed study of the Evangelist's Recitatives
of the St. Matthew Passion, comparing all the versions I could
muster, and constructed an independent version. I then had the
idea of going to Paris to study with the great harpsichordist and
musician Wanda Landowska, at her studio just outside Paris.
That is a story in itself, which one day I would like to tell."

Alas, he did not live to tell this story himself, but fortunately Jean
Hamilton who went to France with him remembers the lessons
vividly. She has written her own version and I am grateful to her for
permission to reproduce it:

"I began work with Steuart Wilson early in 1927. At that time he
used to talk about the Evangelist part of the St. Matthew Passion
and to discuss the possibility of making a thorough study of the
work with Landowska. She had regularly played the continuo
part for Mengelberg in his famous performances in Holland, which
at that time were looked on as the classic interpretation of the
Passion. I too was greatly interested in the work, having performed
it with Sir Hugh Allen at the Royal College of Music and later
with the Oxford Bach Choir, of which I was the accompanist
during the years I was at Somerville.

"I was delighted at the prospect of going deeply into this great
music, but it was not until December 1928 that the chance came
for Steuart to knock off work long enough to go to Paris to have

lessons from Landowska. The reason for his ability to take time off
was the sad one of his illness caused by a recurrent ulcer. He
characteristically took the opportunity of working, from every
known text and score, at the Evangelist part, tackling the very
knotty problem of translation and the relation of English rhythm
and syllables to the notes written by Bach for the very different
length and emphasis of the words in German.   These problems
we used to discuss exhaustively at this time; and when in December his ulcer, at least in abeyance if not actually cured, Steuart
proposed that we should go across to Landowska then and there—
if she could give us lessons—I was thrilled.

"In December 1928 we went to Paris and had almost daily
lessons for two weeks. Mme Wanda Landowska at that time had
her school in the suburb of St. Leu le Forêt about twenty minutes
out of Paris on a suburban railway. 'L'École Landowska' was a
smallish villa, typically French in appearance but with a big
studio-concert hall in the garden that Landowska had built herself. Though we had lessons alone with Landowska, her classes in
general were master classes, the audience paying to listen.

"Wanda Landowska was at that time a woman of about 50.
She was small with raven black hair, a dark skin and wonderful
glowing rather prominent eyes which—when she looked down, as
she usually did, when playing, seemed to be hooded. When she
looked up it was like the lifting of a curtain and the brilliant eyes
shone. Her hands were small and claw-like, and she played with
faultless precision and intoxicating rhythm. She was immensely
vain and egotistical as a person, but an inspired and inspiring
musician and unsurpassed as a harpsichord player. She was also a
scholar and had a collection of manuscripts of Karl Philip
Emanuel Bach's concertos and many others.

"Our lessons from her were amongst the greatest musical
experiences of my life. Landowska was deeply interested in the
Evangelist part of the St. Matthew Passion and had a profound
knowledge of the work—not of course of the problem of the
English translation, and for these lessons Steuart sang in German.
The lessons themselves were conducted in French. Those lessons
were for me a turning-point in my method of work and she tried to
make me promise that I would come back to her to work only at
the harpsichord. When she heard from Steuart later that I had

gone to study with Schnabel (a man she disliked and disapproved of) she was furious and said 'It will be her death'.

Her personality was volatile in the extreme and she would go in a flash from one mood to another, from a profoundly dedicated interpretation of the Passion 'breathless with awe' to extreme hilarity and bawdery as some unprintable episode suddenly crossed her mind.

"It was not only the Evangelist part of the *Passion* that we studied but we played—variously—sometimes Landowska on the harpsichord, sometimes on the piano, the arias which Steuart sang, and even went through the choruses for sheer love of their beauty. I remember that we had a lesson on Christmas Day—snow lying outside—and we played the last bass aria in the *Passion*, with its marvellous swinging 6/6 accompaniment. I shall never forget the excitement of discovering its beauty. It is an aria that was quite often cut in the shortened performance of the *Passion*. From time to time—some phrase suggesting a parallel—Landowska would suddenly play, say a piece by Couperin, Rameau or Scarlatti, as only she could play them, taking our breath away by the magic of it. And then, as suddenly, she would return to the Bach. We gradually realized that she had no fixed version of the continuo part, only a fixed style of interpreting the figured bass. She would alter from day to day the position of the chords so that the tone colour was always changing.

In the end the version from which Steuart and I performed was of our own determining—only the pattern of it came from Landowska. She based her theory of continuo interpretation on the Fantasy of the Chromatic Fantasy and Fugue, maintaining that this was Bach's own way of filling in the indicated harmonies. At that time the idea of a moving accompaniment and of the renewal of the bass note was unheard of—as opposed to the short unrelated chords prescribed by the Novello edition, which was the convention in England. At that time also, no one had really thought about either the Evangelist part or its accompaniment, with the exception of Gervase Elwes who had just begun to be known for his interpretation when his disastrous accidental death brought to it an end. So what Steuart was doing was to break new ground and I was lucky enough to be able to perform it with him.

"When we came back to England Steuart was asked to give a

talk on the Evangelist part to the Society of English Singers. This
turned out to be a collection of all the distinguished *male* English
singers one had ever heard of—operatic and otherwise, and other
musicians too. They met for dinner in the Paddington Hotel and
I was the only woman there. After dinner we went to our performance, I trying to coax an elderly upright piano, deeply
imbedded in a padded Axminster carpet, into some sort of
subtlety. It was not easy for either of us and the audience were
pretty unconvinced, if not actually hostile to these new-fangled
ways. When Steuart had finished, the attack began, and one
pundit after another poured forth destructive criticism which
varied from 'Oh you can't do it that way—it's never been done
like that before' to those who roughly speaking said 'Oh you can't
do that there 'ere'.

"When they had quite finished an elderly man, Dr. Borland,
who had not spoken before said 'Well when I was a young man I
played the piano for Otto Goldschmidt (the founder of the Bach
Choir and Jenny Lind's husband) and Goldschmidt told me that
his teacher Schneider had been told by Karl Philip Emanuel Bach
that the bass must always be 'revived'; and that *his* father (J.S.B.)
had filled the continuo part with movement in the form of arpeggios, scales and melodies.' After that there was no more to be
said but to pack our music cases and go home! It was an un-
answerable vindication of our interpretation and enormously
cheering at that moment to have Landowska's conclusions
confirmed by historical evidence."

From then on, Steuart was in constant demand as the Evangelist
and regularly took part in what he irreverently called "The Passion
Crawl . . . round Easter, often nine or ten in a row, each requiring a
rehearsal with a pianist from my own arrangement." His became the
accepted version and he became the accepted interpreter of the part.

There were annual performances in York Minster and with the
Bach Choir in the Queen's Hall, London. For the most part his fellow-
soloists were Dorothy Silk, Margaret Balfour, Arthur Cranmer and
Keith Falkner, with Adrian Boult or Reginald Jacques as conductors.
Steuart's Ledger shows that each year he travelled from London to
York, to Glasgow and Edinburgh, from Ipswich to Liverpool, from
Birmingham to Southwark, and that his fees ranged from 10 to 20

guineas. Possibly the last performance he gave in public was at the Leeds Triennial Festival in 1937, with Sir Thomas Beecham conducting. Jean Hamilton remembers their going to see Beecham in his suite at his hotel before the rehearsal—Beecham resplendent in pyjamas and silk dressing-gown; there was a fierce argument about tempi and he wanted to make cuts which Steuart equally fiercely resisted.

She told me that "Beecham had never performed the work before and was not interested in the Evangelist part, which he found boring and irrelevant. He had obviously given the matter little thought as in several instances he made suggestions which, if followed, would have ended in the wrong key for the succeeding chorus. This he had not noticed!"

Very many people who wrote to me after Steuart's death—musicians and non-musicians alike—recalled the emotional thrill they experienced when they heard him sing in the *Passion*. I have selected just a few of their comments.

Norman Allin, who often sang with him, wrote: "I recall hearing him at the Royal Albert Hall sing the Evangelist in the *St. Matthew Passion*. I thought I had never heard anything so devotional and beautiful." George Parker, the bass, said "I sang several times with him as the Evangelist in the Minster on Palm Sundays. To my way of thinking his performance was the most moving of any I have ever heard. His voice was so right for this part."

Peter Pears, the tenor, wrote to me: "I didn't meet Steuart until about 1937–8, but I always heard his Evangelist before that whenever I could. He made a great impression on me and I owe a lot to him; indeed his Evangelist was what started me off . . . He gave me a lesson on the *St. Matthew* in 1938, I think, very kindly. It was my ambition to follow in his footsteps in the Bach *Passions*. If I have done something in them, a large part of it is due to Steuart . . . When I started singing lessons in 1933 and professionally in 1934, he was the one English tenor who inspired me (I never heard Elwes or Coates) and I shall always be grateful to him."

CHAPTER SIXTEEN

THE 'INTRUSIVE H'

THERE was one man who did not join in the general praise for Steuart's rendering of the Evangelist. A retired schoolmaster, Mr. M. A. Wheatleigh, of Lynette Avenue, London S.W., was listening to the broadcast of the second part of the *St. Matthew Passion* on Passion Sunday April 2nd, 1933, sung by the Bach Choir, with Steuart as a soloist, and did not like what he heard. He jotted down the number of times he thought he detected the 'intrusive H' which so annoyed him—his tally came to 200. Then he took up his pen and wrote a letter to the *Radio Times*. In this letter, which appeared on 14th April under the heading "Vocal Sins" he said:

"I have just been listening to the broadcast of Bach's glorious Passion music. While on the whole the rendering was excellent, there was one glaring fault that simply ruined the performance of one of the singers and I am amazed that the BBC could engage someone quite so incompetent in his breath control. The intrusive H must have appeared *hundreds* of times. Thus 'Pilate's wife became 'Pigh-highlet's wigh-highf'; 'Potters' field' became 'Po-ho-te-her's feeheeld'; 'High Priest' was turned into 'High-high Preeheest'; 'Purple robe' into 'purple ro-hobe'; 'to' in 'too-hoo' and so on throughout the entire performance.

"It was simply ghastly. It seems to me—much as I admire in broad outline the great work of the BBC that in one respect they are sadly lacking. If they once made the rule that in no circumstances would they engage anyone who was guilty either of the 'intrusive H' or the 'tremolo'—and rigidly enforced the rule—the standard of singing in England would be immeasurably raised in a few years. The two faults I mention are grave and horrible and I regret to say, widespread, and the BBC has it in its power to cure the trouble."

He naïvely sent a copy of this letter to Steuart "in the hope that it might be of assistance to him." The phrase "incompetence in breath control" made Steuart very angry and he regarded it as a slur on his professional capacity. He wrote

"That was what got my goat, and I wrote asking for a withdrawal and apology. I received a short letter refusing either. So I instructed my solicitors to put the preliminary machine into operation to bring a civil action. Nothing more was said on either side, till in June of that year on my way out to Australia by sea, I received a cable from my solicitors to say that I must decide whether I meant to pursue the matter or not. I cabled a reply to affirm my intention."

The case "Wilson v. British Broadcasting Corporation and Another" was eventually heard before the Lord Chief Justice (then Lord Hewart) on 19th June 1934. The story has been told by Mr. Joseph Dean in his book *Hatred, Ridicule or Contempt* (Constable, 1953, reprinted as a Penguin 1968) and the case was fully reported in the press. It was a *cause célèbre* which attracted attention far beyond the musical world.

Steuart prepared his case most carefully. His solicitors, who were also the solicitors to the Incorporated Society of Musicians, engaged Mr. Austin Farleigh as counsel, and his witnesses were invited to give a proof of evidence (i.e. to say in advance what they would be prepared to say in court in answer to questions) "to safeguard ourselves from any possible shattering admissions in cross-examination." Steuart described his preliminary interviews with his counsel.

"He was a confirmed smoker with a cigarette cough of stupendous length and vehemence. Sometimes I wondered if he would ever get round, occasionally if he would get an attack in court! A great deal of the technical point revolved round 'control of the breath'. He, more than once, substituted 'breath control' with an occasional variant of 'birth control'. I had to warn him to be careful, as a juror might easily have been led to a Dr. Marie Stopes conclusion and I could have lost my case."

X. MARY WILSON

1928.

March					470	9	
	20	Birmingham BMS					
		Mendelssohn Lieder.			10	10	-
	21	Leeds Philharmonic.					
		Gerontius[14]			21	-	-
	23	Bradford Festival Choral.					
		Gerontius[15]			18	16	-
	24	Liverpool Welsh Choral					
		Beethoven Mass in D			21	-	-
	27	Derby.					
		B mi[9]			18	18	-
	28	Norwich					
		Schubert Mass in B flat			15	15	
		...					
	30	Hanover School.					
		Judged singing competition.			2	12	6.
	31	Bristol Philharmonic.					
		chorus			15	15	
April	1	York Minster					
		Matt Pass[""]			10	10	
	3	Ipswich or Argyle Tower					
		Matt Pass[12]			15	15	
	4	BBC Bishopsgate Inst.					
		Gerontius[16]			21		
	5	Kidderminster.					
		Matthew Passion[13]			12	12	
	6	Bridgwater. St Mary's Church.					
		...					
		...			15	15	
	10	Bedales. School of Music.					
		Recital (Stock)			10	10	
					690	19	6

XI. THE LEDGER — RECEIPTS

	£	s	d
	131	15	7
pr. Jean Hamilton. 5 gns. *[illegible]*	5	2	4
Danston. Olga Hales. White *[illegible]* 37/6. 1.1.0	5	8	6
Bergan. H. Williams. Brunskill 40/4. 1.1.0. Stephen Evans	5	11	4
Stiles Allen Brunskill. *[illegible]* 42/6. 1.1.0. Coward	5	13	6
Stiles Allen Partridge Cranmer. 65/8. 1.1.0 Bates	4	4	8
Suddaby. M. Russell. T. Jones. 58/4. 1.1.0.	3	19	4
for R.S. Thatcher		10	6
Ibbs. Tillett advertisements a/c Baxter	51	18	6
Silk. M. Russell Heynor Henderson. Fry 54/2. 1.1.0. Buxton	4	0	2
Olga Jones. Parker. 88/8. 1.1.0. G.C. Gray. Slater *[illegible]*	5	1	8
Spong *[illegible]* S. Crocker L. Bennett. 39/2. 1.1.0. Elgar	3	0	2
Hales. Williams		10	6
Glover. Silk. D'Oyly Falkner. 61/8. 1.1.0.	4	1	8
E.V.S. Berry			
Mrs Sully p/c. Doctors organ. 71/8. 1.1.0.	4	12	8
Craston p/c. Rail Taxis. 117/8. Hotel 1.1.0.	2	18	8
	~~184~~	~~10~~	~~9~~
	241	9	3

XI. THE LEDGER — EXPENSES

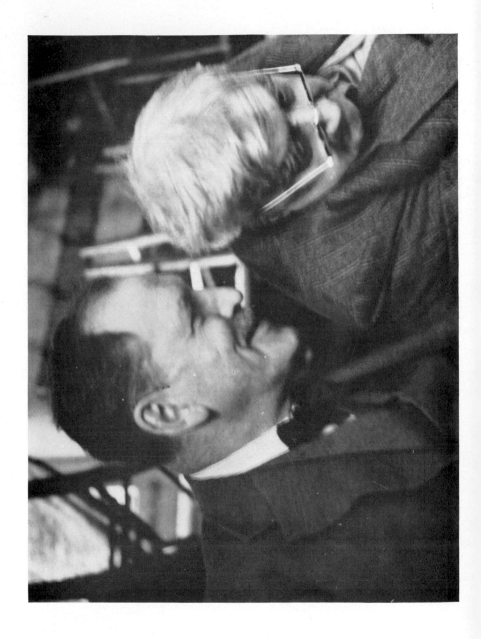

Steuart also took the precaution of getting himself thoroughly examined by a chest specialist. He had heard a rumour that the BBC might allege that because he had been wounded in the lung he was incapable of proper control of the breath. The specialist was not told the reason for the examination until it was over. Steuart wrote: "As I passed the test for breath capacity with a volume that greatly surprised him, I told him the whole story and he agreed, with alacrity, to be called as a witness if my condition were referred to in any way." The matter, however, was not raised in court.

The hearing lasted for three, often hilarious, days. Steuart was not called upon to sing, but he carried on a verbal duet with the BBC counsel, Stuart Bevan K.C., which delighted the packed court-room. This is how it went: (*Times* Law Report, 19th June 1934):

MR. BEVAN: He said that, apart from the use of the 'intrusive H', your rendering of the part was in all respects all that could be desired. That was quite fair?—That is what is called in *Alice in Wonderland* the 'best butter'. (Laughter.) He said that it had ruined the performance.

THE QUALITIES REQUIRED

Mr Wilson said that the part of the Narrator called for exceptional qualities on the part of the singer. It called for sympathy, compassion, indignation, and a highly intellectual performance. He believed that he was generally regarded as possessing those qualities.

It is quite possible, even with the possession of those qualities, to have certain defects. I venture to put it to you that you do exhibit, from time to time, the defects alleged in Mr. Wheatleigh's letter?—I agree that I sometimes do use the 'intrusive H'.

Do you approve of the use of the 'intrusive H'?—I approve of it when used artistically.

You have said that in some 107 instances you use the lengthened vowel during your performance. When you are doing that, is it not difficult to prevent the 'H' slipping in?—That depends on how skilful you are.

K

You have given several instances where Jean de Reszke taught you to use the 'intrusive H'. They were all in operatic music. Do you realize that what is permissible in opera is not permissible in Bach or concert music?—I would not admit that for a moment.

A good deal of licence is allowed in opera?—A good deal of licence is taken. (Laughter.)

I suggest that in Bach and concert music the 'intrusive H' is taboo and that all the great singers are agreed on it?—I do not quite know who sets up the taboo.

De Reszke was an opera singer and taught opera?—Yes, but he taught the principles of singing.

He had never sung at concerts?—I do not think so.

In your examples the language used is either French or German? —Yes.

Can you appreciate that, while the stolid Englishman might tolerate the introduction of an 'H' in German with which he is not very familiar, it would be quite different if he heard his own language distorted in the same way?—The stolid German seems to have stood it all right.

Asked about a statement in Sir Henry Wood's book, *The Gentle Art of Singing*, that aspirated vocalization was a vice, Mr. Wilson said that it was not a vice in general terms.

Was not Caruso the best example of the 'intrusive H'?—He certainly used it a great deal.

As a concert singer he was hopeless?—I have never heard it said so.

Were not his performances on the concert platform quite spoiled by his use of the 'intrusive H'?—I understand that he could fill the largest hall in any country in the world with an audience who had stood all day to get in.

Do you agree that, if you go over all the great works on singing, you will find the same view expressed again and again, with regard to the use of the 'intrusive H'?—Primers of knowledge often fall a long way behind practice and performance. They are aiming at safety all the time.

Is not the use of the 'intrusive H' bad style on the concert platform, but accepted style in opera singing?—Music cannot be divided into watertight compartments. Music is music."

Not reported in *The Times*, but vouched for by the *Musical Times* was this exchange:

Counsel (vigorously tapping his Adam's apple): May we take it that the diaphragm differs considerably with the individual?—No (thumping himself amidships); the diaphragm is the same in all normal people."

Steuart called an impressive array of witnesses "some who would say the statement was a grotesque exaggeration, others that a habit of an 'intrusive H' might amount to a failure of taste, but could not be classed as incompetence." The list included A. H. Fox Strangways, then music critic of the *Observer*, Sir Edward Bairstow, organist of York Minster (where Steuart had often sung the part), the singing teacher W. S. (Bill) Drew and Clive Carey—all of whom praised Steuart's performance and described the criticism as ridiculous. Carey's evidence was particularly authoritative. He said that "inserting an aspirate in groups of two or more notes was a definite part of de Reszke's teaching. It was used sometimes (*a*) for clarity, i.e. to prevent smudging and (*b*) emotional or rhythmical emphasis. It was taught to the plaintiff by de Reszke in my presence . . . The practice of inserting aspirates is nothing whatever to do with breath control. In fact the insertion of an aspirate expends more breath." He added that he had heard it deliberately used by Gigli and Conchita Supervia. Richard Capell, then music critic of the *Daily Telegraph*, who might have been described as a hostile witness, said that the abuse of the 'intrusive H' was "detestable but to say that Mr. Wilson used it hundreds of times on the occasion in question was a gross exaggeration". The singer, Lady Harty, professionally known as Agnes Nicholls, stated that the 'H' was used in both opera and concert singing, and that she had heard it used by Dame Nellie Melba in Tosti's *Farewell* and by Albani in "Rejoice greatly" in the *Messiah*.

On the second day, Mr. Bevan marshalled his witnesses for the defence, which was based mainly on the grounds of "fair comment on a matter of public importance". The 'intrusive H', said Mr. Bevan, could be used voluntarily or involuntarily; its involuntary use was "due to some slight defect in the management and control of the breathing". The jury he said could only come to the conclusion that while Mr. Wilson sometimes did it voluntarily, he sometimes did it involuntarily.

The first witness for the BBC was Dr. Adrian Boult, its music director, whose evidence, as Steuart later commented "might have been given for me instead of against me". Boult who had conducted the performance on 2nd April, said "he had the greatest respect for the powers of Mr. Wilson, whom he regarded as one of the most intelligent singers before the public today, especially as an inter- preter". But, he did have the defect of using the 'intrusive H' rather more often than he himself was probably aware of. "I do not think it is a serious fault," he added, 'but I can quite understand its becoming irritating by its repetition."

There followed this dialogue, in cross-examination by Steuart's counsel:

"MR. FARLEIGH (*cross-examining*): Do you think Mr. Wheat- leigh's letter is a fair representation of Mr. Wilson's singing? —If a person once got the feeling that the 'intrusive H' was an annoyance he might go on listening and become very excited about it.

Was Mr. Wilson's performance ruined?—No.

Have you ever said a word to him objecting to his use of the 'intrusive H'?—I do not think so.

A juror: If you had noticed that anything which Mr. Wilson had done, during all the time you have known him and conducted for him, had spoiled a performance, would you have told him about it as a friend?—It is quite possible.

Did you do so?—No.

Is it possible that through the microphone Mr. Wilson's voice might have been distorted?—I think not."

Other witnesses for the defence were more whole-hearted in their

condemnation of the 'intrusive H'. Sir Landon Ronald, principal of
the Guildhall School of Music, said it was "most offensive" in
oratorio and concert songs; Mr. Maurice Vinden, Trinity College of
Music, thought it "not permissible" in Bach's Passion music. Two
conductors associated with Covent Garden, Charles Webber and
Arnold Perry, agreed in thinking there was "defective breath
control". Malcolm Sargent said he did not approve of the 'H' in
concert singing or in oratorio, and particularly not in Bach's music.
Confessing that he was not a singer himself, "he gave some vocal
illustrations from the witness-box of what he described as the
improper use of the 'H' in certain passages of music."

The *Musical Times* later commented on the wide divergence of
expert opinion, and observed that "too many of the expert witnesses, especially for the defence, were not experts at all";—why had
the defence not called two or three experienced singers, instead of so
many conductors and music critics?

The schoolmaster refused to retract a word. Mr. Farleigh, cross-
examining:

Was it true that Mr. Wilson's performance was ruined?—To me
it was.

When you wrote the letter you were very irritated?—I was
irritated when I heard the broadcast but not when I wrote the
letter.

Is this a clear suggestion that the BBC should not broadcast Mr.
Wilson's singing?—You can take it as that, until he has corrected
his fault.

You made no inquiries from any musician before you charged
Mr. Wilson with lack of breath control?—No.

Did it occur to you that it was a very serious statement to make?
—It was absolutely legitimate criticism.

Did you not consider that, before making a charge of that kind, a
layman would rightly take the advice of somebody skilled in the
art?—No.

The Lord Chief Justice in his summing up was clearly advising
the jury to find in favour of the BBC:

"Great latitude must be given to opinion and prejudice. Here exaggeration or even gross exaggeration does not necessarily make a comment unfair.

"Therefore, on the question of fair comment, you must be extremely liberal when considering matters on which men's minds are moved in things like music and taste and style in music.

"If they use strong language, every allowance should be made in their favour, but they must believe what they say, and that is the question for you. A critic can use ridicule, sarcasm, and irony as weapons so long as he does not use them unfairly."

If they awarded damages, they should give Mr. Wilson a sum that was moderate and reasonable. "It would be a cruel kindness to him to award him an excessive sum," he said.

The jury, however, found in Steuart Wilson's favour and decided to do him a 'cruel kindness'. They awarded him £2,000 damages against the BBC and £100 against Mr. Wheatleigh.

Steuart, describing the events in a letter to his friend Sir William McKie put it picturesquely: "The learned Judge summed up dead against me and the nine intelligent men and three reasonable women said 'Balls to you' and brought in the verdict as aforesaid."

He told me later of a 'dangerous hazard' on the third day of the case.

"In the main corridor of the Law Courts, a man whom I did not recognize came up to me to say he thought it was all going very well. Thinking him to be some musical acquaintance whom I did not remember, I gave him a vague and uncompromising answer, with grateful thanks for his interest. When I went into Court I was horrified to see him in the Jury box! I did not know whether I ought to tell my solicitor and Counsel and plead innocence, or whether I should lie low and wait for the other side to complain. I took the risk of silence and it paid off."

There was another strange incident, which did not get into the papers:

"Before the case came on the Chairman of the BBC Governors, the ex-Speaker the Right Hon. J. H. Whitley, who had been a pupil of my father's at Clifton College and cherished a fervent admiration for him, invited me to visit him privately. He was already a grievously sick man and he told me that he had seen all the papers of the case and that I had no earthly chance of winning and he advised—more, he implored—me to give it up before it was too late. In the circumstances I could only say that I would go and see the BBC's solicitors if he, the Chairman, would arrange for them to ask me. This was done and the letter came making an appointment. The conversation opened with their solicitor, *not* the BBC official solicitor but an outside firm, stating "We hear from the Chairman that you want to withdraw." I was furious at this complete travesty and replied that I was quite ready to compromise on terms that the BBC would pay £5,000 and all my costs. The suggestion was not well received, but I heard afterwards that the story had gathered a good deal of momentum and was repeated inside the BBC that I had visited the Chairman on his sick bed and *demanded* that the BBC should pay me £5,000.''

The outcome of the case inevitably led to a spate of comment in the leader columns of the press, largely revolving round the question "At what stage does adverse criticism become libel?" On the whole the comments were in Steuart's favour. Thus the *Yorkshire Post*: "Today's verdict . . . must be gratifying to his many admirers . . . A critic may say, frankly and even vehemently, that he dislikes a particular performance . . . but if he says that the performer is thereby revealed as a hopeless incompetent, then he is going too far." But the *Birmingham Post* warned that the decision "adds yet one more terror for the life of the writer, whether he be an amateur or professional in the craft of criticism" and represented "a growing menace" to newspapers.

Steuart was himself overjoyed by his victory. To a friend he wrote: "Ha Ha, you see that I won! They will probably appeal against the damages,* but if they do—even if they win—they will lose all their prestige. I am very pleased." And to Sir William McKie: "I'm damned glad I twisted their tail in public. Of course the sniffers all say 'It'll be bound to do him harm and the BBC will never give him a job again.' It will take a lot of harm to outweigh £2,100 and a public duty done, and at the present rate of earning with the BBC it would take me 100 years to earn that money in jobs from them, so I don't give a damn!"

* The BBC did not appeal.

CHAPTER SEVENTEEN

THE LATE 1930s

THE BBC money did not last long. Many people would have providently salted it away in a bank or a building society, but this wasn't Steuart's way. First of all he planned a holiday in Salzburg and wrote to Winifred Fox:

"Is there any chance of persuading you and Vivien to take a holiday with me to celebrate this absurd accession to wealth. I want you both to come to Salzburg with me, starting about Aug 8 or 9. I have always wanted to go there and see what it is like, and I have always wanted to make up just such a party and go there. The fourth would ɒe Fox-Strangways in all probability. He is not quite certain yet. Do *please* cast aside your responsibilities: haven't written to Vivien separately because I want you to talk it over together. *Please* give me the simple and delightful pleasure which this trip opens, and accept without saying that I ought to *save* the money. What more lovely investment could there be than such an expedition.

"I go home shortly, so write there. There will be lots of pretty snippets to tell you about the famous Case. The BBC are *not* appealing and the money should be in my bank on Monday. It was all too superb and too like a novel by A.P.H."

Neither Winifred Fox nor Vivien Russell was able to join him, but his Ledger records that he spent from 8th August to the 19th at Salzburg, after a week at Bernard Robinson's Music Camp.

He was a fairly regular 'Camper', and enjoyed the friendly atmosphere in which seasoned professionals and enthusiastic amateurs tackled major works. He particular relished the opportunity of conducting great orchestral and choral works, among them *Gerontius*, the *Brahms-Haydn Variations* and the Bach Brandenburgs. He started off the Beethoven seventh symphony with the words "No one has ever let me have a shot at this before." He also used to go to Camp Reunions in London, when possible, and on one occasion Bernard Robinson has told me both Steuart and Peter Pears sang in the chorus of the Bach Magnificat.

Not recorded in his Ledger, but very vivid in my memory is the week-end he spent at Ringstead Mill, Professor Cornford's windmill near Hunstanton, where members of the Stewart family and their friends went for music-making holidays. We were all amateurs, except for Sylvia Spencer, the oboist, and it was typical of Steuart to come just for the fun of it. Nearly thirty years later, he wrote to me how well he remembered 'your famous Windmill'.

Steuart decided to spend his winnings on helping his old friend Rutland Boughton who, equally improvidently, had either spent or given away the profits from *The Immortal Hour*, and was living on or near the poverty line, at his home at Kilcot, Newent, on the Gloucester-Herefordshire border. Rutland had arranged music festivals at Stroud and Bath in the autumn of 1934, and Steuart appeared in many performances. He and the other artists gave their services free of charge because as he told Boughton "You don't know how much we owe to you and you must realize we want to show it." Elsie Suddaby, who sang Etain in *The Immortal Hour*, recalls what difficulty Steuart had in mastering some of his lines.

> "He appeared at the dress rehearsal in a white tunic (very mini-mini) sandals à la Grecque, a golden curly wig with a silver band round the head and a star in the front. One night his line to me as Etain 'That I might kiss with my hot lips the white hand of the Queen' was sung as 'that I might kiss with my white lips the hot hand of the Queen'."

Encouraged by the success of the Stroud Festival, Boughton began to plan an ambitious project for a touring company. Long and at times bitter negotiations followed between himself, Steuart and Adolph Borsdorf, the young viola player who was a great admirer of Boughton's music and had urged him to revive *The Immortal Hour*. The venture did not come off, largely because Steuart and Borsdorf found it impossible to do business with Rutland, who did not want to be confined to 'artistic' direction but to have a finger in every pie.

For all his doubts about Boughton's business sense, Steuart still retained faith in his music and decided to back *The Lily Maid* for a short season at the London Winter Garden Theatre.

The Lily Maid ran from 12th to 23rd January 1937. It was produced by Christopher Ede (Boughton's son-in-law) and Steuart himself conducted. The principals included Sybil Evers, Arthur Fear and Frederick Woodhouse: there was a chorus of twenty minstrels and a small chamber orchestra, which had been assembled by Adolph Borsdorf. (The second cellist was Mary Goodchild.)

Whether the publicity was inadequate or whether the London audience of the late 1930s was too sophisticated, or too concerned with the realities of the growing international tension to appreciate the Arthurian legend, *The Lily Maid* failed to spark. It played to near empty houses, and was not well received by the critics. *The Times*, however, noted (13th January 1937) that "Mr. Wilson was making his first appearance as an operatic conductor—his assured beat held the performance well together and proved that there is virtue in putting operatic direction into the hands of a singer who by his own experience knows what is the sort of help the singers want".

In Steuart's opinion, the music was Boughton at his best. He wrote to Rutland:

"I think you have produced a much better work than any of the others (I still cherish the memory of *Alkestis*). The musical strength of it seems to me to be infinitely greater and you haven't lost the power of knocking us down with a fact stated with such simplicity that at first it seems *too* simple."

Later that year, Steuart organized a petition to the Prime Minister for a Civil List pension for Boughton. The signatories included such distinguished and diverse public figures as Sir Granville Bantock, H. C. Colles, Sir Walford Davies, E. J. Dent, Ralph Vaughan Williams, Herbert Morrison, Bernard Shaw, Lady Londonderry and Dame Elizabeth Cadbury. The Memorial, beautifully written and handsomely printed, was successful in achieving a small regular income for Boughton, though it irked him to receive 'charity' in a capitalist society.

The failure of *The Lily Maid* was not Steuart's only setback in the years immediately after the BBC case. He was—as many people had forecast—temporarily ostracized by the BBC. He heard from Patrick Hadley that he (Hadley) had asked for Steuart as a soloist in a new work *La Belle Dame sans Merci* which was to be broadcast in May 1935.

Steuart reacted with a characteristic letter to the *Daily Telegraph*:

"Sir,
    I was recently a successful litigant for libel against the BBC. Before the action was started I used to receive an average of one engagement a year from them; at the end of the case it was suggested to me that even this occasional recognition would cease, but I tried to think better of human nature, even when corporate and chartered. I was wrong.

"Recently a young composer had a work accepted and the date of performance fixed for May 31. He was kind enough to wish me to take the solo part at the first performance, and intimated this to to the BBC. He was informed that my services 'were not available', and he gathered that I was not to be allowed to have a job until July 1. This date is explained by the fact that that will be then a complete year from the date of my obtaining damages in my action against the Corporation.

"The composer protested, but the BBC remained firm; either the performance of his work must be postponed, or else a singer must be found who is *persona grata* to the Corporation. My sentence cannot be shortened by 30 days; the full period of penance must be endured—or rather nine days more, for I obtained my verdict on June 21, 1934.

"I do not ask for sympathy, either for the composer (who has generously given me leave to make these facts public) or for myself, whose period of exile from Broadcasting House may now become longer, but I ask for the completest condemnation of this petty victimization of a successful opponent.

"If the embargo on me were to be permanent, the BBC's action would be spiteful, but as it is intended only to last for a period which is usually deemed suitable for Full Mourning (or two Decrees Nisi) it appears to be merely a ludicrous loss of temper. But it is a warning to others."

Despite the boycotts of the BBC and the Three Choirs, Steuart had plenty of work in hand. He wrote to Anneke in June 1936:

"I have been BUSY with capital letters for so many weeks that I can hardly remember what it was like to feel a man of leisure! What with Easter, then operas to manage and then Festivals and Competitions I have hardly slept two nights running in the same bed. But I have vastly enjoyed it—that is the important thing, and I have been marvellously well and full of good vitality. By the way I have not made any records of the Matt. Pass (the other day a man introduced me to his friend saying 'S.W. is the man who does such a marvellous performance as the Announcer in the Matthew Passion').

Now I am off again on some more opera enterprises which take a lot of planning and make no money—rather the contrary—but they keep us young and hopeful and I have been and I think I still am very happy because I now selfishly live for music alone and don't have to think how it will all appear to someone else. I have no time to worry and whine about my condition or to regret my errors; I've only just got time to get around my job."

He was not, however, making so much money as before. The table of his earnings, reproduced on p. 228 shows that between 1934 and the end of 1937 he averaged £729 a year, compared with £1,253 between 1926 and 1932. He did not, of course, have a wife and family to support. He was then living the life of a gay bachelor at Chepstow Villas, doing his own shopping and cooking. "I go on enjoying my housekeeping," he wrote to a friend. It was in this period that he first acquired the art of cooking, for which he later became famous among his friends.

Then, much to everybody's surprise, he married Mary Goodchild, the cellist in the Macnaghten quartet. He had often insisted that he did not wish "to mix himself up with other people's lives again" and preferred "the pleasures of gaiety and rippling casual friendships."

The exact date of Steuart's first meeting with Mary is not on record, but it must have been in about 1934. Anne Macnaghten and Iris Lemare were then organizing a series of concerts to perform the works of young English composers who were not yet established,

such as Elizabeth Maconchy, Dorothy Gow, Elizabeth Lutyens and
Gerald Finzi. "It was a good scheme and Steuart was generous in
his interest and support," Anne has told me. He wrote to her:

"I would like some time to work really hard at some genuine
modern songs with str. quartet or piano quintet, what Wenlock
Edge was 25 years ago. There is no outlet for that sort of thing now
except your concerts ... I do congratulate your quartet on
playing the new stuff so well."

It was probably at one of the Macnaghten-Lemare concerts that
he first saw Mary. She fell in love with him but he did not at first take
it very seriously. It probably began, on his side, as a mild flirtation
which developed, as these things do, into love and marriage.

Mary was only about eighteen when they first met. She was very
attractive, small, gay and vivacious, with deep-set greeny-blue eyes
and fair hair. Rather spoilt and wayward, she was the only child of
devoted parents who seem to have been rather frightened of her.
Her background was utterly different from Steuart's. Her parents
lived in Sutton and her father kept a high-class tailor's shop (opposite St. James's Palace) making shirts and cravats not only for the
aristocracy but for eminent musicians (I still have in my possession a
collar made by him for Chaliapin). Mary had wanted to be a
dancer, but took up the cello instead. According to Anne Macnaghten she was "very gifted at the cello, but without enough
application or purpose to do more than nicely at it. She found serious
4tet rehearsing increasingly tedious." Mary had studied with the
great cellist Emanuel Feuermann and had been to his school at
Ascona, but otherwise had hardly been abroad at all.

They were married on 12th March 1937 in Kensington Registry
Office. Mary's parents were the witnesses and Steuart gave his
profession as 'Captain K.R.R.C. retired". He was 47, Mary was 22.
They went for a brief honeymoon to the Gleadowes' cottage in
Cornwall.

It must have been something of an ordeal for Mary to be introduced to the formidable Wilson and Padwick relations and to meet
Steuart's critical and intellectual friends, as well as the countless
ladies who adored him and no doubt wished themselves in her shoes!
But if she was overawed, she never showed it and, from the start,
impressed people with her spontaneous gaiety. Steuart was extremely

conscious of the gap in their ages. He wrote to Anneke (23rd April 1937) about summer plans.

"You will be most welcome as usual. There is a difference in my household in that I have got married (I hope you will not think me too foolish), to a girl who is much too young for me and much too kind."

He told of his plans to spend most of the summer down at the bungalow he had bought at Petersfield* 'lazing completely'.

Steuart sought to encourage Mary's interests in art and literature, as well as music, and to 'bring her out' in an almost Pygmalion-like fashion. He advised her on what she should read and how she dressed and did her hair. Mary herself was of an independent turn of mind and had a highly-developed sense of clothes, dressing well, if rather flamboyantly. She had inherited her father's skill and was an extremely clever dressmaker.

Steuart and Mary continued to live at Chepstow Villas, but moved shortly before the War from no. 19 to no. 23. Steuart recalled the amazement of the removal men at being expected to load and unload furniture from one house to another a few doors away—"not a proper move at all" they told him. But, as he was by now beginning to spend more time teaching in Newcastle, they decided to make their home there in 1938 rather than commuting up and down or driving in the large second-hand Chrysler which he had acquired.†

Steuart had a long association with Newcastle music and had often performed for Sidney Newman, who was lecturer in music at King's College and director of the Newcastle Bach Choir. He had taken part in the performances of the *Passion* every Easter and had been judge in the Northeast Music Tournament.

He presented *The Immortal Hour* in the Palace Theatre, Newcastle in the summer of 1936, and himself took the part of Midir. That winter, he started regular teaching at the Conservatoire as a visiting member—£6 6s. a lesson. The Conservatoire had been directed by Dr. Edgar Bainton, who left in 1934 for Australia and was succeeded by Dr. Leslie Russell whose ambition was to make it one of the

---

* He bought the bungalow, Fenn's, standing in about 1¾ acres, half of the land being orchard, for £700 in 1935. It was so called after its previous owner, a riding-school master, Major Fenn. Steuart always used to say that Fenn's had accommodation for eight horses but only two people.

† Steuart did not take up driving until he was nearly 50.

leading music schools of the country; later Dr. Russell took a job in London, with the London County Council, and the Conservatoire at Eslington House, Newcastle, closed down.

Steuart, to whom there was no such thing as a lost cause or a *projet manqué*, took things in hand and found new accommodation in the Studios, 133 Osborne Road, which he christened the "Phoenix School of Music".

The large three-storey Victorian house became the home not only of Steuart and Mary Wilson, but of the reborn Conservatoire. The Wilsons lived in a top flat and brought up most of their furniture from London. The rest of the house was given over to studios and practice rooms and the large basement, lined with mirrors, served as rehearsal rooms for opera and ballet. One floor became the scene of a remarkable venture—Mary's dress shop. Steuart who invented the name 'Popinjay' for it, was anxious to find an outlet for Mary's energies and talents, as well as a possible additional source of income. Jennie Beadle, a young girl from a Durham mining village, was engaged to help in the shop, though she later became an indispensable aide and housekeeper. There was a Tweenie by the name of Sadie, but she was always known as Tweenie.

Steuart took a great interest in the dress shop. He regarded it as his job to seek to persuade the wives of Newcastle businessmen into spending more than they ought to on an evening gown. "Who are you dressing for?" he would say with a wink. And as if his charm was not enough in itself, the process of salesmanship was helped by a huge cask of sherry which was kept at hand.

There is no record of the business results of Popinjay, but as many of the dresses were presented to their friends, it is unlikely to have been much of a financial success. Myfanwy Jones, then a pupil of Steuart's, recalls a gorgeous creation in gold lamé, with panels of red and green satin which Steuart called her 'Stop-Go' dress. Elsie Winstanley, who taught the piano at the Studios and usually accompanied Steuart recalls a "lovely black velvet evening dress."

The centre of the Osborne Road house was the kitchen-cum-dining-room, where everybody who happened to be around—visiting musicians, lecturers, teachers, pupils, staff—would join Steuart and Mary, Jennie and Tweenie, at a long refectory table—acquired for *The Lily Maid*—and enjoy the soup of the day or the stew which Jennie had prepared under Steuart's guidance. No. 133

Osborne Road very soon became the focal point of music in the North-east. Steuart was indefatigable, teaching, coaching, organizing and singing. He organized an opera group which performed excerpts from *Così*, Gay's *Polly* and Vaughan Williams' *Hugh the Drover*. The group performed not only in Newcastle, but, in cooperation with the Tyneside Council of Social Service, toured the mining areas of Durham and Northumberland which were still afflicted by the depression. Jack Hollins, who was then working with the unemployed in the Midlands, brought a party over for a performance of *Così* in the garden of Hardwick Hall. "The miners received it rapturously," he told me. Every possible week-end, Steuart would go walking on the moors and along the Roman Wall, with his friends the Brackenburys. Mary, who didn't particularly like walking, rarely took part in these expeditions.

Because of the abrupt end of the Ledger in 1937, there is no more detailed evidence about the state of Steuart's health or finances. It is, however, clear that he was becoming increasingly worried about money and was looking round for additional sources of income. Unfortunately all the records of his accountant were destroyed in the Second World War.

Shortly before the War Steuart bought a couple of houses in Oakley Street, Chelsea, from an Australian lady, Mrs. Macfarlane, with the intention of running them as guest houses. He installed Miss Smyth, who had been vice-warden of Crosby Hall, as manageress, with the help of the faithful Jennie. Things started off well and Steuart took immense interest in the details of housekeeping and recommended his many friends and acquaintances who wanted somewhere to stay in London. In those days, bed and breakfast cost 7s. 6d., with dinner 3s. 6d. to 4s. 6d. The outbreak of war put an end to what might have proved a good investment. Everybody was getting out of London as fast as possible and nobody wanted to lodge in Chelsea. Steuart had developed an affection for what he called his 'bawdy-houses' and wrote to Valentine Oppé from America: "I hear very little from London—an occasional mournful tale from the Oakley Street boarding-houses which just keep their heads so near to the water line that they are half submerged." He sold the two houses soon after the war; since then they have proved to be extremely profitable.

Another venture which is cloaked in mystery was the purchase of a restaurant in Soho, known as Ali Baba. His accountant does not even remember hearing about it, and the only mention I have been able to find in any of his letters is to the effect that "Poor Ali Baba went smash and we've not been able to save much from the wreckage."

In July 1939, Steuart decided to take the plunge and emigrate to America. He dashed over to New York for an interview and wrote to his friend Myfanwy Jones:

"Prospects are so god-damned gloomy that there isn't much to stay at home for. Now you may well wonder why I'm here. Let me tell you at once that it is a secret in Newcastle that I'm out here at all. It is a flying visit in the hope—a reasonable hope I believe—of landing a job over here at one of the big schools of music. The introduction came my way—knowing how much Americans believe in a personal interview, I decided to risk the money and come over and see the man. I shall be back in Newcastle on Sun. 23rd July. It may be a wild-goose chase but I believe in it at the moment. Singing prospects are lousy and America seems the only hope if only I can land this job!"

He did 'land' the job and proudly wrote to Iris Lemare in September: "I went out to America to 'interview' about a job there and landed it—namely to teach singing at the Curtis Institute of Music in Philadelphia—the swellest job you can imagine."

CHAPTER EIGHTEEN

THE CURTIS INSTITUTE

STEUART and Mary sailed for America on 20th September 1939 on the S.S. *Manhattan*. Steuart embarked with an acute sense of guilt and frustration at leaving England just when war had broken out. From the boat he wrote home:

"I feel rather a pig at leaving everyone in this gigantic mess, but I should be mad to turn down such a chance for the rest of my life just to stay on and be a Special Constable, while I should go bankrupt with complete certainty—whereas I may be able to repay some of my debts with good American dollars. My heart was twisted rather badly when I watched troopships leaving Southampton this afternoon and realized that I was walking away in the opposite direction—actually over age or presumably a crock but not feeling particularly like one at the moment."

And to another friend: "I feel very much of a shirker when I hear what everyone else is doing. Myra Hess refusing to come over to U.S.A. in order to help music in England makes me feel ashamed rather."

He was also full of admiration for the way in which Ralph Vaughan Williams flung himself into wartime activities in Dorking— salvage, war savings, fire-watching, growing vegetables, keeping hens—as well as doing a great deal to assist foreign refugee musicians and helping Myra Hess to start the National Gallery concerts. His sense of guilt was heightened by the knowledge that his elder brother Arnold had enlisted in the R.A.F.

"My brother Arnold did his best to produce the 'better under-standing' that is said always to be the bulwark against war, but he failed and has been the object I understand of a lot of cheap abuse as a 'friend of Hitler'. He has joined up and is very happy at 56 or thereabouts as an observer in the R.A.F. but he is a soldier and is not a person who thinks that war is necessarily always wrong. Nor am I and were I at home I dare say I should have done the same."

When the news came through that Arnold had been shot down in a bombing raid over Germany, Steuart wrote to Clive Carey:

"It was a great tragedy that he—like Chamberlain—should have trusted to an honour in some one else which did not exist. I know his view was, that if that honour did not exist then there was no hope for Europe till it did exist, so that we must foster it and keep on imagining it till the Germans developed it. If we weren't generous no one else would be and the disaster would then come anyhow. Some of his crew in the bomber are prisoners and one of them was buried at Cambrai, but no word or identifica-tion of him has turned up. I have quite given up hope and so I think have all of us."

In spite of his anxieties about the war, Steuart arrived in Phila-delphia, determined to make a success of the job and to make the most of his opportunities in America. The Curtis Institute, one of the most famous of America's music schools, was founded in 1924 by Mrs. Mary Curtis Zimbalist (then Mrs. Curtis Bok) who endowed it with $12,500,000. The Institute was organized on familiar Con-servatoire lines, training about 200 students from all parts of the U.S.A. and from other countries. From 1927 to 1938, the celebrated pianist Josef Hofmann was its director. In 1939 he was succeeded by the composer Randall Thompson, who was responsible for appoint-ing Steuart.

Steuart got on very well with Randall Thompson. "He is a man after my own heart and I know in advance that he wants all the reforms that I want and that he is only waiting for the opportunity—and he is a very good waiter." He also reported: "Luckily for the Curtis, Mrs. Bok, on whose money it all rests, is ideal in respect of keeping out of it until she is asked to take a decision and then she doesn't falter. It might be a hopeless job to beat the whim of a domineering rich old woman. As it is, she turns out to be a good colleague." That was written in the very early stages of his association with the Institute.

"Work at the Curtis is fun. I've never had any pupils continuously so that I could as it were supervise their practice and see exactly what they did. They make them work hard, at solfige and languages but they don't provide accompanists and répétiteurs or coaches and these boys can't teach themselves, the average musical equipment being of a lower standard than we should normally get. I teach 8 boys 2 hours a week and give them certain other classes as well, which is more than my terms of service bind me to, but I haven't anything else to do and I like the job; for they work hard and willingly and are much more stimulating to teach than the more intelligent but less responsive or argumentative English."

Steuart taught only boys. As he wrote:

"Elisabeth Schumann has nothing but girls – either because they wouldn't trust me or more likely because she teaches more by invitation than by general principle and so thinks that women learn from women only and men from men (which opinion I don't agree with . . .) I have certainly never worked so hard in my life – four mornings a week from 9 to 1 are a real revolution in my habits."

After a full morning at the Curtis, he went out most afternoons to a suburb to "teach reading English—I won't call it elocution."

Steuart expressed his opinions about the general standards of the school and its pupils in a letter to Iris Lemare:

"The standards of the school are very high in piano playing, really remarkable and beyond anything that we approach in England. The violins are remarkable, the cellos below our standards, the woodwind all amazingly competent but we think the oboes rather lacking in subtlety after Léon's incomparable pupils—the singers are frankly poor judged by any standard and it's my business to haul the standard up if not to a high level of talent, at least to one of efficiency. They aim at it, but they don't get it because none of the singing teachers in the past has been interested in it and they have merely considered it as 'nice if you had it' but not essential to an artistic career. So the singers thought that you got to the top by singing very loud and that you didn't have to bother about time or rhythm, the 'public' didn't want that—so if they failed—as they generally did—to make an impression they considered that they ought to have sung louder! And so far—it is the only concern they have and they regard sight reading, ensemble etc. as a waste of time. I have done a good deal already to dispel that, because they do admire the fact that I can come down to their chorus group and madrigal rehearsals and be the only one who can read at sight and that I can play the piano for all their lessons and transpose the easy accompaniments and yet can be considered an 'artist'. I like the students and I like their enthusiasm; though their mental development is much behind any European standards they make up for it by much more concentrated desire to learn."

Although he enjoyed the work, Steuart was still nagged by financial worry. He wrote to his friend Sidney Newman:

"Our position is very uncertain here. I think I am being a success and doing what has been badly needed and I think that in a short time I can persuade the Board to have some re-organizing of curriculum and outlook for 1st year students which will be more practical and more suited to their needs and the strange lacunae in their education. But I have no idea if they will raise my salary next year. I'm doing twice as much teaching as the minimum contracted for simply because I've got nothing else to do here—no concerts arranged and no other job. Most of the swell teachers like Zimbalist, Schumann and Felix Salmond come over from New York one day a week and teach for $\frac{1}{2}$ hr. or 40 minute periods."

Life in Philadelphia was expensive but the Wilsons had a fairly hectic social life. At the beginning they lived in a furnished house, 1909 Ringgold Place, in an old and once fashionable quarter of the city.

In May 1940 they moved to new quarters at 1728 Delancey Place, more convenient for the Institute. They very quickly made friends;

everywhere Steuart went, he became the centre of an admiring circle. Mary wrote ruefully to Iris Lemare: "Our circle of friends grows and Steuart is again much beloved, especially by certain dames. I find that in a new existence I can retaliate a bit. Good for him!" Steuart himself wrote: "We both enjoy the social life out here and the friends we have made are pure gold in value."

Both were extremely busy raising funds for war relief. Steuart sold a series of English folk song records to raise $2000 for a 'rolling kitchen', and both he and Mary performed for charity. Mary expressed anxiety about having to organize concerts for stranded British seamen, thinking that her choice of music would be 'rather too highbrow'. She did a lot of quartet playing and found a group who were prepared to tackle all the late Beethoven quartets.

All this took place before Pearl Harbor. Steuart took a rather jaundiced view of American attitudes towards the war:

"America is already beginning to show signs of saying 'If we help you, you must do what we want,' and they cannot understand all the tragedies of their intervention in the last war and the futilities of their innocent statesmanship. They are terrified of becoming involved and of course they are much more hysterical as a nation than the English whom they resemble so little. At the beginning when they felt safe, their attitude was one of vulgar curiosity—but they've changed that. The nice folks here of whom there are a lot—are so eager to help that no day passes without some party raising funds and giving teas and concerts and so on."

They kept open house and gave many parties for their students, Steuart, of course, taking charge of the food and drinks. These parties were much appreciated by the students who thought them a novelty. "They come from all parts and just 'room' here rather uncomfortably and rather poorly, so they appreciate it the more and the girls like a good opportunity for telling Mary all the things about the fashions and their teachers etc. that they want to get off their chest."

The Wilsons also went to concerts as often as possible, and one week-end went on a 'minor jaunt' to New York, where they saw the de Basil Ballet. Steuart was critical of the performance which included *Les Sylphides* and Berlioz *Symphonie Fantastique*.

"The weakness of American taste on the whole is that in art they like exuberance and in music—classical I mean—they like the absence of all faults so that most music over here has only negative virtues, it is not out of tune, it is not shrill, it is not unrhythmical and so on, it comes to you beautifully wrapped up but it has little or no personality or vitality of utterance—in case that should take the sweetness out of the mixture. So I'm always glad to see a rough healthy feeling in any musical job. The orchestra playing in the ballet was pretty useful for a big city. Harp hideously flat in the *Sylphides*, no delicacy in the strings, the woodwind explosive. The trombones in the Berlioz were 'calico-tearers' like old Capt. Hook in Peter Pan. We tried by the way to see Evelyn Rothwell but the N.Y. Philharmonic are on tour and she was away with John [Barbirolli]."

Another jaunt was a trip to Canada in the spring of 1940, where Steuart sang in Dyson's cantata *The Canterbury Pilgrims* with the Winnipeg Philharmonic Choir. This was at the invitation of his cousin James Robertson who had recently become its conductor. Steuart had sung in the first performance of the *Canterbury Pilgrims* at Winchester in 1931. The local papers were enthusiastic both about James Robertson's musicianship and Steuart's singing.

Steuart sang in several concerts under the American conductor J. A. Dash, including a Bach and a Schubert Festival. He gave a joint recital of Schubert songs (in his own English translation) with Elisabeth Schumann. Not all the American audiences took to his singing—perhaps because he didn't sing loud enough for their liking, but the cognoscenti were full of praise.

He and Mary were regular attenders at the Sunday evening parties at the home of Henry S. Drinker and his wife Sophie, the remarkable couple round whom music in Philadelphia revolved. The Drinkers held regular musical sessions, where people just dropped in to sing Bach cantatas and chorales, Brahms *Liebeslieder*, the *Messiah*, the *Elijah* and many modern works as well. It started in 1930 as a 'singing party' for about twenty people—today it would no doubt be called a 'sing-in'—and later took the more resonant title "Accademia dei Dilettanti di Musica'.

Steuart was planning an open air production of *Dido and Aeneas* at Brynmawr for the summer of 1941, with his friend Robin Miller, then assistant music director and organist. Plans were in an advanced state and great enthusiasm had been engendered, when the blow fell. In January 1941 Mrs. Bok suddenly decided to fire the director of the Institute, Randall Thompson, and five or six of the teaching staff, including Steuart. Steuart put it picturesquely "Mrs. Bok ran Amok." From then on, it was a hand-to-mouth existence. Steuart undertook a series of Festival adjudications in Canada and found himself a job teaching singing in a girls' school in Philadelphia: "a very pleasant girls' school, but it can't pay enough and I don't think I shall be a vast success with kids of 8, teaching them solfa and little songs."

He also taught for a time at the New England Conservatory at Boston:

"individual teaching plus a Teachers' Training class, good fun but hellishly difficult as all the pupils come from other teachers; all of them thought they had nothing to learn and that there was only one way of teaching, you said 'Get the voice more forward and that was that!'"

But the "pleasant girls' school" turned out to be anything but pleasant. It proved "an intolerable job."

"I suppose I could have stayed on and fought them, but I got wearied of the struggle and weary of the long journey. I lived in Boston went to Phila. on Monday morning and came back on Thurs. evening, taught all Friday from 9–6 or 7 and part of Saturday. It was a gruelling experience but I learned a lot out of having to teach very small children of 7 years old and up—how to sing and how to start on music generally. Well, it's clear here as everywhere else that individual teaching is going to be damned hard to live off and any concert work here is out of the question—the whole place is jammed full of singers from every country in the world all rampaging around for jobs."

In the end, he decided to give up the unequal struggle and come home.

Just what he would do when he got back he had no idea. But he thought he would perhaps be able to straighten out his finances if necessary, by "washing up and making beds in Oakley Street." He wrote to Clive Carey:

"As to my singing—well I'm 53 and out of practice, it's useless to think that I can bawl my way through a big work again and *I'm not going to try*. I can teach—I can't be methodical and give everyone just the same exercises and songs and so on but I can develop something natural in them if they will allow themselves to understand what I'm after—and not be put out by the fact that it is new to them."

PART THREE

ADMINISTRATOR

CHAPTER NINETEEN

THE ARTS COUNCIL

WHEN Steuart arrived back in London on 19th September 1942, the future seemed very bleak. "We are all bankrupt, tottering on the edge of eternity," he wrote to Clive Carey. He found it depressing to "see how many second-rate people are muscling in on the job—all the punk conductors there on the bill. I think I shall go and be an honest cook in a nice home."

This mood didn't last long. He had only been back a few days when he met his old Petersfield friend Ronald Biggs, who told him there was an organizing job going in Manchester. Suddenly out of the blue came an invitation from Sir Arthur Bliss, then director of music at the BBC, to join the Corporation. Steuart wrote to Iris Lemare:

"I have renounced Manchester—didn't go up for an interview in the end because I have accepted an offer of a job in the BBC through Arthur Bliss and I start work there as soon as possible, perhaps tomorrow, to learn the routine job before Leonard Isaacs whose dept I take over goes to the Army.

It was all very quickly arranged, but I decided after some vacillations that I could do something in the B.B.C. in the end when the War is over that might equal what I could do in Manchester and I hope I shall turn out to be right."

He started on 11th November 1942, 'learning the ropes', and a month later became European music supervisor. In January 1943 he was appointed Overseas Music Director, a post he held until March 1945 when he left to join the Arts Council. He came back to the

BBC on 1st January 1948 as Head of Music, and resigned in August 1950.

In order to save duplication, and even at the expense of chronological exactitude, I am taking his two BBC periods as *one* chapter, covering his general attitude towards the Corporation. And since his second term there was the more important, we may turn immediately to the Arts Council and all its works.

Music was kept alive in England throughout the darkest days of the war, in defiance of bombs and black-out and in spite of the complete breakdown of normal social life. People could not get to concerts—there was little public transport, petrol was rationed and most halls had anyhow been commandeered by the military—so concerts had to be taken to the people. This was the job of C.E.M.A., the Council for the Encouragement of Music and the Arts. Established in January 1940 by the Pilgrim Trust with some Government support, C.E.M.A. organized concerts in air-raid shelters, rest-centres, hostels, factory canteens and mining villages. Its Music Director was Dr. Reginald Jacques, conductor of the London Bach Choir. He resigned in April 1945, to return to his professional career after five years' devoted service. The drama director, Lewis Casson, who had also been in C.E.M.A. since the start, resigned at the same time. Casson was succeeded by Michael MacOwan, Jacques by Steuart Wilson.

In 1945, C.E.M.A. was given a full exchequer grant and Lord Keynes was made its chairman. That same year it became the Arts Council of Great Britain, with a Royal Charter. Keynes said that he had deliberately chosen unpronounceable initials which could not be made into a portmanteau word. He had been amused to hear that a letter had been addressed to the Council for the Encouragement of Music and Darts.*

The Arts Council's terms of reference, announced in Parliament on 12th June 1945 by Sir John Anderson, then Chancellor of the Exchequer, were "to carry the arts throughout the countryside and

---

* This recalls a story in Hugh Dalton's reminiscences *High Tide and After* which Steuart was very fond of quoting. Attlee, Bevin, Dalton and Dai Grenfell (then Secretary for Mines) were discussing who should handle a coal problem which had arisen. "Attlee asked Bevin: 'which of us shall handle it?' Bevin replied. But was it 'You and I?' or 'Hugh and I?' Or 'You and Dai?' or 'Hugh and Dai?'" The only flaw Steuart detected, which he pointed out in a letter to Winifred Fox, was that Bevin would have surely said "You and me."

to maintain metropolitan standards." The Council would be an independent body financed by a grant-in-aid from the Exchequer. Lord Keynes said in a broadcast (*The Listener*, 12th July 1945) "State patronage of the Arts has crept in . . . At last the public Exchequer has recognized the support and encouragement of the civilizing arts of life as part of their public duty." Keynes stressed the determination of the Council to "decentralize and disperse." "Let every part of Merry England be merry in its own way," he declared.

Steuart Wilson was a natural choice for the post of Music Director. Mary Glasgow, the Council's secretary-general, who was seconded from the Board of Education in December 1939, wrote to Keynes in February 1945 about the agenda for a forthcoming executive meeting: "I imagine that the first matter for consideration is the appointment of Dr. Jacques's successor. We already have a list of promising nominees, of which the most popular appears to be Steuart Wilson, now at the BBC."

Steuart got the job, and his appointment was widely welcomed. He did not have much experience of desk work, but the Arts Council job called for qualities amounting almost to those of a crusader—which he possessed to the full. As Frank Howes (music critic of *The Times*) pointed out (*Musical Times*, March 1951):

> "His experience as a professional singer, a working artist who knew all about long train journeys, bad hotels, cold halls, wrong-pitch pianos and organs, small fees, the vagaries of conductors and the tempers of fellow singers, was now put to work from the other side."

Steuart's appointment as Music Director was announced in April 1945. A few months later, the Arts Council report said that he was "driving straight for an active peace-time policy with many new ideas and experimental programmes," and his approach had "given the staff new vitality." Mary Glasgow confided to Keynes: "S.W. is of course a delight. He is gay, efficient and speaks with authority. He gets on with his plans—in alarming numbers and at an alarming speed, but never fails to keep me informed."

The two assistant music directors were Mona Tatham and Ian McPhail. Steuart relied very much on them and on the eleven regional directors and their staffs for carrying out central policy and developing local activities.

C.E.M.A. had originally been housed in the Board of Education's wartime offices in Kingsway; later it moved to 9 Belgrave Square. In September 1947 the Arts Council found the home which it was to occupy for twenty years in Lord Astor's beautiful and dignified house at 4 St. James's Square, which the owner had sold to the Ministry of Works on very generous terms. Steuart described the new quarters in a letter to Audrey Mildmay. "We are palatially housed in Lord Astor's mansion. Some of us, like myself, are in the servants' quarters, others housed palatially like Mussolini in the middle of a ballroom, half a day's route march away from the door. We like the splendour."

In 1945 the Treasury made a grant to the Arts Council of £235,000—an increase of £60,000 over that given to C.E.M.A. The following year, the figure was increased to £350,000, double the original C.E.M.A. grant of £175,000. (In 1968-9 the Treasury grant totalled about £7 million.) Of the total grant, expenditure on music and opera accounted for about half, and by far the largest share was taken up by opera.

The Arts in general, and the Arts Council in particular, suffered a cruel blow with the death of Lord Keynes, on Easter Sunday 1946. His had been the inspiration behind the Council's creation; he had provided the faith and drive which led to its establishment as the focal point of cultural life in post-war Britain and guided it through the difficult formative months. Steuart felt the loss keenly. He had grown to have a great respect, amounting almost to affection, for this shy, acerb man, whom many regarded as an unapproachable economist, but who had a deep understanding of human values. King's was a bond between them. Keynes liked Steuart and respected his judgement. His letters to Mary Glasgow often refer with approval to "Wilson's plans" for this and that, usually adding the caution "But don't let him overspend." Even while he was immersed in complex financial negotiations in America, Keynes found time to take a detailed interest in the affairs of the Council. "Yes, I would like to be bothered while I'm away," he told Mary.

Steuart and Keynes held the same views about the purpose of the Arts Council and they agreed about the way it should be run. Keynes insisted there should be a minimum of red tape. "We have been wonderfully free from cut-and-dried organization so far and I hope we shall stick to it," he wrote to Mary Glasgow. He wanted to keep things as informal as possible and for this reason opposed a suggestion that the Council might appoint a Press officer. "They only make foolish remarks, get you false publicity and generally speaking coax you into doing things which are better not done," he wrote.

Lord Keynes was succeeded as chairman by Sir Ernest Pooley, a former vice-chairman of the Old Vic and Sadler's Wells Board of Governors.

Steuart outlined his policy in the official *Bulletin*:

"The work which has been done as a National Service by C.E.M.A. musicians will have been fruitless, if it does not lead to a wide increase of professional music all over the country. We hope that out of the special audiences of wartime may spring many new permanent organizations, managing their own affairs and engaging their own artists at normal professional fees. The Council will readily give advice and financial support where necessary to all concert-giving societies established on a suitable basis."

The demand for organized concerts after working hours dwindled as industry returned to normal and the army of wartime workers dispersed. Instead, the Arts Council lent its full support to the formation and development of local music clubs and appointed a team of specialists known as "industrial music advisers." To encourage the 'club' atmosphere, members' meetings were arranged, with brains trusts (then at the height of fashion) gramophone recitals and lectures. The Arts Council also continued to provide concerts in industrial areas, at the express request of the Ministry of Labour.

The success of the Arts Council's mission "to carry the arts throughout the countryside" can be gauged by a look at the long list of fixtures arranged month by month in its fourteen regions. To take one month at random—July 1945—some ninety concerts were given in factories, churches, institutes and schools, as well as those for the Forces and the symphony concerts.

The concerts served a dual purpose. They continued to satisfy the growing thirst for music in England and they provided much-needed work for musicians, giving many who had just returned from war service the chance to regain their confidence and refresh their rusty techniques. Most of the works performed were classical and traditional, rather than modern and adventurous. This was, by and large, what their audiences wanted. But the Arts Council attached great

M

importance to fostering contemporary music and to helping young British composers. One of the earliest ventures with which Steuart was associated was a Festival of Contemporary Music, sponsored by the *News Chronicle*—then under the enlightened editorship of Gerald Barry. Steuart attended a lunch given by the paper and reported: "There, no doubt inflamed by wine, I enunciated the general principle that the Arts Council would be prepared to finance the performance of British works by British artists." His action was not altogether approved of. Mary Glasgow noted: "I am afraid it is another case of the Music Director being too forthcoming in the beginning."

The Festival ran for a week in July 1946 and included works by Prokofiev, Stravinsky, Hindemith, Schoenberg, Béla Bartók, Webern and by British composers, such as Benjamin Britten, Alan Rawsthorne and Elizabeth Lutyens. It made a loss of £705. 9s. 7d., which the *News Chronicle* bore. It was a brave venture, but possibly ahead of its time.

Steuart was more cautious about a second appeal for Arts Council help in sponsoring the cause of international musicians, which reached him that autumn. It came from Dr. Alfred Kalmus, who put forward a scheme for an International Music Association, with the idea of improving international understanding "since the language of music is one of the easiest means of *rapprochement* between nations". The scheme was blessed by Malcolm Sargent, but Steuart was cagey. He wrote a characteristic minute, with the inevitable Biblical reference (Luke xvi 3) criticizing the syntax and declaring that "the combination of legal language and Kalmus seems to me to end up in several Total Eclipses".

Steuart and his music panel were determined to strengthen national symphony orchestras. He pointed out in an Arts Council report that "the country was facing for the first time the cost of supporting a type of first-class musical institution which in the past had been left to fend for itself, or to depend on private bounty". The question of fees and salaries for orchestral players was discussed with the Musicians' Union, with apparently satisfactory results. At any rate, by March 1947, the Arts Council was fully supporting four symphony orchestras—Birmingham, Hallé, Liverpool Philharmonic and London Philharmonic—and four chamber orchestras (New London, Boyd Neel, and the Jacques and Riddick string orchestras).

Eight other orchestras were associated with the Council for certain approved concerts.

Arts Council support was given only after the most searching and stringent investigation of musical standards.

As can well be imagined, there was always a long queue of applicants and supplicants knocking at the door of the music director, begging for money and patronage. The burden of advising Yes or No, which fell on Steuart, was an onerous one. It often meant disappointing people who had been closely associated with him in the past, but he was determined both to maintain the highest possible artistic standards and to encourage only the genuine and worthwhile enterprises.

One cause which was very near his heart was that of the International Folk Music Council, of which Vaughan Williams was chairman. Steuart had presided at most of the meetings of its inaugural conference, in London in September 1947 and when its secretary Maud Karpeles wrote to the Arts Council requesting help, he backed her. Vaughan Williams wrote to Eric Walter White (the Arts Council assistant secretary) in December: "Miss K is asking for £500. When is this likely to come up, so that I may be there to advocate it?" A non-recurrent grant of £300 was given and Steuart was nominated the Arts Council's official observer on the Folk Music Council. "From our point of view there could not be any one better." Miss Karpeles observed.

The next year—when Steuart was no longer with the Arts Council —the grant was withheld. Vaughan Williams was furious. "I was dismayed to hear that the A.C. had turned down Miss Karpeles' appeal for help," he wrote to Mary Glasgow. "It does seem to me to be rather a cat and mouse policy to give £300 one year and withdraw it the next."

Despite Vaughan Williams's advocacy, the Arts Council declined to reverse its decision, though it did agree to help finance an international Folk Festival in 1952. "Les folkloristes" came from all over the world to a conference at Cecil Sharp House, where Steuart took the chair. According to Eric Walter White: "There was a moment of gorgeous confusion when the maximum amount of misunderstanding was caused by the inadequate translation of such French words as professeur, chaire, école normale etc. and the Anglo-Saxons had no idea what the French-speaking parts of the conference were

getting at; but Sir Steuart ironed out these differences with relent-
lessly suave amicability." (This was to be Steuart's apprenticeship
for the much bigger task he later assumed of presiding over
UNESCO's International Music Council).

All the time he was at the Arts Council, Steuart was indefatigable,
touring the regions, giving lectures, arranging concerts and attending
a multiplicity of committees and conferences. He was the official
representative on the standing conference of county music committees sponsored by the National Council of Social Service, a body
responsible for organizing musical activities in forty counties in
England and Wales.

Steuart was keen to encourage local groups to perform opera. In
October 1947 he gave what he himself described as a 'sales talk' on
opera to the standing conference. It was packed with practical
advice and hints on matters ranging from the choice of works to
production, scenery and lighting, and the kind of help the Arts
Council and its experts could give them. His advice to budding
amateur operatic societies was, not to think solely in terms of Gilbert
and Sullivan, but to put on imaginative works, though they might
have to fall back for 'bread and butter' on such favourites as *Faust*,
Cavalleria Rusticana and *Pagliacci*. "We want to show people that
amusing opera is not necessarily bad music, nor is dull opera
necessarily good."

He was involved in many negotiations with local authorities, who
had been given powers under the 1948 Act to subsidise entertainment and the arts from local rates, but who were not always taking
advantage of these. Steuart appealed to members of the Incorporated
Society of Musicians at their annual conference:

"Each member must make it his business in his own sphere to
preach the gospel of Good Entertainment and to encourage every
Councillor and Alderman to enquire for professional advice on
how to get it ... Let it be known that you are a professional
musician with a professional standard of how things *should* be done,
and that you know where to get advice on how they *can* be done
and what they will cost. Could you convene a meeting within
your area to discuss with any authority who has the powers, how
they will use those powers? Do you owe that to your profession or
would you rather stay outside and offer no advice? I beg of you to

go back and use every shred of prestige or position you can put forward to make Authority listen to you."

An immediate problem facing musicians was the shortage of suitable halls for concerts and recitals. Early in 1945 the *C.E.M.A. Bulletin* had described the situation: "Performances of all kinds have had to be given in town halls and country houses and camps, cathedrals and churches, hotels and restaurants, shops and commercial showrooms, in fact in almost every kind of building except one properly designed, equipped and decorated for the purpose. The Arts should be honourably housed." The Council's regional officers were always on the look-out for possible premises and were, in some cases (e.g. King's Lynn and Bridgwater) successful in acquiring them for the Arts. Steuart himself was responsible for acquiring the Wigmore Hall in London for the Arts Council, an achievement of which he was justifiably proud. Negotiations had started in 1945, with Keynes's full approval, and the first licence was granted by the London County Council in August 1946, on condition that the necessary structural improvements, fire precautions etc. were undertaken. Steuart conducted a running battle with the Ministry of Works, which at first refused a licence. The reference number CL 5/189556 must have been a very hot potato on the civil servants' desks because Steuart, as was his wont, would not take 'No' for an answer. "No—that's only a beginning," he would say whenever he became embroiled in a battle with bureaucracy.

His campaign was successful—the licence was granted, Steuart enlisted the help of Sir Kenneth Clark to advise on decoration and borrowed pictures from the Royal College of Music to hang in the foyer. A letter to H. T. C. Brickell, the Hall's manager, dated 3rd March 1947, illustrates his meticulous attention to detail:

... "I am anxious to get on with the platform plans. I think it is very important that the heating duct should be divided so that there is no screen immediately under the front of the platform, but that the heat should come out into the sides of the auditorium. That will prevent the hot blast of wind that used to disturb singers ... If you notice the arrangements made at Covent Garden for the symphony orchestras, you will see that the curved shell which they place behind certain instruments is seldom more than 8 feet high before it begins to curve. The height of the cupola must be more like 14' before it begins to curve comparatively gently.

"I very much trust Sir Kenneth's judgement on decoration. He completely reorganized the National Gallery and is a person of extremely fine taste, and being interested in music is not likely to want to spoil a Concert Hall for the sake of decoration. Moreover, his wife has just as good a sense of the sort of place in which the well-dressed handsome woman looks her best, so we shall be safe-guarded on all sides."

Steuart wrote to Mr. Brickell in September 1947: "Everything seems in good shape at the Hall, and I am going tonight to see what it looks like at an actual concert. So far as I know, the users have been pleased."

An early performance in the Hall was of the opera *L'Amfiparnaso*, redesigned for puppets with the Lanchester Marionettes and the New English Singers, whose voices were recorded so that the show could go on tour. This delightful story of Pantaloon's adventures by Orazio Vecchi was translated by E. J. Dent, who helped in the production. *Amfiparnaso* was a tremendous success, both in London and the provinces.

Steuart left the Arts Council in December 1947 to become Music Director at the BBC. The Council's official report stated, "It is no exaggeration to say that he is irreplaceable." All in all, his two and a half years with the Council were undoubtedly the most productive and personally satisfying of his administrative career. It was in recognition of his services to music, while at the Arts Council, that he was awarded a Knighthood in the Birthday Honours of 1948.

His first year at the Council was, however, clouded by ill-health and by the recurrence of his old enemy, the Ulcer. John Denison, who was to succeed him as music director, has recalled how Steuart used to lie on a big couch nicknamed 'Nuppers' in his office, dictat-ing, telephoning, interviewing and generally conducting his normal business, taking occasional swigs from the bottle of milk at his side. Most of the time he was in pain, and his then secretary Eileen Wisdom remembers his looking 'absolutely grey' and thinking that he would surely not survive.

On 7th May 1946 Steuart wrote to E. J. Dent about possible successors to Lord Keynes as chairman of the Covent Garden Opera

Trust and added: "Have had further trouble and have decided to go into Hospital to have some surgery attempted. Go to Nuffield House, Guy's this afternoon."

Two days later, he again wrote to Dent, this time from his hospital bed, discussing the arrangements for *Amfiparnaso* and his ideas for model art centres in smaller towns. He included a full progress report on the state of his stomach:

> "I am just undergoing a series of test meals, rubber tube down the gullet and samples of cold porridge drawn up by siphon every 15 minutes. Tomorrow may have more fun and games in store. Meanwhile the Augurs are gathering for a conclave on the Viscera and we may expect some 'Auspicium'."

The operation was successful and the ulcer was finally tamed. Steuart went, with Mary, to Dartington to convalesce and returned to the office full of vigour and apparently completely restored in health.

It must have been about this time, that Steuart started knitting, presumably on his doctor's orders, as a therapeutic exercise. David Franklin, the singer, has told me how he remembers meeting Steuart with a long, grey shapeless object at the end of outsize knitting needles. "*What* are you knitting, Steuart?" he asked. "I'm not knitting a What," was the reply, "I'm just knitting."

As a postscript to this chapter it is worth putting on record a correspondence in the *Daily Telegraph* of August 1957, in which Steuart criticized the Arts Council's tendency to look after the big fish and neglect the smaller fry.

> "One large cheque to one large concern and everything is tidy— 50 smaller cheques take too much time to investigate, so let the Societies die . . . We now tend to measure culture only in terms of tourists coming to Festivals. I would like to go back and measure it again by a smaller unit of those who want it in small doses for their own consumption at home. Let only those take up music who feel in some indefinable way a dedication. Let those who want money dedicate themselves likewise to an exacting career."

John Denison replied that in the ten years from 1947 to 1957 the number of local societies assisted by the Arts Council had increased from 90 to 450, so that it was not true that they were being allowed to die. Steuart came back: "I would like to congratulate Mr. Denison on his answer. . . . Like the well-trained official he stresses figures and statistics, showing that a very much increased number of musical societies in the National Federation share a not nearly so much increased share of money." He particularly deplored the decision to disband the regional organizers who had done so much to keep music alive in the provinces and fulfil the Arts Council's original mission "to carry the arts throughout the countryside."

CHAPTER TWENTY

GLYNDEBOURNE AND EDINBURGH

THROUGHOUT Steuart's time at the Arts Council, and even before he joined it and after he had left, the problem of John Christie and the future of Glyndebourne loomed large. Even though there was no corpse in the library, and no Poirot to unravel the tangle, the 'Christie affair' had all the elements of a thriller—drama, plots, personalities, intrigues and even a threatened duel! The full story of Christie's persistent efforts to win financial support for his ambitious plans to re-establish Glyndebourne after the war as a National Opera House, has been told by Spike Hughes and by Wilfrid Blunt in their books.* They tell it necessarily from Christie's angle; the Arts Council's version will have to wait for some official historian to dig into its archives.

Steuart Wilson, as music director, was at the centre of the protracted and often acrimonious negotiations, which were to prove so frustrating to Christie and so time-consuming to the Arts Council. He wrote letters and minutes and attended meetings where the problem was discussed endlessly. On one occasion, Mary Glasgow recalls, Christie, who was suffering from gout, arrived in a National Health Service ambulance, which he kept waiting outside the Arts Council office, while inside he argued long and bitterly with Steuart and herself. In the end, Steuart lent his full weight against any proposal to subvent Glyndebourne. "I should not be able to recommend to the Council that I could take on any financial responsibility for the Glyndebourne season out of the existing Music budget," he minuted in April 1947.

* *John Christie of Glyndebourne*, Wilfrid Blunt; Geoffrey Bles, 1968. *Glyndebourne*, Spike Hughes; Methuen, 1965.

As long ago as 1942 Christie had written to Sir Stafford Cripps, outlining grandiose schemes which would need government money. Cripps' laconic advice was: "Keep in touch with Keynes." In 1944 Christie approached Sir John Anderson, then Chancellor of the Exchequer, asking for "state aid pure and simple" and mentioning a figure of £1 million a year to be spent on music. "We are thwarted by the Treasury, by Keynes and by C.E.M.A.," he complained. "Keynes refuses to see me and I believe that he is there, with the satisfaction of the Treasury, in order to keep me out." He planned to buy the freehold of Covent Garden and to establish it as the "headquarters of England's Art" with Rudolf Bing, Glyndebourne's general manager since 1935, to run it. The scheme collapsed when the Opera House was leased to Boosey and Hawkes, the music publishers. Keynes, the chairman of the Covent Garden Opera Trust, rebuffed him in the summer of 1945, with what Spike Hughes has described as a "rough and ill-mannered rejection."

About the same time, however, we find Keynes writing to Mary Glasgow: "John Christie is holding out to me a very amicable, leafy and well-grown olive branch. I am preparing to accept it." Sir Thomas Beecham, who had likewise failed to come to terms with Covent Garden, then put forward a plan for running an opera season at Glyndebourne at which, it was agreed, *The Magic Flute*, *Figaro* and *Carmen* would be presented. But the clash of their two eccentric and self-willed personalities, plus Beecham's exacting demands—he objected to the proposal to bill Kathleen Ferrier as Carmen—caused this idea to be dropped.

Soon after this, Steuart, another temperamental and forceful character, entered the lists. He was first approached by John Christie at a luncheon early in 1946, when he (Steuart) was giving a talk on the rôle of the Arts Council in Opera.

"Christie's question to me, three times repeated in almost identical words," Steuart wrote later, "was 'What is the Trust going to do about creating ideal conditions for the conductor or the producer of Opera?' Three times I repeated in almost identical words 'Nothing'."

Steuart had very definite ideas about the future of opera in England and Christie's Glyndebourne just didn't fit into his pattern. He wanted opera for the people and not for the select few. From the Arts Council, he wrote to an American musician who was asking about opera in England:

"Glyndebourne . . . is the project of a rich individualist, who believes in doing everything in the original language with a lot of elaborate and careful preparation in a large country house 1 hour from London, with prices scaled only for the rich. Before the War, this had a definite place in social life—it's beginning to feel a little out of it with the change in habits. Mr. Christie is just an individualist and it's difficult to get him into co-operation with anybody else."

Christie's views were expressed in a long Memorandum to the Arts Council which concluded:

"I am quite sure that an organization must exist which aims at the sky. It is not a question of doing your best (in your circumstances). It is something quite different. It is a question of doing the best that can be done under ideal conditions and this means forcing the World or the Country to supply the right conditions. That is what we set out to do at Glyndebourne and at Edinburgh."

To this Memorandum, Steuart replied:

"Mr. Christie's last paragraph is the clue to his thoughts. He forgets that at Glyndebourne he started with a complete blank space and he could design everything to fill it. He filled it in many ways to perfection (though I doubt if his stage plan is anything like perfect) because he only attempted a very small fraction of the operatic repertoire, and because he made no attempt whatever to satisfy certain social problems. His was an opera for the rich and the leisured in gala style of remarkable quality.

"He appears unable to see that the operatic problem can be seen from another angle of sight: first the commonsense angle, that you cannot start your opera scheme by destroying Covent Garden and building a new 'ideal' theatre. While an iron is hot is the time for moulding it and the British people—many of whom had scarcely heard of Glyndebourne and none of whom had ever been able to afford to visit it—were ready to hear opera. Secondly, that the social changes that had taken place would make it utterly impossible to recreate the 'Gala' scale of pre-war opera. Thirdly that there is a strong bias of opinion that if opera is ultimately to take root among the less educated people it must be sung in the vernacular, for the most part.

"Lastly, as a general concern, it seems to me that Mr. Christie, who has never been closely in touch with any opera-goers except the Glyndebourne-goers, has got entirely out of touch with contemporary social views if he believes that it is possible to force the world or the country to re-create the Glyndebourne conditions which are the only opera conditions which he really knows."

Wilfrid Blunt wrote that "The quarrel continued for several months, John calling Steuart Wilson a liar and Steuart Wilson calling John a fool and proposing (though doubtless not seriously) a duel; what is surprising is that John did not accept the challenge."

There was a subsidiary row between the two men to which Mary Glasgow referred in a letter to Keynes:

"Did you know that Steuart Wilson is having a violent quarrel by letter with Christie? Steuart, with three others, was asked to advise the Sadler's Wells Governors confidentially about the appointment of their Opera director. Candidates were Roy Henderson, Stanford Robinson, James Robertson and Rudi Bing. The experts advised against Bing. James Robertson was appointed. Christie has accused Steuart of giving false evidence against Bing."

The hatchet was to some extent buried when, in February 1948, John Christie received, and accepted, an offer to serve on the Arts Council's newly-created panel for opera and ballet. Steuart had by then moved to the BBC but remained a member of the seventeen-strong panel, whose composition suggests not only the inclusion of leading opera experts, but a rich blending of personalities, many of whom had barely been on speaking terms, as well as a modicum of committee men who could be relied upon to keep the peace.

There was also, many years later, a ceremonial burying of the personal hatchet. John Christie invited Steuart and Mary to his box to hear Bellini's *I Puritani* on the eve of their departure to India in May 1960. Mary wrote to her mother "Steuart is so pleased to have made up an old quarrel."

In 1950 the Treasury made a grant towards the production of four Mozart operas in 1951, to mark the Festival of Britain year. The grant was for one year only, but the State guarantee of £25,000 against loss was, in Christie's eyes, deserved, if overdue, recognition.

The Arts Council had refused to subsidise the Christie ventures, either directly or in collaboration with Beecham; but it came in two important ways to be associated with Glyndebourne in the immediate post-war period.

On Rudolf Bing's initiative, Glyndebourne agreed to present a season of Benjamin Britten's new full-length opera, *The Rape of Lucretia*, with Carl Ebert as artistic director, Eric Crozier producing, sets by John Piper, and Ernest Ansermet and Reginald Goodall sharing the conducting.

The Rape of Lucretia was given its world première on 12th July 1946 and had fourteen performances. The Christie administration sponsored and encouraged the season, but it was not artistically responsible.

In accordance with its policy of supporting works by British composers, the Arts Council, on Steuart's recommendation, made a grant of £3,000 to support performances of Britten's works not only at Glyndebourne, but at Sadler's Wells and in the provinces. There seems at one stage to have been considerable misunderstanding about the precise arrangements. At any rate Britten wrote a rather querulous letter to *The Times*. Ralph Vaughan Williams wrote a very contrite letter to Steuart:

"Dear Steuart,

"I am fearfully sorry I believe it was all my fault. I was talking to Audrey and took it for granted that John had *let* Glyndebourne to the promoters of the Opera. It is, so far as I can remember partly C.E.M.A.'s fault, because I feel sure that Glyndebourne was never mentioned at either Council or Music panel and I can't remember it appearing on the minutes of the EC."

Steuart poured oil on troubled waters all round and wrote to Britten: "We want you to write the music and leave it to the rest of us who cannot do that to organize finance." He himself went to Glyndebourne to see *Lucretia* on behalf of the Arts Council and told Britten: "I was profoundly moved by it last night and felt the strength of its emotional and philosophic appeal."

Kathleen Ferrier made her operatic début in the title role, and Steuart wrote to her:

"I should like to tell you how very much I was moved by your performance. I know that you are not an experienced opera singer, but you gave no sign of lack of confidence on the stage and the whole performance was deeply moving and satisfying."

She was touched by his letter and replied: "I can't tell you how it cheered me up . . . I have been very worried by my automaton-like extremities, so your letter helped me more than I can say."

The opera was sung by two different casts, which included Peter Pears, Joan Cross, Owen Brannigan and Margaret Ritchie. They were soon to form the nucleus of the English Opera Group, and later of the Aldeburgh Festival. Despite its artistic success, and the Arts Council help, the 1946 season made losses which Christie described as 'startling'—so startling that, although he offered the Group house-room at Glyndebourne the following year, he declined to become financially involved. Faithful to Wagner and Mozart, he did not really like Britten's music nor did he like the singing or the sets. Notwithstanding Christie's negative attitude, the 1947 Glynde-bourne season presented nine performances of Gluck's *Orfeo*, nine of Britten's new comic opera *Albert Herring* and three of *The Rape of Lucretia*. Steuart, who was the official 'assessor' for the Arts Council, was enraptured by the production of *Orfeo*. To Kathleen Ferrier he wrote (27th June 1947):

"Your Orfeo is the nearest thing to the armchair dream that most of us will ever see. The music is my 'Desert Island' choice. If I never heard anything else in my life, I should choose the whole Opera. If I were limited to 20 minutes music, I would pick the Hades and Elysian fields 'Che puro ciel'."

He was also entranced by *Albert Herring*, the comedy based on de Maupassant's *Rosier de Mme Huisson*, with the scene transferred from Caux to Suffolk. He wrote to William Parsons, who played the part of the country clergyman: "I am afraid that I am without influence in the Church of England, otherwise I would immediately recom-mend you for any good country living that was vacant."

After Glyndebourne, the Group went on tour to Switzerland and had an enthusiastic reception. Steuart noted in a pencilled minute: "Lucerne papered! Zürich concert v. good, impression excellent."

He was so impressed that he recommended that the Arts Council should increase its grant for 1948 to £5,000. "Britten's music is the important thing," he noted. It was essential that the Group should form a company to exploit it and he didn't think it desirable to go on with the existing Glyndebourne arrangement. The Council duly raised its grant and Anne Wood, the Group's general manager, wrote to Steuart, thanking him warmly for his help. The following year— after Steuart had left the Council—the grant reverted to the original £3,000, but, largely thanks to Steuart's advocacy, the English Opera Group had established itself on firm foundations and found a permanent and satisfactory platform for Britten, at the Aldeburgh Festival.

By the end of December 1949, it was reported to the Arts Council that the English Opera Group had given ninety-nine performances of three Britten works—*Lucretia, Albert Herring* and *Let's Make an Opera*. It had acquired an impressive list of sponsors, with Lord Harewood as President and Oliver Lyttelton (later Lord Chandos) as chairman.

The second link between the Arts Council and Glyndebourne was the Edinburgh Festival, first held in August 1947. The idea for such a Festival (its full title being the Edinburgh International Festival of Music and Drama) sprang from the fertile mind of Rudolf Bing, who realized its potential advantages for the Glyndebourne company. The Lord Provost officially requested the support of the Arts Council in January 1946. Keynes was said to have poured cold water on the scheme, and Steuart at first was sceptical.

The Arts Council, however, eventually agreed to support the venture on the understanding that "every step was taken to ensure that British music and British performers were in the forefront of the plans". Bing went ahead with his plans, recruiting Moran Caplat and Ian Hunter as his principal assistants. After all the flaps and frenzy which inevitably attend the launching of any such enterprise, the Festival opened on 24th August.

The programme was indeed a rich feast of music and drama for a world only just beginning to recover from the effects of long years of cultural starvation. The Glyndebourne Opera Company presented *Figaro* and Verdi's *Macbeth*, both under the artistic direction of Carl Ebert. (In view of the Arts Council's concern about British singers, it may be noted that in *Macbeth*, Owen Brannigan [Banquo] and Walter Midgley [Macduff] had important subsidiary roles. The parts of Figaro, Susanna, the Count and the Countess were all played by overseas artists and the subsidiary roles by British singers.) The Old

Vic company took over the King's Theatre for *Richard II* and *The Taming of the Shrew*, and no fewer than six orchestras, including the Vienna Philharmonic under Bruno Walter, gave concerts. A list of internationally famous performers, among them Schnabel, Szigeti and Fournier, gave chamber music and solo recitals.

Steuart sent in a full report to the Arts Council, in which he admitted that some of his earlier misgivings had proved unfounded. "Everyone in the city seems to wish the whole thing well and to be determined to make it a success," he said. "As that was one of my gloomy fears I am all the more glad to record that I was wrong." He was critical, however, about the lack of social amenities. It was impossible, he complained, to get any refreshments in the Usher Hall, a lack which "turns concerts into somewhat intellectual and sober events". But he was full of praise for Bing's ability to make a success of the social receptions held after the concerts. On the musical side, he said that only the Jacques String Orchestra had provided a really enterprising programme, while in the chamber concerts, the combination of star performers who had not played together before was not always happy. "The quartets were nervous, Schnabel started off the Brahms trio with wrong notes and none had played in public in this combination, but they warmed up to it."

The Wilsons stayed at the home of their old friends of Newcastle days, Dr. and Mrs. Sidney Newman, travelling up to Scotland in a small car borrowed from the Arts Council. Steuart wrote: "We will bring rations and, if necessary sheets, because I expect you are just as hard up as everybody else"—a considerate gesture which illustrates both Steuart's thoughtfulness and the extent to which the nation was still suffering under austerity. His official representation at the Festival (confirmed by a note from Miss Glasgow approving his expenses) was to be his last major job for the Arts Council.

He resigned in December 1947 to become Head of Music at the BBC.

CHAPTER TWENTY-ONE

STEUART AND THE BBC

S TEUART was as sorry to leave the Arts Council as it was sorry to see him go. He had been happy there and, professionally, fully stretched. But when he was offered the job of Head of BBC Music, he felt it was a challenge from which he could not flinch, and he was never a man to resist a challenge. He also believed that he could influence a wider public and do more to advance the interests of the musical profession than by staying with the Arts Council.

His appointment, in succession to Dr. Victor Hely Hutchinson, was announced on 20th December 1947. I have been told that Sir William Haley, then Director-General, did not know, or had forgotten about Steuart's famous libel action against the BBC. Whether he did or not, the BBC certainly did not operate a black-list and Steuart had, after all, already worked for the Corporation in its overseas department.

He sent out a round robin letter on New Year's Day, 1948:

"Please excuse my inability to write a personal letter to all my friends whose congratulations and good wishes do much to fortify me when I need it most.

"I can only hope to justify their expectations—if they are not too high—and to deserve their praise when I come to the end. I can't add more!"

Over the years, Steuart had developed what can only be described as a love/hate relationship with the BBC. He wrote to Clive Carey in 1927:

N

"The BBC provides an absolute paradise for the third-rate singers who can get a lot of jobs at 3 to 10 guineas, but they have no use for me at all!"

And in his autobiography, he described his efforts to get more BBC work. He was staying in Aberdeen at the home of his 'ex-godparents' George and Lillian Adam Smith.

"Lady Adam Smith was on the BBC Council for Scotland and I told her that I should very much like to get more broadcasting, but it didn't come my way. She said she would see what she could do. Some months later I was summoned to meet the Director-General, already the legendary figure of Reith—who I imagined was going to offer me more engagements.

"He thought I had come in search of the job as Regional director of Scotland! I deprecated all such high intentions and ambitions. The interview was carried out in typical M.I. 5 style, me in a low chair with a strong light on me, and the great man in a high chair already towering above me. When I made it clear what I wanted he rang up the Music Head, whom I knew perfectly well, and without telling him why he wanted to know the answer, put leading questions and repeated to me in my chair the answers. 'What sort of voice?—a light baritone—not much good for any popular work, I see' and so on."

Steuart's own Ledger shows, that despite this unpropitious opening, he did in fact get quite a lot of engagements from the BBC during the late 1920s and early 1930s.

In an article in *Music and Letters* "Olympic Music" (October 1931) he outlined his views on the right relations between the BBC and professional musicians and called for some form of reciprocity:

"Seriously, the BBC must consider well how they can help music in the country in the widest sense, as well as how they can collect the finest orchestra that we can produce. They must consider the rock whence all this music was hewn, and the pit from whence it was digged. In other words, they must be at great pains to help provincial music by frequent broadcasts of choral performances, even at the expense of their studio hours; their regional directors must be charged with the urgent duty of caring for every musical activity in their region, and of coming to their rescue wherever possible. Similarly, it is our duty, on our side, to communicate our difficulties with the greatest candour to the BBC and to search jointly for a solution of our joint problems. Surely we are not begging any question by saying that it is a 'joint problem'. The BBC has greater resources financially than any other musical body we ever dreamed of. It is a Maecenas who can play Queen Elizabeth, Ludwig of Bavaria, Caracalla and Nero all rolled into one—the greatest potential power for good that has appeared in our times. If occasionally it reminds us of Nero more than Maecenas, do not let us lose patience with it; tomorrow it may be Ludwig. But above all things let us learn to think parochially occasionally, and let Olympic rivalries pass away."

The burden of his complaint was that the BBC engineers were allowed to lead policy rather than follow it and that more attention was paid to studio than to outside broadcasts.

"Whether this article comes to their (the BBC's) eyes or no, is immaterial. Its purpose is rather to help performing musicians to see how they can put their case for help to the BBC, to show them a future line of policy when everything seems very dark, and finally to encourage them to regard the BBC as a dragon which, when tamed, will be an excellent animal to have in the house, and to the heading of this article should be added, perhaps 'Hints on Dragon-Taming'."

Just who was the Dragon and who was the Tamer when Steuart finally landed up at Broadcasting House is still not quite clear!

In June 1935 he wrote a highly critical article in *The Nineteenth Century*, explaining "the case against the BBC, as professional musicians see it." His charge was that nobody with musical knowledge or expertise was on the Board of Governors, while the post of Controller of Programmes (responsible for all music, which amounted to 80 per cent of programme time) was until recently held by a former secretary of a golf club and at that time by a regular soldier. "The Director of Music is an inferior servant of theirs. There is not at present and there never has been any governor who had any *real* knowledge of music in this country from any but the most amateurish standpoint." The Music Advisory Committee was allowed only to advise, and not to initiate, while programme planning was left to a committee of BBC officials. "There is only one person who deserves the confidence of practising professional musicians by reason of his experience and that is the Director of Music Dr. Adrian Boult."

"Why we are 'agin the Government' is because we cannot think that the government knows anything about music . . . We demand that the programmes be chosen as in the old Prom days, Robert Newman and Henry Wood chose them, to lead a public into new tastes to a sympathetic guidance, not by alternate pandering to the crowd by incessant light music and cringing to the extreme modernists who cannot listen to any music but that which comes from Berlin and Vienna. We cannot any longer adopt the attitude the BBC wish us to take up—that of the fireside cat whose privilege it is to look up at his regal master. We may play on catgut, we may make night hideous with our cries, but we have not forgotten that the lion and the tiger are also of our race and our claws can still be unsheathed at will."

After this outspoken challenge, and frank acknowledgment of his prejudices, it is not surprising that the musical public was astonished to learn that Steuart Wilson had been offered and accepted a job with the BBC. Presumably he did so on the principle "if you can't beat them, join them". Thus his daughter Margaret in a letter (undated) writing to thank Steuart for his birthday wishes: "I'm amazed to hear you're working for the BBC—an organization I always understood you loathed!"

Steuart's first BBC job was in the overseas department, which was run from 35 Marylebone High Street. It had the task of pumping out music for almost twenty-four hours on end, on four networks all over the world. This meant very erratic hours for the director and his staff. The department had to cater for the very varied tastes of Africans, Indians, Americans and Australians. Thanks to Steuart's habit of scribbling notes for his lectures and articles on the back of old BBC schedules we can gather some idea of the kind of music that was fed to different parts of the globe. Thus in one week, programmes on the African Service varied from Robert Casadesus playing Chopin and Ravel to the Melachrino strings; the Eastern Service, slightly more highbrow, had the BBC symphony orchestra and a Liszt tone-poem. For the Pacific, there was a Rubbra symphony, Reginald King and his Courtiers and the Melachrino Strings.

Steuart had a fairly free hand in programme planning, as the overseas department was never subject to the same kind of control as the national network. But even there he found hints of trouble ahead. He wrote to a friend:

"My new job is working out in quite an interesting fashion—but we all have our difficulties in the BBC. Your immediate boss wants to help but far above the clouds is someone whose decision is final on what is called High Policy, the height depending on how far away it is from a knowledge of the ground-structure of fact—and they torpedo things equally ruthlessly and then say like Pilate "What I have written" and almost ceremonially wash their hands. I haven't had to fight it in person yet, but sooner or later it comes."

Harold Rutland, then a member of the overseas staff, has told me: "Steuart usually came to departmental meetings with a list of topics he wished to discuss, and his radical fresh approach to matters brought life to the meetings and often caused a stir. Once after an official luncheon party, he and I walked off together and he said 'Harold, a great deal of poppycock is talked in my office and I expect it is in yours too'." When Steuart became Head of BBC Music, one of his first actions was to give Harold Rutland the opportunity to undertake more creative work than he had hitherto been engaged in.

Julian Herbage, as chairman of one of the numerous BBC committees which Steuart attended as head of overseas music, was a bit more dubious about this 'fresh approach'. He has written:

"These meetings provided me with a grandstand view of Steuart's responsible and logical wildness as an administrator. Any rule or decision was for him made to be challenged or broken if he disagreed with it. On occasions he made my position as Chairman very difficult, but if he was conscious of this it made no difference to the fact that we got along together very well as friends."

But Sir Arthur Bliss was in no two minds:

"He was a tower of strength in every way. He was a splendid person with his colleagues, curiously enough because he was generally very much of a lone wolf, meticulous about paper work and so on. He was certainly not awkward to me or anyone in the department. He was very much admired. He had no fear of the high-ups which was one of the things in the BBC that one despaired of. I think he was regarded as a great Godsend there."

Steuart left the Overseas department in March 1945; George Baker has recalled that on the morning of the very day his appointment to the Arts Council was announced:

"With a wave of his hand and laughing good-bye he was off. The same afternoon I became his successor. By a wonderful mathematical calculation of his own, he claimed and got his last month's salary without putting in one single official appearance. Only a man with Steuart Wilson's fearless temperament could have got away with it without leaving a trace of ill feeling."

Back with the BBC three years later, as its Head of Music in the same offices in Marylebone High Street, Steuart had more direct contact with the hierarchy. He had many friends in the department's headquarters and regions—among them Kenneth Wright, Basil Lam, Gerald Abraham, Maurice Johnstone, Walter Stanton, John Lowe, and he was on very good terms with George Barnes, head of the Third Programme which had just started. He seems to have got on reasonably well with Haley, and with R. J. F. Howgill, the Controller of Entertainment whose job was to plan the entire output of classical and light music and drama. Mr. Howgill told me: "I got on well with him and he consulted me constantly. His only fault was that he too often tended to bat on the other side!"

Steuart soon fell into the routine of the office. Normal hours were 9 to 5.30 but he would often take homework back to Chepstow Villas—although he did not have a radio there—and there were often concerts and conferences to attend in the evening.

He had regular weekly meetings with the Controllers and with the committee responsible for planning programmes.

He also fell easily into the routine of minutes and memoranda, and the habit of using incomprehensible initials which was, and still is, the practice of the BBC. For example a Music policy and output meeting in November 1949 had before it a memorandum circulated to DHB, CHS, CLP, CEnt, HM, AHM, RC in R, ACOES, OPP. concerning the planning of the Proms. This followed discussions between Steuart, the Controller of Entertainment, Malcolm Sargent and Rafael Kubelik over dinner at 23 Chepstow Villas. One result of this meeting was the acceptance of Sargent's suggestion that young conductors should be encouraged, as well as young composers.

At one departmental meeting, when Steuart was in the chair, the discussion turned on a proposal for a concert in honour of Sir Thomas Beecham's 70th birthday. Relations between Beecham and the BBC had at times been strained, to put it mildly. "This concert may bury the hatchet," said Steuart, "though I expect that after a short time it'll be dug up again, as bright and shining as ever."

He also had to deal with a very distinguished Central Music Advisory Committee.* Steuart had been invited by Haley to join this in February 1947 while he was still at the Arts Council, but had declined on the grounds that it would be limited to advising on programme policy matters and would not deal with such questions as the BBC's relations with artists and orchestral policy on which he held strong views. Despite the eminence of the men on the Committee, he clearly did not think much of it, for he told a BBC 'Any Questions' programme some years later:

"While I was occupying the post of Head of Music, there was a thing called the Central Music Advisory Council [sic] and the difficulty was to give them anything to advise about, because they only met about twice a year being busy people. Unless they are in constant session they can't advise except on such broad lines as that it would be better for us all if the programmes were brighter or some nonsense of that sort. That is all they can do."

Steuart was involved in a curious, and rather embarrassing, incident during the early part of 1950, concerning the future of the BBC orchestra. Sir Adrian Boult had been its conductor since 1930 and had built up a very fine orchestra which had, before the war, earned the praise of Toscanini. Some of the high-ups in the BBC detected a falling-off in its standards after the war—this was surely inevitable when so many players had departed or had become rusty in their techniques—and thought it would be a good idea to bring in a fresh conductor. Sir Adrian's contract ran out in April 1949 under

---

* There was a separate Committee for Scotland. Steuart was always amused at the way in which the Scots were segregated and used to tell about the BBC Schedule which carried the phrase 'Lighten our Darkness—Not in Scotland'.

the BBC age limit of 60, though he was still in the prime of life professionally. There was some bitterness and Boult thought, quite wrongly, that Steuart had something to do with the decision. Frank Howes, then chairman of the music advisory committee, had to mediate. According to those who were close to him in the BBC, Steuart was *not* personally involved, but he was concerned with finding a successor. Several names had been suggested, among them that of Sir John Barbirolli, conductor of the Hallé Orchestra.

Steuart approached Barbirolli privately at the Cheltenham Festival in June 1948 and conversations continued sporadically for some months.* The BBC asked for a reply, but although Barbirolli said he would like to "put the bloke (Wilson) out of his misery" with an immediate reply, he asked that he should have until the end of the year to make up his mind. On 28th December 1949 he wrote to Steuart, declining the BBC offer. The news of the negotiations had been widely reported in the press. Malcolm Sargent was appointed chief conductor of the BBC in July 1950.

In 1949, the music department moved to Yalding House, in Great Portland Street. Whether in Marylebone High Street or at Yalding House, Steuart insisted that people should come and discuss business with him in his office, and not over lunch. He was determined to break down the idea, then prevalent, that jobs went to people who gave the BBC producers and executives the best lunches. "To hell with the lunch parties," he would say. "Let them come and talk to me in my office." This did not mean that he did not believe in as much discussion as possible with the members of his staff, both in his office or over a sandwich in the Rose of Normandy or, later, at the George which was then (and still is) the favourite BBC pub. He would always invite suggestions and listen to them, and only after intensive questioning and discussion give his own ruling. He was, as at the Arts Council, enormously kind and understanding towards those who worked for him.

He could also be ferocious. Basil Lam told me that when he had planned a series on the History of Music for the Third Programme, he sent a copy of his outline to Steuart, but omitted to consult him beforehand. Steuart sent for him, much in the manner of a headmaster, and, with a torrent of expletives, tore up the memorandum

* See Michael Kennedy: *The Hallé Tradition*, Manchester University Press, 1960.

and threw it into the waste-paper basket. Basil went away duly chastened, but next morning he met Steuart in the lift. Steuart put his arm round him and said 'My dear boy, we were in the middle of a discussion yesterday—will you come round to my room this morning and continue it?" After that, all went well and the programme was broadcast in due course.

Marjorie Pratt, the New Zealand girl, who was his secretary at the BBC wrote me:

"I was always conscious of his amazingly complex, fascinating personality, and of how little I could contribute—though you may be sure I strained every nerve to help him with his gargantuan task at the BBC. I was full of admiration and love for him." Steuart much later wrote a reference for her:

> "There could have been a great deal of worry about papers, timetables etc. In fact there was none and I must say that if I don't owe that to you I owe it to Providence and I would rather give *you* the credit. . . You had to bear the burden of my bad temper for making me do what I had told you I wanted to do . . . In addition to this I had more than the usual capacity for losing papers."

He elaborated this theme on Any Questions: "Large concerns like the BBC wouldn't really function at all if somebody didn't muddle up the papers from time to time. I speak with experience of that."

How far was Steuart able to fulfil his twofold ambition of helping professional musicians and raising the standards of performances? Even his fiercest critics will agree that he revolutionized the system of auditions, no doubt remembering his 'non-audition' with Reith.

In February 1948, the Incorporated Society of Musicians sent a deputation to the BBC criticizing the manner in which the Corporation selected artists for broadcasting engagements and asking for a new system of auditions. Steuart arranged for a panel of outside experts whose names would be made public and would command the confidence of the profession. The panel would not know the names or details of the performers, who would be described only by number. This principle of anonymity, he wrote in a memo, "will be a safeguard against lobbying." He wrote personal letters to some thirty distinguished musicians, among them Myra Hess, Louis Kentner, Lionel Tertis, Arthur Bliss, Gerald Moore and Astra Desmond, urging them to accept the invitation as a public duty, despite the low fees proposed (1 guinea per hour, with a minimum of 3 guineas and extra for subsequent attendances at committee meetings). He got enthusiastic replies. Thus Louis Kentner: "May I congratulate you on this really brilliant idea and the zest with which you are carrying it out?" Myra Hess wrote from New York: "I feel like sending you a cable of congratulations—It is an answer to all our prayers." To which Steuart replied "Heaven knows I need your prayers."

The new procedure* started in September 1948 and a year later Steuart reported "I believe that the system is sound and is working well." He told an ISM conference that about 2,500 auditions were given annually, resulting in 85 per cent of the successful applications being given a 'test date' within a year.

By the time Steuart arrived at the BBC, the Third Programme had been in operation for over a year. He had been concerned with it, while he was at the Arts Council and had suggested Alfred Deller, then a lay clerk in Canterbury Cathedral, as one of two counter-tenors in Purcell's cantata "Come ye sons of Art" which was performed at the inaugural concert on 29th September 1946. He thoroughly agreed with Haley's dictum that the Third Programme "must reflect the world of the living as well as the dead artists and stimulate the new as well as sustain the old."

One of the first programmes which he introduced on the Third was the series *Music for Worship*, which he dubbed "Mus for Wush." It began in the autumn of 1949 and was designed to present music used in the worship of different denominations, ranging from the Roman Catholic choir of Westminster singing plainchant to the Salvation Army, from Wesley and the Methodists to Vaughan Williams's edition of the *English Hymnal*. The series had a great following and Steuart put an enormous amount of research into it. A correspondence with the Lady Abbess of Stanbrook Abbey (an old friend of Canon Wilson) on an obscure theological quotation eluci- dated a point of doubt. Steuart wrote to the Lady Abbess, "Your

---

* It was the same procedure that had operated at the Arts Council. Gerald Moore has recalled that on one occasion, when he was on the auditors' panel, a personal friend of his turned up and played the violin very badly. "Steuart," I said, when we were alone, "this is a friend of mine. I know it is bad playing, but when she receives an official letter saying her services will not be required, she will telephone me in high dudgeon. What shall I say to her?"—"My dear boy, put it all on me. Simply say that Steuart Wilson said that she cannot play the fiddle and never will be able to."

triumphs are quite secure! You have now added the BBC reference
library to the list of your grateful friends and admirers," and in a
minute to the BBC Librarian Miss Milnes: "Here we are—the
nuns have turned up trumps. Please return to me and when in
further trouble for patristic quotations, remember the Nuns of
Stanbrook."

Early in 1950, Steuart found himself deeply involved in planning
for the Festival of Britain 1951. In a memo dated 1st February, he
argued the need for including as many British composers and artists
as possible. With the possible exception of Bruno Walter and
Stokowski, all the conductors should be British and the works performed, he suggested, should include Vaughan Williams' *The Pilgrim's Progress*, and works by Walton, Britten and Rawsthorne. He
was a firm champion of the Festival and on an Any Questions programme, where Bob Boothby and Michael Foot were engaged in a
savage argument about whether it was a waste of time, he quietly
interjected: "As the only one of the four people here intimately
connected with providing a considerable part of the entertainment
in this Festival, I say that the idea is that quite a lot of people should
have FUN on a large scale."

All the time he was Head of Music, he had constant battles with
the BBC high-ups—some of them on trivia and some on points of
principle. He maintained that the music department ought to have
more autonomy and its Head more authority. He resented the fact
that it was purely a 'supply' department, without its own budget,
and that every decision had to be referred higher up.

A BBC reply to this would be that the Corporation has to cater for
a wide variety of viewers and cover the whole spectrum of public
taste—from sport and gardening to music and drama—and that
central allocation and control of funds and time is the only way to
avoid in-fighting between the various interests.

Steuart also insisted that the Administration was not qualified to
judge programmes or standards on artistic grounds and that this was
solely the job of Head of Music. Sir Lindsay Wellington, then Controller of the Home Service, has recalled an argument he had with
Steuart about a certain programme in which Steuart wanted to
include some modern work while he (Wellington) wanted to limit it
to classical music. "I suppose you are going to tell me next that the
viola is out of tune," was Steuart's scathing remark. But Sir Lindsay,

himself a keen amateur musician, did not take offence. He had the highest regard for Steuart and told me that if Steuart had joined the BBC earlier, or stayed longer there, these pin-prick rows would have faded out. Steuart often crossed swords with William Streeton (Head of Programme Contracts) and with Basil Nicolls, (the Director of Home Broadcasting) whom he accused of interfering in his province. He objected to Nicolls criticizing his symphony concert plans on any grounds other than economics, and described his criticisms as "uninformed, prejudiced and worthless". This was not the sort of statement calculated to make for smooth and harmonious relations, but Steuart did not mind, so long as he made his point. In the end, of course, the BBC machine won—machines very often do—but Steuart had fought a gallant rearguard action in defence of what he believed to be right. The Music Programme today and the extent to which music is recognized and honoured by the BBC may, indeed, owe something to his pertinacity of twenty years ago.

Kenneth Wright wrote in *Ariel*, the BBC staff magazine, in January 1967:

"To the Establishment he may often have been an irritant, for he was firm in his views and forthright in expressing them. To his staff he was a true leader, sympathetic, encouraging, yet relentless in eradicating amateurism and denouncing incompetence and humbug; while always 'the Boss', at Christmas he nevertheless became the punch-brewing host, complete with gorgeous tartan waistcoat and ringed cravat, making us feel more of a family than for twenty years. He was the first Head of Music who defied Director of Home Service Broadcasting on purely musical matters and won. This important step led, after Herbert Murrill's interregnum ended by his untimely death, to the creation of Music Division and the recognition of the true status of music in the broadcasting world."

To my mind—and I think many people would agree—Steuart's main contribution to the BBC lay not so much in his battles against the hierarchy, as in the quality of the scripts and programme notes which poured from his pen. He compèred many operas and gave talks on folksongs, Shakespeare songs, the Elizabethans and Purcell, and wrote some lively pen-portraits of contemporary composers. He made the music of Beethoven and Verdi intelligible and living to the ordinary listener, as it were compelling him not to switch off, but to enter a new world.

Thus, on the Verdi *Requiem* (for a performance conducted by Malcolm Sargent in the Albert Hall in December 1951) he wrote:

"There will still remain some who contend that opera is all very well in its right place, but that right place is emphatically not the Church ... If any listener to Verdi's *Requiem* is going to object to 'operatic' style in sacred music, let him take his leave at the very outset of the work."

And on the *Dies Irae*:

"Verdi treats the Hymn in one great movement without a break and lavishes on the design all his wealth of imagination, as did the medieval designers of the great West windows which so often contained the pictures of the Hell which they imagined to be exact and authentic. This is not music which will stand up to questioning by an emancipated agnostic; if there are no terrors of the imagination for you there will be no thrill in this magnificent outburst of fear and hope."

The note concludes:

"Man, not the individual, is at the bar of judgement. This great and impassioned picture comes to a close with a quiet prayer for eternal rest (Pie Jesu Domine). The terrors of death and judgement cannot outweigh the hope of mercy: the flames die down, the passion is spent, the individual is merged into the general and with a single simple 'AMEN' this tremendous musical experience comes to an end."

He was a master of the microphone. He spoke as beautifully as he sang, taking immense care with his diction, so that every word was given its weight and his phrases were marshalled to the fullest possible effect to give in the best possible sense a word picture. Take for example a talk on Schubert songs:

"Let us take a preliminary walk with Schubert, the hypothesis in this case being that it is spring time and that the dog is also out for a walk, sniffing in the hedges at smells which are 'supersonic' to us, but simply delicious to him, while we watch the fish in the stream, the reeds blowing in the wind, and if we are lucky we shall catch sight of a curl or two of flaxen hair and a dirndl skirt, disturbed by the same playful breezes."

This evocative piece was followed (need you ask?) by a record of 'Das Wandern', from the *Schöne Müllerin*, sung by George Henschel. But for sheer dramatic content, and for conveying the sinister atmosphere of suspense and intrigue in contemporary terms, it is difficult to beat Steuart's interval talk on *Tosca*:

"Scarpia is the embodiment of cunning, cruelty and cold-blooded lecherous villainy—the worst character ever drawn, the Himmler of Naples . . . Scarpia goes across and writes the permit—Tosca sees on the dinner table the sharp pointed, gleaming knife. This is to be her kiss, and Scarpia shall die, gasping, choked with the blood of his victims . . .

"When this opera was new fifty years ago . . . there was no torture, no conspirators, no spies. All that belonged to the 'cloak and dagger' days. Today one has the uncomfortable feeling that this torture business is too near the bone. How many people in the audience today know someone whose relations went through what Angelotti went through, political prosecution, gaol, escape, arrest, suicide—or Cavaradossi: no politics, just painting, help a chap who's up against the police, then comes arrest—examination—torture—and then what?"

CHAPTER TWENTY-TWO

COVENT GARDEN

T HE dramatic intensity of Tosca's death scene, as told in Steuart's BBC script in the last chapter, provides the key to his decision to join the Royal Opera House in 1950. Opera had always fascinated him—as a small stage-struck boy he had been thrilled by the big theatre when he was taken to see *Ben Hur* at Drury Lane and he had performed in opera on every possible occasion. When his days as a professional singer were over, he took every opportunity to produce and conduct operas and to encourage amateurs to be adventurous in their choice of works. The chance of being directly associated with productions at the national opera house was not to be missed—it was a challenge which he could not resist. He had also heard rumours of impending changes at the BBC which he feared might place more limitations on his authority.

Steuart had been associated with Covent Garden since his days at the Arts Council. He was one of the original members of the Opera Trust* formed in February 1946 under the chairmanship of Lord Keynes, and remained a member until July 1950.

The Opera House had re-opened in February 1946, thanks to the prompt action of Messrs. Boosey and Hawkes, the music publishers, who took on a short lease of the theatre to save it from becoming a permanent dance hall. David Webster, a Liverpool businessman and

* The original members of the Trust were Lord Keynes, Samuel Courtauld, Sir William Walton, Professor E. J. Dent, Leslie Boosey, Ralph Hawkes, Sir Kenneth Clark, Sir Stanley Marchant, Sir Steuart Wilson. Lord Keynes was succeeded by Lord Waverley in August 1946, when the Hon. James Smith also joined the Trust. After the death of Samuel Courtauld and the retirement of Ralph Hawkes, Sir George Dyson, Lord Wakehurst, the Hon. Edward Sackville West and Sir Barry Jackson were appointed in 1949.

former chairman of the Liverpool Philharmonic Orchestra became general administrator and the Austrian-born conductor, Dr. Karl Rankl, a former pupil of Schoenberg, was appointed musical director in 1946.

Early in 1950, the Trustees were considering appointing a deputy administrator, to relieve Webster of some of his work-load. To everybody's surprise, Steuart volunteered. James Smith, a fellow-trustee, has recalled that David Webster told him: "What do you think, Jimmie—Steuart Wilson wants to become my deputy." James Smith replied that it was up to Webster to choose the man he wanted, though he himself had doubts whether a man of Steuart's experience, temperament and seniority (he was several years older than Webster) would make a suitable second-in-command. As it turned out, James Smith was justified in these misgivings. Steuart was not a natural Number two. As he himself once wrote to his father when his sister Margaret was having some trouble in her religious community: "We Wilsons are no good unless we are at the *head* of a community."

The appointment, however, was made and Steuart started in September 1950, at a salary of £2,500 a year. There does not appear to have been any definition of what his responsibilities would be as deputy general administrator.

Sir David Webster himself told me that there was no clear line of demarcation. "Steuart was my deputy—he was in charge when I was not there." Steuart worked closely with the general manager of the Opera Company, Pat Terry, and did a lot of casting and coaching, and worked on versions of operas. As at the Arts Council and at the BBC, he was responsible for auditions. He gave general advice on artistic standards.

Steuart entered upon his new job—as he had on his previous jobs with the Arts Council and the BBC—full of hope and enthusiasm, and with the glint of battle in his eye. He wrote to Anneke (17th November 1950):

"You can think that there is much to be enjoyed in my new job and that I am having fun with a real large live theatre. It is true that the roof leaks when it rains hard and that opera singers are more trouble than ordinary singers and that everyone in a theatre gets more excited and suffers from higher pressure than they do anywhere else. But there is great reward in seeing a good result on the stage and seeing people develop into artists from being just beginners."

Shortly before he joined the Opera House, Steuart had a bitter clash with Sir Thomas Beecham over its policies. At the Incorporated Society of Musicians conference at Brighton in December 1949, Beecham launched a savage attack on the Covent Garden Trust and was scathing about the lack of musical qualifications of its members. He called for a public enquiry: "Let everything about the Trust be brought into the open," he said. "The press must be made fully aware of the intense resentment against, and even disgust with, the strange and un-English way of doing things. Let them see the evidence of how the vast sum of £100,000 has been spent in one year with so little to show for it." He criticized the appointment of Rankl and described the choice of "an alien, and especially one bearing a German name", as incredible and fantastic. He also attacked the composition of the Arts Council's opera panel, and made a personal onslaught on the music publishers Boosey and Hawkes.

Steuart was inflamed by this attack and replied in the same coin and from the same platform two days later. The *News Chronicle* reported under the headline "Sir S replies to Sir T":

"Sir Thomas Beecham's attack on the Covent Garden Opera Trust was described by Sir Steuart Wilson, musical director of the BBC at Brighton yesterday, as 'irresponsible and foolish'.

"'It is a pity Sir Thomas did not take advantage of the information which would have been available to him of the exact relations of the trustees before launching a rather light-hearted attack on their honesty,' said Sir Steuart."

He replied in detail to Beecham's attack, pointing out that Boosey and Hawkes had rescued the opera house for the nation and had in fact lost many thousands of pounds in doing so. Covent Garden received an Arts Council grant of £120,000, compared with the £600,000 given to the Paris Opera house and the guarantee against loss in Vienna. It had a total staff of about 600, compared with more than 800 in many other opera houses. Its running costs were about £400,000 a year, excluding production costs and it was not true to say public money was being squandered. Finally, said Steuart, "What

o

is rather sad to me in this controversy is to recall that the British
National Opera Company broke up largely because we were unable
to persuade Sir Thomas Beecham to believe in English opera singers.
He threw his hand in, paused a little, and then went in for international grand opera."

Statements in defence of the Trust were also made by Lord
Waverley and Leslie Boosey, and Beecham got a bad press. But he
had had his fun.

The policy adopted by the Covent Garden Trust immediately
after the war was to make the Royal Opera House a really *national*
institution, presenting works by British composers and engaging
British artists. This policy was described by David Webster in the
Arts Council *Bulletin* (January 1946) on the occasion of the re-open-
ing of the theatre with the Sadler's Wells ballet presenting *The
Sleeping Beauty*:

> "It augurs well for the new régime at Covent Garden that its first
> company should be one whose dancers and choreographers are
> British, whose productions are largely designed by British artists
> and many of whose scores are contributed by British composers.
> While foreigners will not be excluded from the (Opera) company,
> British artists will be given first chance; the operas will be given in
> English; every encouragement will be given to our own com-
> posers; the Opera Trust will on its own behalf and on behalf of
> Opera in England combine with other authorities to set up a first
> class school of training."

This was absolutely in accord with Steuart's own views and with
those of E. J. Dent, who was also a Trustee. During the first post-war
decade, nearly every opera was given in English—including *Fidelio,
Carmen, The Magic Flute, La Bohème, Tosca, Tannhäuser, Die Walküre,
The Flying Dutchman, Der Freischütz,* and Verdi's *La Traviata, Il
Trovatore* and *Aïda.*

The tradition of singing in English continued until well into the
mid-1950s but gradually it was found that as more and more international artists were being engaged, it was more sensible to sing in
the original language. It seemed rather nonsensical to expect
Renata Tebaldi to sing Violetta in *La Traviata,* or Kirsten Flagstad
Isolde, in English. This trend sorrowed Dent, who was getting rather
crotchety and increasingly deaf—he told Steuart he wanted to get

"a really big ear trumpet which he could brandish at Sir John Anderson, so that he could retreat into an Anderson shelter". Dent wrote to his Manchester friend Lawrence Haward in 1951: "I must say I feel a good deal hurt at the way C.G. keeps me at a distance when I am actually one of the Directors."

Steuart, however, backed him on several occasions, for example in a row with Erich Kleiber (then a guest conductor) over Dent's translation of *The Magic Flute*. Dent wrote:

"Steuart told me that Kleiber has started altering my words without consulting me. He has exercised his authority and stopped it ... S rather like a cat on hot bricks. ... However it all ended happily. S says that Kleiber likes artists but not administrators and was much surprised when S told him that a conductor had no right to tamper with the words of a translator."

In the late 1940s and early 1950s, many English operas were produced at Covent Garden—Purcell's *Fairy Queen* was one of the earliest ventures, with Constant Lambert conducting—Arthur Bliss's opera *The Olympians* had its first stage production in 1949. Of this production Bliss told me; "It was one of those frightful occasions when everything went wrong—the conductor Karl Rankl and Peter Brook, the producer, didn't get on together and the cast was not assembled until the last moment and the thing was really awful." Steuart, then at the BBC, arranged for the opera to be broadcast and "was a great help. I didn't care for Covent Garden," Bliss added, "it was rather like a sponge—you press it in here and it goes out there." Britten's *Peter Grimes* was produced in 1947, after its successful production at Sadler's Wells; *Billy Budd* was given its first performance in 1951 and *Gloriana* as part of the 1953 Coronation celebrations.

Walton's *Troilus and Cressida* had its first production, with Malcolm Sargent conducting, in December 1954 and Tippett's *Midsummer Marriage* was put on, with John Pritchard as conductor, in January 1955.

Of all the English operas presented while he was at Covent Garden, Steuart was most closely associated with Vaughan Williams's *The Pilgrim's Progress*, based on Bunyan's allegory, an opera on which R.V.W. had been working for many years and which he finally completed in 1949. The production was planned to be

Covent Garden's principal contribution to the Festival of Britain year, 1951. Nevil Coghill was the producer and at Vaughan Williams's specific request, a young English conductor, Leonard Hancock, was selected. Vaughan Williams wrote: "L.H. will be all right—he knows the score well and is able to listen and evidently the orchestra likes playing under him. Steuart is doing me like a prince— he gave a lunch today to L. Hancock and his pretty little wife, who is to be the woodcutter's boy." Leonard Hancock has told me:

"Steuart and Vaughan Williams attended a great number of rehearsals, from the very early musical ones through the routine production rehearsals up to the final stage rehearsals; I have a memory of Steuart singing no fewer than three roles at one rehearsal because the singers were absent through illness or other causes. I also remember a somewhat hilarious tea party at a work-men's café in the Holloway Road, when V.W. and Steuart insisted on taking the whole cast and staff out to tea during a break in a rehearsal at the Northern Polytechnic, which in those days was one of Covent Garden's regular outside rehearsal rooms."

Inia te Wiata, the New Zealand bass, who played the part of John Bunyan and was one of Steuart's favourite pupils, remembers many sessions at Chepstow Villas, where Steuart coached him in the role.

For all the beauty of the music, *The Pilgrim's Progress* was not a commercial success. It was panned by most of the critics—for example Richard Capell in the *Daily Telegraph* described the production as "so wanting in the dramatic element—so anti-theatrical". Michael Kennedy wrote later*: "The worst aspects of the production were the appalling costumes and the unimaginative lighting. The critics, almost to a man, admired the music but failed to find the work suitable for a stage setting." The day after the first performance, Vaughan Williams wrote to Steuart:

"My mind goes back forty years, also on a musical occasion when I first met you and ever since then my music and any success I have in it has been connected with you, and now comes the climax. I know that I owe last night to you (probably in face of strong opposition) and I do hope you do not feel that you have

* *The Works of Ralph Vaughan Williams.* Oxford University Press, 1964.

backed the wrong horse. It was, every one says, a splendid performance and I feel most grateful to everyone."

The Pilgrim's Progress was dropped from the repertoire at the end of the season and has not been performed on a professional stage since that date.*

Steuart did a great deal of regular coaching and himself sang at many rehearsals where singers were absent—he even sang the bass part of Monostatos at a *Magic Flute* rehearsal. He made himself responsible for auditions policy, and introduced a new system, very much on the lines of the one he had established at the BBC. He also carried out many administrative duties. One of these was to find 'extras'. Mr. J. Hurren, a London headmaster, has recalled that his school was called on to supply four boys as midshipmen for *Billy Budd*. One of the boys was knocked down by a car on his paper round and taken to hospital, but insisted on appearing on stage that night. As a reward Steuart arranged for the boy to be taken to *Il Trovatore*, took the trouble to find where he and the headmaster were sitting and said, "I hope you haven't been knocking any more cars about lately." Another of his jobs was to find 'props'. He managed to get hold of an old broken-down, beerstained piano for Alban Berg's *Wozzeck* (1952) and to his horror, found that one of the opera house experts had decided to tune it!

He was an indefatigable and enthusiastic guide to the opera house, taking parties of school children and his own young friends behind the scenes and explaining the stage mechanism. On one occasion, he escorted Queen Mary round the wardrobe, and the staff still remember how she insisted on examining every item, down to the last button that had to be sewn on to costumes.

Steuart's Ledger during this time shows that he did a great deal of entertaining of visiting conductors and artists, both in restaurants and at Chepstow Villas. His record of expenses includes dinner to Vittorio Gui and his wife, a lunch party to Erich Kleiber and 11 guests and "flowers for Mrs. Kleiber". He accompanied the company on many of its provincial and European tours.

Covent Garden was not without its lighter side, and it is a pity that

* A very successful performance of *The Pilgrim's Progress* was given by the CUMS in Cambridge Guildhall during 1954, with Boris Ord conducting. (Allen Percival took over for three performances when Ord had a dislocated shoulder.)

Steuart never wrote down his recollections of some of the incidents. I remember him telling me about the first production of *Gloriana*, when the assembled Royal family were clearly 'not amused' and the Duke of Gloucester was reported to have said as soon as the curtain went down on Act I "Get me a drink, for goodness' sake." This reminded Steuart of the story of H. H. Asquith having to sit through a performance of *Aïda*, when the horse brought on to the stage had found its way outside and was discovered chewing up cabbage leaves in the Market. "The horse, more fortunately placed than I, made good his escape," Asquith was reported to have remarked. Then there was a stormy incident, involving Maria Callas and James Johnston the Belfast tenor, which caused Madame Callas to threaten to walk out. Steuart was called upon to make the peace and placate the irate singer and her equally irate husband, Signor Meneghini.

There is no evidence to show at what point Steuart's relations with the Covent Garden administration began to turn sour. It was probably a cumulative process. He felt that he was not being sufficiently consulted or informed about plans and programmes. Lord Harewood, for instance, has told me that his own appointment as administrative assistant to the general administrator in the autumn of 1953 came as a complete surprise to Steuart. Steuart wrote him a rather sharp letter, but nevertheless the two men remained good personal friends. He was feeling frustrated and confided to Martin Cooper, his friend on the *Daily Telegraph*, that he was "unhappy about the set up". He was particularly concerned about the influence of a homosexual clique in the opera and ballet companies. There was never open warfare, but the position grew increasingly uncomfortable and, from all accounts, Mary Wilson voiced her opinions in an embarrassingly frank manner that Steuart ought to be the Number One. Sir David Webster has told me "He wanted my job—and Mary egged him on."

Matters came to a head in the spring of 1955, when the Board of Directors became involved. Lord Waverley, the chairman, adopted a rocklike attitude and refused to countenance any of Steuart's criticisms of the administration. The tension developed to such a pitch that Steuart was asked to leave at the end of April, four months before his contract would normally have elapsed. Arthur Bliss, who by then had joined the Board, was given the unenviable task of breaking the news to him. Steuart recorded in his Ledger: "At the end of April I went on leave from the R.O.H. on salary until the 1st September 1955, the office and position of Deputy Gen. Administrator being discontinued." A public announcement was made to the effect that as Rafael Kubelik had been appointed musical director (a position which had been vacant since Rankl's departure in 1951) Steuart's post had been discontinued.

On 24th July 1955, a paragraph appeared in the Sunday newspaper *The People*, to the effect that Steuart was going to lead a campaign against homosexuality in British music and quoting him as saying "There is a kind of agreement among homosexuals which results in their keeping jobs for the boys." *The People* quoted David Webster as condemning this statement as 'nonsense'.

Steuart wrote to the Board on 22nd August 1955, regretting the statement in *The People*, which he said he had not authorized. Nevertheless he returned to the charge the following year and circulated a memorandum on the subject to members of the Board.

Lord Waverley called an emergency meeting of the Board at his office at the Port of London Authority (of which he was chairman) and it was decided to ignore the memorandum. As far as I know, all copies have been destroyed. Steuart wrote a letter to the *Daily Telegraph*, calling for a full investigation into the affairs of the Royal Opera House (9th July 1956):

"The time has surely come when the public has a right to be given full and reasoned statements about the following:
1. The powers at present wielded by the Administrator of the Royal Opera House, Mr. David Webster, uncontrolled by the Board of Directors,
2. The constitution of the Board of Directors in which the amateurs and patrons of the Arts outnumber by 6 to 2 those with real musical knowledge and experience,
3. The system of engaging artists by which the Opera House insists on a singer abandoning the concert platform without guaranteeing his regular appearances at Covent Garden when he may remain weeks or even months unemployed. . ."

The *Daily Telegraph* in an editorial backed the idea of an enquiry, because the Royal Opera House was "a national institution of international fame" and because it was that year receiving a Government grant of £270,000. "The Board of Directors can hardly ignore the criticisms made by their former Deputy General Administrator" it concluded.

The Board did ignore the criticisms—many of which were an echo of those made by Beecham six years earlier. Steuart wrote again:

"The Covent Garden oracles are dumb—they will not reply to my letter or to the leader in the *Daily Telegraph* of a fortnight ago . . . I am not just a dismissed servant with a grouse. I reported in 1953 that the management needed improvement . . .

This report was discussed with Lord Waverley, Lord Wakehurst and Mr. Webster, but I found out that it was never mentioned to the Board then, nor to the new Board who terminated my appointment. I therefore sent to each member a copy of the report of 1953 and various other criticisms—some of them admittedly personal. While I was in the Administration I defended it—I told Lord Waverley that I had 'whitewashed until my bucket was empty'. On the later documents I have not been questioned: either the Board disbelieves me or they prefer to leave things as they are . . . The 'autocracy' of which I complained tends to operate through a clique. All cliques are dangerous, whether political, religious or old-school-tie: the special dangers of this clique cannot yet be safely particularized in a newspaper."

Of the composition of the Board Steuart wrote:

"Two out of eight members are professional musicians, with some knowledge of how the music profession of this country works. The remaining six have many other tasks of great importance— the Port of London, Northern Ireland, a Bank, a financial newspaper, an All Souls Fellowship. In the world of great affairs they are great men—in the world of the theatre they are amateurs lost in the back-stage area. That is why a public enquiry would be justifiable."

The oracles remained dumb.

The episode was an unhappy one and, writing nearly fifteen years later, when public attitudes have changed so completely, the whole affair seems rather unrealistic. Steuart was not particularly sensible in his choice of battle-ground but, having decided to make the challenge, he went through with it showing inflexible determination and belligerence.

Steuart thereafter never went back to Covent Garden if he could help it, though he had many good friends among the staff. One of his cherished possessions was a tie-ring presented him on his departure by the music department:

"This tie-ring is sent to you with the affectionate good wishes of the music staff, past and present, as a small token of our appreciation of your many kindnesses to us.

"Signed: Edward Davies, Norman Feasey, John Gardner, James Gibson, Peter Gellhorn, Reginald Goodall, Leonard Hancock, Robert Keys, John Matheson, Eric Mitchell, Douglas Robinson, Emmanuel Torry."

CHAPTER TWENTY-THREE

THE COMMANDING HEIGHTS

I T seems absurd to talk about Steuart Wilson belonging to any Establishment, when he spent so much of his life fighting the powers-that-be. Yet, by virtue of his status, his eminence and his achievements, he had by the 1950s reached such a pinnacle of public fame that he could be regarded as a pillar of the music Establishment. So it is perhaps appropriate to devote a chapter to the many side-line activities and interests which developed out of his official positions and which took up an increasing amount of his time and energy during the decade. These activities are faithfully recorded in his Ledger, which mysteriously starts again in August 1950, after a break of thirteen years. They read rather like a Musical Who's Who.

Steuart may not have walked with kings—he certainly talked with them. When he and Mary were staying with friends in Norfolk, they were invited to lunch with King George VI and Queen Elizabeth (the Queen Mother) at Sandringham. Steuart later recalled that the King was very shy and he (Steuart) had to put him at his ease.

When the Queen Mother attended a function at Dartington to mark the twenty-first anniversary of the music festival, Steuart referred to the tremendous growth of musical activity throughout Britain: "If your Majesty should walk from Balmoral to Windsor—which Heaven forbid—you would be able to have a music lesson in almost every county you passed through." The Queen Mother was delighted.

As chairman of the Royal Concert Committee of the Musicians' Benevolent Fund from 1953 to 1958, Steuart had to escort the Queen, or whichever member of the Royal Family decided to attend. He once told me that it meant a big drop in takings if the Queen didn't attend in person. For example, in the winter of 1953, when she and the Duke of Edinburgh were in Australia, there was a profit of only £1,618 compared with £3,850 in 1952 when both were present.

Steuart was a member of the small executive committee which arranged the concerts and chose the programmes to suit the royal taste; its membership included, at various times, Frank Howes, John Denison, Herbert Murrill, David Webster and Frank Thistleton.

Steuart had been a member of the Benevolent Fund's executive committee and its chairman before the war. In 1956 he again became chairman and remained a member of the executive until his death. He was anything but a paper chairman, and Muriel Williams, then assistant secretary, recalls how the day after his election he spent hours in the office, browsing through the account books and files, and talking to the staff about future plans.

Though never a president of the Incorporated Society of Musicians, he played a very prominent part in its activities and was tireless in his efforts on behalf of professional musicians. He regularly attended I.S.M. conferences, either as a speaker or a 'rank and file' member.

Steuart joined the Corporation of Trinity College of Music in 1950. At the College, he taught a few selected pupils. Among these were Amy Shuard, Phyllis Mander and Inia te Wiata.

Dr. Wilfred Greenhouse Allt, who was then principal of the College, was the moving spirit behind the creation of the National Music Council, an 'umbrella' organization which aimed to co-ordinate the activities of the various musical bodies in Britain. Steuart became one of its vice-presidents. He was also prominent in the council of the Central Music Library, which he had been responsible for launching while he was still at the Arts Council.

A scheme very near Steuart's heart was the Council for Music in Hospitals, which had been devised by Sheila McCreery, when she was working for the Arts Council in the north-west. Its purpose was to give concerts in mental hospitals and to encourage research into the therapeutic value of music for mentally disturbed patients. Steuart arranged for many artists to perform—among them Mary, Inia te Wiata, and Phyllis Thorold—and he also enlisted the support of many leaders of the profession. Frank Howes and Malcolm Sargent joined him as vice-presidents. At Steuart's invitation, Lord

Harewood became President and the Wilsons gave a party for him at Chepstow Villas. There, leading mental health specialists and musicians met to discuss how this very valuable work could be extended and to imbibe Steuart's very special wine punch.*

Steuart subscribed £100 to the Council, in memory of his son Jonathan who had been killed in the war. He continued to be actively interested in Music in Hospitals all his life.

Steuart used his position of authority and influence, not only to extend the frontiers of music, but to help individual musicians, especially those who were in difficulty. The list of people whom he helped is far too long to be recounted, but one outstanding example is the Polish composer, Andreas Panufnik. Panufnik escaped to the West from Zürich where he had, to his surprise, been allowed to conduct a concert. The Polish Government had never let him leave the country to attend meetings in Paris of the International Music Council, of which he was vice-president. Panufnik arrived in London in the summer of 1954, penniless and literally with nothing but a conductor's baton in his knapsack. He met with a chilly reception, but Steuart befriended him and got up a fund among leading British musicians to help him. Steuart himself reported to a friend:

"Panufnik—all goes well with him. I raised £400 as guarantee for overdraft, but I think he won't need it. R.V.W., Willie Walton, Bliss, R. Mayer, Arthur Benjamin all agreed. Alan Bush refused! I told him that I wasn't surprised but didn't like to take his refusal for granted. If ever he wanted to sample Poland I was sure I could raise a similar guarantee for his expenses in moving!"

Andreas Panufnik has told me: "The first real step of my new life in my adopted country was no doubt achieved through Steuart's understanding, friendship and assistance. He was the first Englishman who understood my position artistically, politically and financially and who held out his hand to me."

* "Sir Steuart Wilson's own recipe for Wine Punch: For every quart bottle of cider, take a bottle of white wine. The best wine for this purpose should not exceed 8s. a bottle. South African and Australian wines are admirable. (Do not buy a sweet or expensive Graves.) Peel fine two lemons and leave the rind to soak, pouring in the lemon juice strained. Add Pimm's No. 1 and brandy—this should not be liqueur brandy but tough stuff—until the required alcoholic strength is reached. If it is desired to have a hot Punch, use a red wine but make lemonade out of lemons and boiling water. Allow cloves to steep, six to the quart, add such spices as may fall conveniently to the hand. Serve as hot as possible and taste as often as seems desirable."

Steuart was not concerned with the colour of a man's politics, and hated the intrusion of politics into music. This was shown in the celebrated Russell case. It is a rather complicated story, but the gist of it is that in the summer of 1952, the London County Council decided to withdraw its £25,000 grant to the London Philharmonic Orchestra. Members of the orchestra said this was because Thomas Russell, L.P.O. chairman and managing director, was a member of the Communist Party and had recently visited Moscow. *The Times* music critic wrote that the L.C.C. had been influenced by "personal and political animosities." This was denied by I. J. Hayward, Leader of the L.C.C., and Steuart took up the cudgels on Russell's behalf, challenging Hayward to produce in public evidence to refute *The Times* allegation.

In a letter to *The Times* on 12th June, Steuart wrote that Russell had never obtruded his political views and that the L.C.C. decision would mean "the murder of the L.P.O. by calculated starvation and the depletion of all other London orchestras". He ended his letter with a characteristic flourish:

"In common with most people I detest witch-hunting. In common with many others—including the overwhelming majority of the L.P.O. members—I share a complete failure to appreciate Communist politics and methods. But if we are going to have a witch-hunt let us hunt in the open and without recourse to Mr. Hayward's device of saying that 'it is not in the Minutes'. Of course it is not: who would be so unwise as to leave it there? The cat is out of the bag. Let Mr. Hayward chase it—not in committees and minutes—but round and round the Royal Festival Hall where we can all see it."

Steuart was an international as well as a national figure. In 1947, at the suggestion of John Maud, he was invited to attend a conference in Paris to discuss how U.N.E.S.C.O. could "raise the interests of artists and writers". He did not go to this conference, which in 1949 resulted in the formation of the International Music Council, but was selected to represent Britain on the I.M.C. in 1951 and became President in 1953.

He presided over the General Assembly in the Hotel Majestic, Avenue Kleiber (the building which had been used by the Gestapo as their wartime headquarters and was to be the scene of the Vietnam peace talks in the late 1960s). International musicians and U.N.E.S.C.O. staff alike were impressed with his firm, but fair, chairmanship. Jack Bornoff, the I.M.C. secretary (incidentally Steuart's own nominee for the job) told me: "I always used to look forward to meetings with Steuart in the chair. He knew what he was doing and how to express himself." On one occasion, Steuart championed the right of Hardie Ratcliffe, secretary of the Musicians Union to be represented on the Council. Some of the more academic members were afraid that the M.U. would use it as a platform for trade union propaganda.

Steuart often had arguments with Edward Clark, the representative of the International Society for Contemporary Music, over the extent to which the I.M.C. should support ultra-modern music. "I can't imagine anything more old-fashioned than *avant-garde*," he once said. "Twelve tone writing is all right, but don't take twelve tones to be the ten commandments."

Steuart paid great attention to the detail of paper work and was largely instrumental in re-writing the statutes and rules of procedure to make them "less bureaucratic and more realistic" as Bornoff put it. At an early stage, he battled for an increase in the U.N.E.S.C.O. grant.

"At present we carry an extensive programme of hopes and ideals with a very small budget with which to realize them—an inverted pyramid. The growth of our Council implies increased communication, but we have cut our operational expenses for next year to a point so dangerously low that we may not be able to afford to communicate effectively with our own members. We are on a three-pronged fork:

"*Either* we do not attempt to expand,

"*Or* we expand membership and reduce efficiency,

"*Or* we must abandon some of our few *real* activities and fall back on 'hopes and ideals' with which we are already overstocked.'

Steuart was determined to keep the I.M.C. down to earth. Its committees he divided into those which were "active, inactive and actively inactive" and he wanted to encourage the active ones. He was against prestige window-dressing and of a proposal to appoint an Honorary Committee for a Council conference he wrote: "I suppose it is necessary to have one, but one must reflect that it seems a mere façade to any business and not any *use* at all. Of those names, Sibelius and Vaughan Williams are over 80 or near it. Honegger and Milhaud are invalids."

Steuart was a magnificent representative for British and Western music at the Manila conference of the newly formed National Music Council of the Philippines in November 1955. In his presidential address, he dealt with what was clearly a difficult and touchy problem of East versus West. "Music," he said, "is an international language . . . The East and the West have been able to translate each other's literature and understand each other's visual arts far better than their music. It is time that we from the West learned to hear the quieter tones of the music of the East. It is time that you of the East came to teach us and that we come to you to learn." He praised the initiative of the "brilliant and energetic Filipino" Dr. Ramon Tapales in seeking to "build the bridge between Eastern and Western music" by organizing the conference.

Steuart's correspondence with Jack Bornoff during his period of office reveals his close interest in the day-to-day activities of the International Council and all the behind-the-scenes moves that seem to be inevitable in any international organization. From Madras on the way back from Manila, he wrote to Bornoff:

"I had a chance of meeting X and Y at a dinner given by the British Council. They scarcely speak to each other. Mary put her foot well in by thinking that Y had been in Manila and he was furious and scarcely said goodbye. He brought his very charming wife, who had never been out to dinner before! She sat next to me at a small table with Y not there and he was wildly jealous and kept on getting up to see that we weren't petting under the table."

When the time came in 1956 for the re-election of the President, Steuart was under strong pressure to stand again; but he was a firm believer in the principle of rotation or 'changing feet', and said that no president should hold office for more than two years. "I am afraid of the President-Dictator," he said. He was succeeded by the Chilean composer, Domingo Santa Cruz-Wilson, with whom he claimed distant cousinhood—though there is no evidence in the family tree that the Wilsons of Cumberland ever got to South America.

Steuart's trip to Manila as I.M.C. president was an unqualified success. The same cannot be said of an earlier mission to Latin America which he undertook on behalf of the British Council in the autumn of 1954. He visited Peru, Chile, Argentina and Brazil and found that in most of these countries, everything had to be referred back to the appropriate Ministry and there was political interference everywhere. "The work is running on like a decapitated chicken," he reported.

He was also making unofficial soundings about the possibility of bringing out the Covent Garden opera company to perform Walton's *Troilus and Cressida* and Britten's *Peter Grimes* in Buenos Aires, Rio de Janeiro and Montevideo.

It was a strenuous tour and unfortunately he was taken seriously ill with acute tachycardia (rapid heart movement) and gastro-enteritis and spent a fortnight in the British Hospital at Buenos Aires. Nearly all his Argentine engagements had to be cancelled, but he insisted on continuing the tour and arrived in Rio looking 'very shaky' according to the British Council representative Ronald Bottrall. He picked up strength and went through with four lectures, two press conferences, a radio interview, as well as innumerable cocktail parties and receptions. "He made a most favourable personal impression. His good humour, tact and patience were outstanding," said Mr. Bottrall.

During the next few years Steuart's health continued to trouble him, but he did not let it interfere with his very full programme. Both before and after he had left Covent Garden, he was busy teaching, lecturing, broadcasting and adjudicating and as he wrote to a friend: "I need two of myself and at least one more secretary all to myself." And so it continued until at the beginning of 1957 he received an invitation to become Principal of the Birmingham School of Music.

That is a saga which merits a chapter to itself.

CHAPTER TWENTY-FOUR

BIRMINGHAM

THE news that Steuart Wilson had been appointed Principal of the Birmingham School of Music was received with great enthusiasm by music-lovers in the Midlands. J. F. Waterhouse, music critic of the *Birmingham Post* wrote: "His tempestuous presence is the healthiest thing that has come to Birmingham's world of music during my years with this newspaper. Long may he dwell among us!" And George Baker, the baritone, wrote in the *Music Teacher*: "Look out, Birmingham; when the wind blows from the Wilsonian quarter it blows at near gale force, but it is invigorating and clears the air."

Sir Adrian Boult had been associated with the school for many years and it was on his suggestion that Steuart was invited to become its head, in succession to Dr. Christopher Edmunds who had resigned in 1956. The appointment was formally confirmed by the Council of the Birmingham and Midland Institute on 8th March 1957.

In view of the bitter controversy that developed later, it is worth recording the terms of Steuart's engagement. The appointment was for a period of three years, at a salary of £2,000, with an annual expense allowance of £300. It was a full-time job, but with "reasonable freedom to accept outside engagements". It was stipulated that the Principal would be responsible to the School of Music committee for:

1. The musical and educational standards of the School.
2. The planning of the syllabus and the direction of studies.
3. The appointment of examiners and the conduct of examinations.

P

4. The development of corporate life in the School.
5. The fostering of external musical and educational relations.
6. The performance of such duties as shall from time to time be prescribed by the School of Music Committee after consultation with him.

Steuart explained why he had decided to accept the job in a letter to Marjorie Pratt, his former secretary at the BBC. He described the set-up at the Institute:

"Yes, it's true that I took over this job—the Music School—in March. The Institute is a queer old (100 years old) body that was pioneering adult education and took incidentally to music. All the technical, chemical, metallurgical, etc. things have gone to the new Tech. College. All the languages to the new Commercial School, but Music has stuck. The last Principal, Chris Edmunds, really tried to sell the place to the Socialist Council on the City and resigned as a sort of defiance. It failed—there was a fearful row and scandal and after nearly a year I came in (at the age of 67 plus) to sort it out—to reunite the staff, to defeat the City and to get started again. It is a bit of a change for me, but I couldn't resist the challenge to raise this body out of the mire and clay and set its feet on the road again. So I'm back in an office in the most extraordinary old building, trying to be kind here, firm there and brutally rude somewhere else . . . I'm busy and I'm happy and I feel well, though two days ago I entered my 69th year!"

Excited as always about a new challenge, not even he could have foretold the appalling administrative difficulties which impeded him at every stage. The trouble arose from the 'divided control' between the administration of the Institute and that of the School of Music. The Institute was governed by an elected Council consisting of a President, two vice-presidents, a Treasurer and thirteen Governors, and it was this Council which determined the composition of the School of Music committee—a body of seven individual members and five representatives of local education authorities in the Midlands. No fewer than fifteen different L.E.A.s were concerned. The Secretary of the Institute was also secretary of the School of Music Committee. Few of the members of this committee had any knowledge of music.

Steuart said much later that he had "accepted the situation in general good faith that I would be given an effective voice." He saw his relations with the music committee as being much the same as they had been with the various committees of the Arts Council or the BBC, and he had become an expert in dealing with committees. But in Birmingham he found that the Principal of the School of Music was circumscribed by the music committee and subordinated to the secretary of the Institute. Nor was he the sort of man to submit meekly to the rulings of a committee when he disagreed with them, or to accept the shackles of petty bureaucracy.

Things started well. Eric Knight, the secretary of the Institute, wrote a warmly welcoming letter: "I look forward personally to some years of pleasant association with you in this work." A series of cocktail parties was given to introduce the new Principal to the committee members and to Birmingham notables. Mr. Knight wrote: "The cocktail parties were a great success in my opinion and I cannot help feeling that we have made a very good start." At the beginning Steuart stayed in a hotel, travelling up and down from London, until he had arranged to sell his house in Chepstow Villas. The Wilsons actually moved, with their furniture and their dogs, in September 1957 to a flat in Edgbaston.

The 'cocktail party' atmosphere did not last long, but Steuart started off, as a very new broom, determined to exert his authority and retrieve the fortunes of what had once been a great school of music. In a circular letter he told the staff that he intended to make "the collective part of the school work important" with the emphasis on orchestral, choral, opera and ensemble work and making it compulsory for all pupils to take part. Discipline, he said, must exist and be enforced in every artistic matter. "The Principal must have the final voice if he is to control. This is a School and not a co-operative group of teachers." He must also have the power to introduce new teachers and to make it worth their while to come. "That is what makes a School, and in a School co-operation and discipline are essential." He planned to cut down the number of part-time pupils and increase that of full-time students.

Within a month and in his first report to the committee, he announced plans for a new syllabus and a new examination in order to raise the standards—"Indifferent standards shall carry no recognition or mark of the Birmingham School of Music"—He promised to seek "new and attractive" teachers who would attract a better "top layer" of students. He also reported on his talks with the Lord Mayor of Birmingham and some of the main education authorities, and on his plans to visit them all, in order to dispel the general "aura of uncertainty" about the future of the School. He talked about a new contract for teachers and declared his intention of listening to every teacher at work, and hearing all the pupils individually. His basic aim was to vest the School with the status of a Conservatoire.

By the autumn, when the first academic year opened, there were 56 full-time and 538 part-time students. For all his emphasis on discipline, Steuart was in favour of practical democracy, and welcomed the formation of a Students' Union. One of his earliest appointments to the teaching staff was David Franklin, the Glyndebourne and Covent Garden opera singer. He also arranged for master classes to be given by Denis Matthews, Archie Camden and Frederick Grinke. Opera, of course, was given high priority and we find him laying plans for *Il Seraglio*, Purcell's *Dido and Aeneas* and *Sumida River*, a work by Dr. Clarence Raybould, who had a long association with the School as student and teacher and who acted as Principal in the interregnum between Christopher Edmunds and Steuart. The *Il Seraglio* performance was a tremendous success and Steuart borrowed costumes from Sadler's Wells for the occasion. He also arranged for some distinguished figures in the musical world to come up to Birmingham—Astra Desmond, Douglas Guest, then organist of Worcester Cathedral, and Larry Adler, the harmonica player.*

Everything seemed to be going swimmingly, but suddenly in the late summer of 1958, the situation deteriorated. We find a note from Mr. Knight to the Principal in early October complaining that he was using one of the Institute rooms for music-making on Sunday evenings "without any official arrangement having been made". This was the first of a long series of acrimonious exchanges. Steuart was always ready for a fight, but he liked to do battle in the open and not in the twisted atmosphere of intrigue that characterized the Institute at that time. There were constant rows about such matters as the allocation of rooms, the library, practising times, the lending of

* It was through Steuart that Larry Adler met Vaughan Williams who was so impressed with the young American that he decided to write a work for him, the *Romance for Harmonica and Orchestra*. It received its first performance in New York in May 1952.

instruments, pianos and delays in paying teachers' salaries. The situation revealed in the various memoranda and letters would be comic if it had not been so tragic.

The main cause of the midsummer storm was Mary. Steuart, concerned at the lack of cellists, arranged for her to give lessons to two pupils, with the full concurrence of Anthony Pini, the cello master. Almost casually, he mentioned this in his report on 16th July. The music committee not only took umbrage—it took action. It decided to ban Mary from taking part in any school activities apart from social ones. Steuart was furious, and retaliated by asking for an injunction in the Vacation Court and deciding to enrol Mary as a student—of the harp! The committee refused to accept her enrolment and Steuart placed the whole matter in the hands of his solicitors.

On 22nd October the music committee decided that "in view of the general attitude of the Principal during recent months, any further suggestion of a compromise was not worth pursuing. It therefore recommends that the Principal be dismissed." This resolution, I understand, was carried by one vote—the casting vote of the chairman.

The minutes went on: "The Principal had indicated his unwillingness to accept the authority of the committee and its chairman, and he has also failed to co-operate with the Institute administration. In the absence of the co-operation the committee expects, it is felt that there is no further hope of amicable relations between the Principal and the committee, and it is therefore necessary in the best interests of the School to press for his dismissal."

This decision was communicated by Mr. Knight to Steuart, who was invited to attend a special meeting of the full Institute Council "with a friend if you so wish." Steuart made a full and detailed statement to this meeting, asking for details of his alleged non-co-operation, and blaming the Institute administration for *their* failure to co-operate with the School of Music.

"The Institute must make up its mind that the School of Music is a major activity," he wrote. "The Council may be surprised to know that I have never been invited to an Officers' meeting to discuss any points concerning the School of Music, neither its equipment nor its financial needs nor its administration. I have to

put any arguments to them through Mr. Knight and I have to
rely on him to press any point." He concluded: "I came to this
School in March 1957 after a considerable upheaval here and
when I spoke to the members of the Institute at the Members'
Concert I said that I would be proud to be known as 'the servant
of the servants of music'—I am still a servant, but I find it difficult
to believe that I am serving 'the servants of music'. I came here to
put on its feet a School that was failing because of its disputes—
now it is proposed 'in the best interests of the School' to dismiss me
because I am not afraid to say when I find things wrong and to
stand up for my opinion."

Fortunately, there were sensible people on the Council who said
that to dismiss Steuart peremptorily would make the Institute look
utterly ridiculous. One member commented: "I think that the
Principal is arrogant, autocratic, contentious and cantankerous. He
is also a very senior man of pronounced artistic reputation and
temperament . . . I do *not* think that this is the right or the opportune
moment to bring it (his term of office) to a swift and premature
conclusion." The voices of reason prevailed and the dismissal resolution was negatived. Steuart was laconically informed (7th November
1958), "The Council at its meeting last night decided not to insist on
your dismissal." There was no hint of any apology or regret.

In spite, or perhaps because of the Council's decision, relations
between the Principal and the secretary of the Institute got steadily
worse, and the issues raised more and more ludicrous. There was the
incident of the ladies' lavatory. According to Steuart, he was asked
by the foreman to suggest a colour scheme for re-decorating it and
naturally asked Mary's advice. But again, this was a case of 'Lady
Wilson interfering' and angry minutes followed. The incident ended
with "a more appropriate colour scheme" being chosen.

Then there was the incident of the Principal's dog. Steuart was
rebuked by the chairman of the catering committee for bringing his
golden cocker spaniel Argo into the canteen. "The continuation of
this practice is very undesirable and a matter which calls for tolera-
tion and forbearance on your part." Steuart replied:

"I gather that you produced at the Council meeting a statement
that the dog had been observed to foul the canteen; this I understand you are now not prepared to substantiate, and also a further

general proposition that 'the students had objected'. That statement was completely denied by the Union of Students Committee ... You then fell back on another general proposition that dogs in canteens were 'unhealthy' and in some ways 'improper' ... You have had, after your personal interview with me, an opportunity to let this 'sleeping dog' lie, but you clearly do not wish to do so. I must request therefore that you will allow me an opportunity to put my side of the case before the Council."

Mr. Knight's memos got progressively more acid and Steuart's more explosive. Here is a sample:

KNIGHT: I have received your two extremely objectionable notes dated 25th June, one of which I regard as nothing short of insulting.
WILSON: "We are here to make this School work ... I don't want to demand a showdown. You are here on a long-term job, I on a short one. But I'm not going to endure any longer your pin-pricks. If *you* want a showdown *I* too shall have one, on my own terms this time and I warn you that I can be as savage as I can be friendly."

After this, it is not surprising to find that the two men barely spoke to each other. A note from Mr. Knight reads:

"In order to avoid yet another source of irritation and bad feeling, may I ask you to give a little more consideration to the privacy of my personal office. Perhaps you do not appreciate that you make a regular habit of walking into my private room unannounced ... On several occasions you have walked in when I have had a visitor and have thereby created an embarrassing situation for me. There is an internal telephone which you could use to find out if I was free to see you or, if you are already in the general office, it would be perfectly easy to enquire if I was disengaged. I reckon to make myself extremely accessible but I think I am entitled to make my own decision as to when, and whether, I am immediately available."

To Steuart, who always kept his office door wide open and was always available to teachers and pupils, this was the last straw.
Though the proposal to dismiss him in October 1958 had been

kept out of the press, it was becoming increasingly difficult to keep the squabbles out of the public eye. Mary herself was always outspoken; she felt bitterly angry at the way both she and Steuart were being treated and openly showed her contempt for the Institute's Council and its members. The Chief Master of King Edward's School, the Rev. R. G. Lunt, a Governor of the Institute, brought the whole thing out in public at a meeting of the City Education Committee in February 1960. The *Birmingham Post* reported his speech in full:

"It has been for a long time now that I have kept these troubles under my hat. I have been terribly shocked at the government— or rather the misgovernment—of the School of Music.

"Today I am driven to using strong words, but they are considered words. I feel pretty strongly about these things, having been through some 18 months of misery and frustration. . . .

"I have been driven to the conclusion that the leadership of the Institute just tolerates the School of Music and does so only for the sake of the money it brings in. And that is a tidy sum: £13,000 a year for the management of the school.

"Here is I think a unique cultural and educational feature of this great city . . . it is in a sorry state, moribund, riddled by intrigue and run by internal manipulation preferring hole and corner methods to the light . . .

"The present Principal has done much good to the cause of musical education in the Midlands. This summer he comes to the end of his appointed term. It has been good for us in Birmingham to have had him even for a short time."

The fat was well and truly in the fire. Letters poured into the paper confirming the Chief Master's statements and an editorial called for an immediate public enquiry.

Steuart asked to be released earlier from his contract, due to run until the end of July, so that he could go on an examining tour in India. The Council agreed, adding a somewhat hypocritical note of "appreciation of his services to music in the city during his period of principalship".

These developments and the difficulties of the School were fully reported in *The Times*. Steuart, an inveterate *Times* letter-writer, took up his pen (23rd March 1960):

HARMONY AT MUSIC SCHOOL

Sir—A paragraph in the report, in an edition of *The Times* on March 17 from your Birmingham correspondent needs one correction and one amplification. I did not resign: my contract was for three years from March 1957. By letter it was agreed that the termination date was to be July 30 1960. But the annual report officially stated December 31. As I was not asked whether I would continue I made other arrangements and finally obtained leave to terminate on May 30 in order to start an oversea examination tour.

The 'petty squabbles' to which reference is made include such things as the 'right' of the Principal to attend the meetings of his committee to which formerly he had been 'invited' and his theoretical subordination to the secretary of the Institute. Likewise the habit of delaying, for as long as three months, payments due to teachers.

I have had four chairmen in three years and every year an entirely new committee of the council may begin their labours in the middle of the academic year. This committee have twice voted for my immediate dismissal and one of my previous chairmen, at their last annual general meeting, publicly thanked God that they had only six more months of me to endure. But I definitely did not resign.

Your obedient servant,

Steuart Wilson

He followed this letter with a longer and more detailed explanation to the *Birmingham Post*. The basic argument was the same—the divided control at the top and the domination of the music school by the Institute council and its secretary.

"I do not like municipal enterprises for reasons which are too long to state and I accepted the offer of Principal of this School in order to keep it reasonably independent. After 3 years' experience of the government of the Institute and their management, I now would prefer any municipality to be in charge."

This was in fact to be the eventual solution. The School of Music was hived off from the Midlands Institute and now comes directly under the City Education Authority. The 100-year old building in

Paradise Street has been pulled down, but the Institute continues to function on a very reduced scale, in the former Birmingham Library building, pursuing various cultural activities (lectures, art shows, poetry readings etc).

Steuart left Birmingham without regret. He wrote to a friend: "I shall be glad to forget this place for a month . . . I think I feel 70 now and occasionally physically well over."

It should not be inferred, from the foregoing somewhat sordid story, that Steuart's time at Birmingham was unproductive or that they were three wasted years. There is abundant evidence from members of the teaching staff and from his former pupils that he made a real impact on the musical standards of the School. When he announced his decision to go, his pupils organized a petition asking him to change his mind.

J. F. Waterhouse wrote in the *Birmingham Post* (23rd May 1960) "My feelings are too bitter and savage for these decent pages. I regard Sir Steuart's departure . . . as the most deplorable thing that has happened in Birmingham's world of music."

Steuart had certainly done much to encourage music-making in the Midlands. He had lectured, adjudicated, sung and spoken throughout the region. He had presented very successful per-formances of *Figaro* and *Il Seraglio* and had brought many dis-tinguished musicians to Birmingham. As at Chepstow Villas, the Wilson home at Edgbaston had been the scene of many parties for students and teachers.

He also did much to raise the status of the teaching staff. Allan Bixter, his number two, the director of studies, told me how Steuart fought a long battle with the Council to get his (Bixter's) meagre salary raised. Steuart always made a point of discussing problems with the staff and with his secretary Della Hawkins, who was utterly devoted to him. One day Steuart was due to interview pupils (of both sexes) when he upset a bottle of ink over his oatmeal-coloured trousers. Bixter heard a torrent of four-letter words through the communicating door. "Milk, get me milk," Steuart called, peeling off his trousers while the bowl was being prepared. He conducted the interviews sitting behind his desk in his underpants.

There were happy week-ends and holidays in Wales, staying with his step-niece Ann Pennant and her husband Arthur, at St. Asaph, or at Beguildy, in Radnorshire with Jack Hollins, his great friend of the

1930s who was, like Steuart, an accomplished cook. Jack often accompanied Steuart at concerts and festivals and in between times they would talk endlessly about madrigals and sauces. The Wilsons spent one holiday in Portmeirion, on the Merionethshire coast, where Steuart somewhat surprisingly approved of the Italianate atmosphere created by Clough Williams-Ellis. He made many friends in Birmingham, none closer than John and Rachel Waterhouse. John, a member of the music school committee and its chairman from January 1959 to January 1960, was a staunch champion of Steuart and his ardent advocacy exacerbated relations with the officials of the Institute.

Although Steuart was always glad to re-visit the Waterhouses and their family, he never went back to Birmingham without a shudder.

CHAPTER TWENTY-FIVE

INDIA

WHEN Steuart set out on an examining tour in India for the Trinity College of Music in May 1960, he was approaching his 71st birthday—an age at which it might be thought he could sit back and relax rather than undertake an arduous mission in a hot climate. But Mary had been suffering from rheumatism and he thought the change would do her health good. They spent a few days in Rome, staying with their friend Mary Cavaletti in a lovely villa on the Appian Way and found it a refreshing break. Mary Wilson wrote to her mother: "Steuart is certainly rested and free of all his wretched worries and there's no inclination to think of them." They arrived in Bombay on 16th June, exhausted, according to Mary after a brush with the Customs and "rather a gay voyage" on a Lloyd-Triestino boat. "I wish you had seen S. and me coping with the baggage which slid all over our cabin; in one desperate lurch Steuart's sarong fell round his ankles and I had to put both my arms round his middle to hold him upright ... The cello came to no harm."

Steuart spent a fortnight examining in Bombay, and one of his letters to Dr. Greenhouse Allt, Principal of Trinity College, illustrates the troubles besetting a visiting examiner. On his arrival at the Bengalee Girls School, he found that the piano had fallen to bits, and he had to jam it with books and folded newspapers. "In my opinion," he reported, "this piano would not stand up again to the severe test of six hours a day and more with young fingers hammering on it in hot weather. By the way no provision was arranged for cleaning the keys."

The Wilsons went on to Colombo, where a hectic social round awaited them. The High Commissioner, Sir Alexander Morley, was an enthusiastic clarinet player and was delighted to entertain visiting British musicians. He threw a big party for them at his Residence, where Steuart sang the *Dichterliebe*.

Steuart immediately plunged into a whirl of local musical activities. Mary wrote that he "had his nose to the grindstone too much . . . all for love and prestige of the U.K." Steuart himself wrote to Grace Hutson, of Petersfield, who was acting for him in legal and business affairs: "This is a strenuous life in some ways. Call at 7 a.m. Start exams about 4 miles away in Park Road Bungalow. Take a sandwich lunch and come back about 4.45 to 5 p.m. Bath and a swim. It is dark by 6.30 here. Then sleep till dinner about 9 p.m. Thank God Ceylon hasn't gone prohibitionist yet," he added, "so that one can get a drink of beer. With humidity round 85 + whatever you do you break into a sweat."

Steuart took on the conductorship of the Ceylon orchestra, which meant rehearsals every Sunday morning, and they gave a concert in August which, according to Mary "got terrible notices in the local press". The people of Ceylon were fond of Western music and had not developed their own indigenous music in the same way as the Indians. It used to be considered part of upper and middle class education for daughters to learn the piano and the violin and to take the diploma of one of the English institutions. The result was that there were far too few cellos and hardly any woodwind—apart from Sir Alexander Morley. There was quite a strong pro-British element, although politics just then were a bit tricky, as Mrs. Bandaranaike had succeeded her husband as Prime Minister and was seeking to oust Western culture and ideas from the island.

Steuart conceived the idea, in co-operation with Sir Alexander, of establishing a permanent school of music in Colombo. In a memorandum to the High Commissioner, he pointed out that the present standard of teaching varied "between the capable to the extremely low" and he thought the emphasis should be on improving "the teaching (which *can* be taught) rather than the production of performing talent (which cannot be *taught*)." He felt there was an urgent need for some focal point for musical activities, which were often carried on in completely watertight compartments and depended too much on the talent and enthusiasm of a few individuals.

The school, it was envisaged, would be run by a Director, from outside Ceylon, and a full-time secretary. It would be largely financed by fees from the students and teachers. Steuart wrote to Dr. Allt to get his general blessing for the project. Steuart himself would have liked to become director, with Mary as the cello teacher, and the appointment was tentatively discussed. But the Colombo School of Music remained a pipe-dream.

The Wilsons left for India at the end of October, having given a final concert with the Brandenburg concerto No. 5 and music by Ireland, Boyce and Britten. This concert, unlike the first one, was a success. The orchestra presented Steuart with an inscribed silver salver. Mary wrote home: "We are both brown as berries and I am rather slimmer. I think Steuart is also. I made him have a white dinner jacket because he couldn't sweat around in his thick black one. He is proving an excellent conductor of amateur orchestras and choirs and I think he enjoys it."

For the next few weeks, there was a programme of hectic travelling, examining in schools and convents. It was their second tour of India, as Steuart had been on a similar examining visit in the winter of 1955, on his way back from the International Music conference in Manila. On both visits they had stayed as long as possible in Colombo and were enthusiastic about the arrangements made for them by the British Council.

The Council's representative in Ceylon on their first visit was John Kelly who, with his wife, became firm friends of Steuart and Mary. Mary spent about six weeks with them while Steuart was touring in India. The programmes on both occasions seem to have been extremely arduous. Mary wrote in a kind of 'travelogue': Darjeeling . . . Benares . . . Lucknow . . . Simla . . . Delhi—always the same drill, Steuart examining, broadcasting, lecturing while she went shopping or swimming, "organized liquor supplies" or practised. "Went to buy S another sarong and one for me . . . Were nicely swindled by taxi . . . S had satisfactory row with driver." At one convent Steuart amused the children with "Oh No, John", and made the Irish sisters weep over the Famine song. But he had several bouts of tachycardia, especially at high altitudes.

Mary's last letter to her mother was written on 19th November 1960 from Madras. "We have had a gruelling but interesting three weeks travel by all sorts of conveyances. Steuart seems well and loves

this country and its people." Next day she was taken ill. She had
picked up a fatal germ.

She was taken to a nursing home and looked after by a Dr.
Somasekhar who, Steuart said, "was all that I could have wished."
There seemed to be no special cause for anxiety so he decided to fly
to Bangalore on 24th November to continue his examining. The
following morning he was recalled by a telegram which told him
"condition deteriorating", but, after consultation with the doctor
and with Mary who was no longer in acute pain, he returned to
Bangalore at the week-end. At 7.45 a.m. on Tuesday 29th November, he received a telegram to say that she had died at 4.30 a.m. of
heart failure. He sent a wire to her mother, Daisy Goodchild, at
Petersfield: "Mary died early morning no press notice please till
letter received." In two long letters to Daisy, he gave a full account
of what had happened and ended: "Had she lived I fear it would
have been at very great cost to herself; she couldn't have recovered
very much and the cello would have been impossible and an agony to
see ineffectual attempts towards recovery."

The death certificate gave the cause as "acute infective poly-
neuritis, Landry's type, cardiac failure". Mary was only 46 when she
died. On the same certificate Steuart registered himself as "Musician—no religious affiliation."

In a later letter, just before Christmas, from Madras, he went on to
discuss his plans. At no point did he even contemplate coming home
or abandoning the full programme.

"I go on to Poona and Karachi and return here about Dec. 20th.
Then to Colombo. I shall soon make up my mind what to do for
the future. I feel I must do Hong Kong in February but beyond
that I can't at the moment tell. I had promised to go on to
Australia from April 1961 to Christmas and I must look into that
carefully.

"I realize very much now that even since the beginning of the
year I have deteriorated physically a good deal and I can't concentrate at work continuously and when I am tired, I have difficulty in writing correctly—not legibly so much as the wrong words
come out. I don't like to have to exhibibit (there you are—there's
one for exhibit!) and I am increasingly deaf in conversation and
a bad guesser—that makes me a poor participant in parties. For

all this I was increasingly dependent on Mary as well as for the practical as for the social things, and that's why I can't take on the job that I was virtually offered of conducting the Ceylon Orch. and running some kind of school of music. I have got too old all of a sudden and it is better that I should realize it too soon rather than too late . . . I must admit to being very tired. Christmas goes on here with children's parties and a vast Indian music festival at which we took part 5 years ago. I can't go now I'm done in."

Sir Alexander Morley, who saw Steuart in Madras soon after Mary's death, told me that he was "utterly broken", lost and sad, but determined to carry through his programme as arranged. Steuart told Morley that he couldn't, however, carry on with the scheme for a music school in Colombo. As he wrote to Daisy Goodchild:

"I realized that I hadn't got more than another year, if as much, of work left in me and that I must try to establish something for Mary to hand on to her, and this Music School in Colombo would have been exactly the thing. Not only I *can't* do it alone, but there isn't any point in my beginning it at my age and I have no heart for the job. So I mean to come home as soon as I decently can."

To Trinity College, he wrote that he would proceed with his plans for Hong Kong, Singapore and Malaya, which would bring him back home about the end of April, but he said he could not face the prospect of the Australian tour which had been suggested (1st January 1961):

"I don't think I am capable of it physically. At the end of a long day not only do my feet and legs give way under me but I can't write the words I'm thinking of and no one can read them) . . . My tachycardia is very much better, almost no trouble except in the hill stations. Menière's Disease can be tiresome and I'm generally unsteady on my pins and balance badly—need a stair rail and all that and I find I can't walk a mile on the flat without exhausting my thigh muscles. Main thing is that I funk a collapse. In Karachi I had a duodenal haemorrhage of some size, fainted dead off at 2 a.m. in the bathroom and woke up with a cut on the eyebrow, on the floor. I was at the Convent and they fed me soup and milk for 2 days and I didn't die of it, and it seems to have cleared

XIII. STEUART WITH MALCOLM SARGENT

XIV. UNESCO MUSIC CONGRESS — 1956

XV. STEUART WITH ARGO — 1958

up and no sensation of pain, but it doesn't mean that the little
bugger isn't just round the corner still."

In spite of this attack, he did a fortnight's travelling, by air, to
Bombay, Delhi, Bangalore and Madras before coming back to
Colombo for a rest.

He left Colombo on 17th February . . . "This is a sad leaving,
because I was really looking forward to the long-term future here."
He then set sail for Hong Kong, to adjudicate at the annual Schools
Music Festival. He complained about the bitter cold—"You need
an extra blanket and a hot water bottle." But he was enchanted by
the place. "This is a wonderful island. I've done my first morning's
work in the Festival, 94 children playing Beethoven's *Romance* in G.
This evening 'Harmonica Band' and 6 little cellos. A short evening
and another long morning of 100 children on the piano."

His mission in Hong Kong, Singapore and Malaya was to revive
the Trinity College examinations which had lapsed since the war.
In these countries, the Associated Board alone conducted examinations in practical subjects. (Perhaps a note of explanation is needed
here. Music examinations fall into two groups—those of the Associated Board (Royal Academy, Royal College, Royal Manchester
College and Royal Scottish Academy) and those of other schools, not
bearing the title Royal, of which Trinity College is the oldest and
alone conducts world-wide examinations.) Steuart wrote in advance
to the various education authorities, explaining his objective:

"The Board of Trinity College believes that the teaching of music
of the Western European type is in general a cultural asset to any
country whatever be its indigenous musical history and that their
progressive examinations are admirably fitted to suit the teacher
who is grateful for an expertly prepared course and the pupil whose
interest is continuously stimulated."

His initiative met with a mixed reception. The authorities in Hong
Kong were not interested. In Singapore, although he found an
enthusiastic local representative in Mr. Anciano, only three teachers
turned up to the meeting to hear his plans. He fared better in Bang-
kok—"situation here very promising" and in Kuala Lumpur "good
meeting, with about 20 present." In Rangoon, he stayed with the
British Ambassador, Sir Richard Allen (son of the musician Sir Hugh
Allen), and was given a cocktail party by the British Council. The

Q

chief difficulties he met were raised by education authorities, because they did not want to have to alter their working arrangements. In one centre, the chief education officer was "an expatriated Yorkshireman from Leeds who believes in being 'rugged and downright' which comes to be synonymous with 'offensive and obstinate'". He spent a great deal of time writing to convents, which didn't reply, and interviewing Mothers Superior: "Can you look up for me the names of the Convents in all the places you mention in your letter, in particular Penang, Taiping, Ipoh and Kuala Lumpur? These are the most likely sources of information," he wrote to the Secretary of T.C.M.

He left Rangoon by air on 6th May and arrived back in England, stopping *en route* in Istanbul, on 19th May. He went straight to Petersfield, where Mary's mother was living. He had been away from home for almost a year.

He was broken in health and in spirit, and for the first time he looked his age. What had started off as a happy and hopeful tour had ended in tragedy. Shortly before they left, Mary confided to a friend that she was afraid something disastrous would happen, but it was for Steuart, not for herself, that she feared. He had always expected to die first and had indeed made over his entire estate to her, as he was worried about her future security.

It is difficult for me to write about Mary, whom I never met. She was obviously not a person you could be neutral about—you either did or did not like her. Many of Steuart's older and more 'intellectual' friends did not like her and held her lack of discretion responsible for most of the trouble during his Covent Garden and Birmingham periods. (Steuart once told me that when he was about to be knighted he didn't warn Mary about it. The first she heard was when a friend rang up to congratulate them. "It slipped my mind," he told her later). Steuart could say outrageous things and get away with it—Mary could not. But many people, whose views I respect, thought she was right for him and that it was a fundamentally happy marriage. Mary sparked off the fire in Steuart, where a more placid partner might have damped it. She was temperamental, sometimes imperious, sometimes kind, alternately gay and moody, but witty, and a good hostess although she did not like domesticity. They quarrelled incessantly, and often violently (especially over each other's driving) and some friends who frequented Chepstow Villas thought that a break-up was inevitable. Mary could say wounding things, but Steuart was utterly loyal to her, and protective. On her side, Mary was passionately devoted to Steuart and fought for him like a tigress.

I think he himself summed up their relationship in a letter to Anneke shortly after her death: "I used to have constant rows with Mary over all sorts of things, but it didn't disturb something settled in us. There is a phrase in Jane Austen's *Mansfield Park* about the row over theatricals. I forget how it comes in now, but the phrase is 'unintelligibly moral' and that was my fault if I didn't make it intelligible. But there was never a blank wall."

PART FOUR

RETIREMENT

CHAPTER TWENTY-SIX

AT LAST YOU ARE HOME

STEUART's third marriage was born out of tragedy and resulted in happiness. My first husband, Leslie Hunter, died in December 1961 in very tragic circumstances and I, too, was 'utterly broken'. Out of the many letters of sympathy I received, none gave me greater comfort than one from Steuart who had read the *Times* notice of Leslie's death. He recalled that he had last met me some thirty years before "at your famous windmill".

"I never kept up with you but that was my fault, but I couldn't forget you and the impression you made on me. Now I return to England from a year abroad in the Far East, examining music, rather decrepit in condition, rather reduced in energy and having lost in India by sudden illness, my much younger wife Mary whom you didn't know or perhaps hear of. And now I hear that you too are battered by fate. So I want to say that if you are *too* heavily battered, you have one profound sympathizer."

I was prompted by this letter to telephone Steuart and go over to see him at Fenn's, his home at Petersfield, where Mary's mother Daisy Goodchild was looking after him. I found him, as he had said in his letter "rather decrepit and reduced in energy". He had put on weight and looked unhealthy and puffy, although he still had his famous twisted smile and wonderful speaking voice. The flame was burning low and he himself told me that when he went to have his beloved spaniel Argo (then over 14) put to sleep, he asked the vet: "Will you do two for the price of one?"

We met frequently that spring. He came over to Brockham Green, in Surrey, where I was in the middle of selling the house and we both felt like goldfish in a bowl with the flood of people who had come to view. It was typical of his great generosity that he offered to *give* (not lend) me money to tide me over the time until Leslie's finances had been sorted out—Leslie had not made a will. "I could do £250 easily and promptly as I really spend *no* money now, and it would be *such* a pleasure." But I was earning reasonable money on various writing jobs and knew that I would get a good price for the beautiful little Georgian house on the village green. Steuart's advice was not to sell. "You'll never find a more attractive place . . . I fell for it completely" he wrote. However, I wanted to move away from a place with so many associations and I found a flat in London.

On 11th April 1962 Steuart invited me to share his life, working in London and spending the week-ends in Petersfield. It was arranged that Daisy should go to her sister's in Colchester. I expressed doubts to Steuart about whether this was fair on Daisy who had lived at Fenn's for nearly twenty-five years. I received a typical "Make up your mind" letter from Steuart—"Accept or put the whole thing off." I was on my way north to visit a steelworks and telephoned at once from Sheffield to say it was On.

Daisy Goodchild was most kind and understanding and I am sure she never bore me any grudge. She was at this time nearing 80, and while still physically and mentally active, she realized that she could not cope indefinitely with the burden of caring for Steuart or give him the companionship he needed.

Steuart at the start was inexorably set against marriage. "You must realize that I may have not much more than five active years of a very restricted activity," he wrote me. "But you have a life in front of you still . . . You can't spend your life looking after an old man and I won't allow you to give up your life to looking after my slow decay." To my mother, he wrote on 22nd May:

"Dear Mrs Stewart,
"I have fallen in love with Margaret, which was thoroughly improvident of me because I am too old and too inactive to match up to her youth and energy, but she has agreed and it is perhaps improvident of her . . . At our time of life and with our past experience I think we are *not* bound to a legal and formal marriage

and we are agreed on that, though it was my suggestion—in fact my stipulation.

"You can, I'm afraid, tell that I'm not physically what I was—my handwriting has deteriorated and I am clumsy in every way. She knows that and refuses to be daunted. . . . She will live here as Margaret Stewart, which is a name she has made well known and important and I should hope that she will go on with that side of her life long after I have slid into oblivion . . . I am fairly well house trained and can manage cooking and we can get some help. I think we can manage all right.

"You have in the past welcomed me so often and I think your charity will extend to me again. My past record is bad and not proposing what would be generally considered a 'reformed life' I don't want to risk bringing her into trouble.

"May I come and see you in Cambridge with Margaret soon?"

Steuart wrote round to his friends, telling them of his changed circumstances and explaining why he didn't want to get married. Thus, to Anneke:

"I have taken a new step in this last month or so. I have joined up with an old Cambridge girl whom I knew as an infant when I was an undergrad almost. She is a professional journalist and an expert on trade unions and labour relations, Margaret Stewart (with a W). She has a busy freelance life still and I do not intend to shackle her with marriage."

A serious blow fell in August. Steuart's doctor ordered him a complete rest in a Portsmouth hospital to get his blood pressure right. "We must bale him out," the doctor told me. So there was I, occupying Fenn's in solitary state, driving down daily to Portsmouth in the Mini we had just bought and feeling altogether rather anomalous. Steuart recovered quickly and was allowed out long before the doctors and nurses expected, with an enormous selection of variegated pills. Then he said he wanted to go to the Three Choirs Festival at Gloucester. I felt I couldn't face the Bishops and the clergy on a 'sharing' basis and Ursula Vaughan Williams wrote suggesting there were advantages in 'certification'. Steuart finally agreed and within a few days, on 31st August, we were married at the Town Hall, Petersfield.

The witnesses were Ronald Biggs and Grace Hutson, and the only other wedding guests at Fenn's afterwards were my sister Frida and her husband, Jonathan Knight, Cecile Biggs and Kathleen Merritt. Steuart baked an outsize loaf as a wedding cake.

We spent our honeymoon at Ross-on-Wye and drove to and from Gloucester, but Steuart found the seats in the cathedral unbearably hard and we played truant a lot. It meant my missing the Trades Union Congress for the first time for about twenty years, but, as I told him, "You are more important than the T.U.C."

We quickly settled down to a fairly routine life. Steuart had the 'harness room'—one of the outhouses of the old riding school—converted into an office for me, installed an electric typewriter and the refectory table from *The Lily Maid*, and I kept busy, while he did the cooking and most of the shopping. He got progressively more ambitious in the kitchen, experimenting with spices and garlic, and was delighted when he produced a really successful soufflé, or Zabaglione, or tripes à la mode de Caen. He was rarely out of his huge red apron, except when he donned his butcher's blue one to do a bit of gardening or wood-chopping.

"In our union there is no demarcation," he wrote to a friend. "She *can* cook and I *can* write." This life he described in a talk we gave to Woman's Hour, on the general subject of "How to be useful though retired."

"My philosophy for retirement is that you should do something not necessarily active and not necessarily in the job which you were brought up to. You see many people who've been school-masters, they think the way to be retired is to be the Chairman of an Education Committee. I don't think so. Your way to be useful, though retired, is to start something you know nothing about—and send your wife out to work like I do."

It was a charming broadcast, though I must confess to some embarrassment when they left in the bit about his washing and ironing. "If she's busy writing an article for the International Labour Office, why shouldn't I iron her pants?" Steuart cooked an excellent lunch for the two BBC producers, Mollie Lee and Theresa McGonigle, and we played a vicious game of croquet and listened to some of his 78-r.p.m. folksong records. To end the talk, the BBC played a record of him singing 'The Crocodile'—one of his favourites.

In August 1964 the Petersfield Labour Party selected me as their prospective parliamentary candidate. There were only about six weeks before the election; there was no proper organization, and only one and a half functioning local parties. But Steuart threw himself into the hustings with a fervour which would not have disgraced an American Presidential campaign manager. He cooked huge meals for the election workers, and he came out canvassing in the highways and byways of this vast, scattered rural constituency.

He toured in so-called motorcades—usually our Mini plus one other car—bawling slogans through the hand loudspeaker we had bought for the occasion; he took the chair at meetings; he investigated the scandal of the tied cottage and bad rural housing which made the main plank of my platform; he manned the telephone and organized the committee rooms in the old co-op bakery; and he acted as host to some of the V.I.P.s who came down to speak—John Freeman, Ray Gunter, Harold Collison, Vic Feather, Ritchie Calder among others.

He got on famously with my agent, the veteran party worker and former baker 'Robbie'—Scipio J. Robinson, who was the same age as Steuart, nearly blind, without a telephone or a car, but nevertheless a splendid campaigner who knew the region like the back of his hand. "Comrade Lady Wilson" he addressed me at election meetings.

The results were, of course, abysmal. I came bottom of the poll with 8,477 votes and the Tory Joan Quennell romped home with over 23,000. The Liberal, Colonel Digby, who had been working up the constituency and had an efficient organizer, came second, and a fourth candidate, an Empire Loyalist, lost her deposit. I think the fact that Colonel Digby was fighting three women may have helped him! Anyhow, I comfortably saved my deposit, and raised the Labour vote, whereas the last Labour candidate at a by-election saved his by only 15 votes.

I fought again in 1966 and managed to poll 10,000 votes, with a big local swing to Labour—the name Wilson was a great help in those days! I was again pipped into second place by Colonel Digby (and 57 votes) and Miss Quennell got even more votes than she had in 1964. Steuart did not take such an active part the second time, though he continued to sustain my stomach and my morale and turned up at the eve of poll meeting wearing an outsize red rosette— "I feel like the horse of the year," he told the audience.

He had never before taken much interest in politics, but he was always naturally on the side of the under-dog, and he had never in his life voted Tory. He regarded himself as an old-fashioned Radical, brought up on the *Manchester Guardian*.

Even after the election, Steuart continued to help the local party. We entertained Tom Driberg and Lena Jeger, who came down to speak: and he often opened fêtes and jumble sales. We used to entertain the committee at Christmas: "I have been making a really good Russian bortsch," he wrote to Iris Lemare, "and last night we had a party of mulled wine and cheese for the Labour Party committee, nearly all of them retired and middle class (Tony and Brenda Gillingham by far the youngest)."

Politics apart, the great excitement in our lives arose through my work for the United Nations and the I.L.O. In 1963 we spent six months in Geneva, where I was engaged as one of a team of writers boiling down about 1 million spoken or written words at a U.N. conference and trying to put them into readable English. My particular chore was "Industry and Transport". I went out ahead, but Steuart kept me fully posted about what he called his 'inactivities'. His letters were full of details about his meals: "lunch of bread and cheese, rice pudd and prunes, with a good dollop of porridge for breakfast; mushroom packet soup tonight with toast and canned peaches. Perhaps some Whiskey to wash it down." (He always drank Irish whiskey for preference.) Or: "Am now writing on the pastry board in bed. By the way I've not got the bread right—too yeasty and the top crumbles away, oven too hot. I'm quite fed up. I used to get it perfectly well." The letter I treasured most said: "Bless you my dear for making my life start again when I thought it had stopped."

And Ursula Vaughan Williams, with whom Steuart had been staying in London, wrote to me: "The only pity is that you are not here too—but in a sense you are, for Steuart looks so well, so beautiful and so happy, that I feel your presence and influence. It is such a joy to see this renewal in him and to hear the planning—'we are going to'—this and that—and I feel so delighted for you both."

This, indeed, is the only excuse for this chapter, which does not bear much relevance to Steuart's musical career, but does show his resilience, his zest for life, and his ability to take on new interests and engage in new ventures.

In Geneva, I found an extraordinary flat in the centre of the town, belonging to a Polish lady and her musical husband. I took it because it had a grand piano, but Steuart refused to play. The carpets and rugs were on the walls, not on the floor; the double bed was so narrow that I had to sleep on a divan; the bathroom geyser was temperamental; and Madame hoarded stale bread—every time you opened a kitchen cupboard a whole lot of old rolls came tumbling out.

I was a temporary international civil servant, paid handsomely in dollars, so we had no need to worry about money. But we lived fairly frugally, and Steuart used to go round the market with a string bag buying grammes of butter and cheese, vegetables and fruit. Every week-end we took the car out to the Jura or Annecy, where he could dispatch me up a mountain while he sat at the bottom, reading or sleeping; when I got down I would find a marvellous spread of paté and cheese and a bottle of white wine, cooled in a mountain stream. Geneva, we both agreed, was a good place to get out of. But we heard some wonderful concerts—the whole of the Beethoven quartets, Karajan conducting the Brahms Fourth symphony and a Music Festival at the spa of Divonne on the French-Swiss border.

We spent the last six weeks of my assignment at a pleasant, slightly crazily-run, hotel on the edge of the Lake at Coppet (the home of Mme de Stael). The theory was that Steuart would spend the morning writing his memoirs, while I drove into Geneva, and would come in on the steamer to meet me in the late afternoon. In practice, he would sit on the terrace drinking coffee and looking at Mont Blanc, and little if any writing got done, I think he thought that my output of wordage was more than enough for us both.

We travelled home slowly, by way of the Franches-Montagnes, enjoying the rolling parkland of the Swiss Jura and the wild horses at Emibois, and returning through France on a 'cultural crawl', which included Bourges, Vézelay, Chartres and the Châteaux of the Loire (which Steuart loathed).

Steuart was the ideal travelling companion. We shared the same tastes in food and wine and liked modest, but comfortable hotels; with his appreciation of the beauties of the countryside and his knowledge of history and architecture he introduced me to much that was new and wonderful.

In 1965 we went to Yugoslavia, where I was doing a tour of instructor training centres for the I.L.O. We stayed with the British Ambassador in Belgrade and Duncan Wilson has recalled an amusing mix-up. Both he and Steuart were known by their second names. Duncan Wilson writes: "I was informed that 'Margaret Stewart would be accompanied by her husband, Sir James Wilson' while he learned that 'Sir Archibald and Lady Wilson would be glad to have them to stay'."

It was not until we arrived at the Residence for breakfast, after a night on the Orient Express, that Steuart realized the Ambassador was in fact his friend Duncan Wilson, with whom he had sung madrigals during the war. The Wilsons were most kind and hospitable; they put the Embassy Rolls at our disposal to be driven round the city, and entertained us royally. The first night they had arranged a dinner party for us to meet leading Yugoslav and Embassy personalities. Steuart who always travelled in nineteenth-century Grand Tour style with an inordinate amount of heavy luggage found that his best suit was stuck in the Belgrade customs shed and he could not get it out in time. But he sat unconcernedly through this very formal diplomatic dinner-party in his dirty old corduroys and sports jacket. He delighted the Embassy kitchen staff by giving them a demonstration of how to use the Kenwood mixer, which had just arrived from London.

The only drawback was the bitterly cold weather. Luckily Steuart had borrowed back the huge American air-raid warden's coat which he had lent to John Kelly, the British Council man in Warsaw, to face a Polish winter. It weighed about a ton and reached to the ground, but with his famous fur hat (bought in the Portobello Road) he kept warm even in the snowstorms at Sarajevo. We both liked the Yugoslavs enormously and had a royal reception wherever we went, though at times the language difficulties were insuperable and the Training Centre had omitted the elementary precaution of providing an English or French-speaking interpreter. Our personal interpreter, a handsome Serb, couldn't speak any language except Serbo-Croat, so Steuart assumed that he had been attached as a bodyguard, to make sure we didn't see anything we weren't supposed to and that the people we met didn't tell us anything they ought not to.

The highlight of the trip was a week-end at Opatija on the Adriatic, once a resort for Austrian aristocrats and now a holiday centre for Yugoslav trade unionists. Our hotel was a centre for training catering workers and when we arrived there was a course in progress for bar-tenders. It started at 8 a.m. with a lecture on Gin!

We came home via Venice, where Steuart recalled his first visit in 1925, when he sang the *Daniel Jazz* to Professor Dent's 'Zoo'. We sat out on a bright cold February morning, in the Piazza San Marco, deserted except for the pigeons and the disconsolate souvenir men, reduced to selling picture postcards to each other.

The same year, we did a similar trip to Poland, to look at a management training centre run by the I.L.O. This was less enjoyable. We found Warsaw grey and sad; the hotel, although the best in the city, was poor, the food monotonous and the service appalling, while winter set in prematurely and Steuart hadn't got the Kelly coat. Nor was the job so interesting—it involved mastering the language of a computer and the intricacies of the production of chemicals. Thanks to the kindness of the Embassy people and to Jack Veitch, the 'computer man' who was training the Poles to use an I.C.T. 1300, the visit was made less dismal. We both enjoyed a visit to Cracow, to see the famous Wawel tapestries.

Between these foreign trips and in the intervals of cooking, Steuart did quite a lot of work. He gave many talks, including a lively lecture for James Robertson at the London Opera School, and some of his best broadcasts—on Plunket Greene, the *Enigma Variations* and Gervase Elwes. He was still on the committee of the Musicians' Benevolent Fund and we used to go to the St. Cecilia dinners in the Savoy, he resplendent in tails, decorations and best white waistcoat, the whole effect slightly marred by the gymshoes he always wore. We attended many functions and conferences of the Incorporated Society of Musicians.

Steuart was on the committee of the Southern Orchestral Society, of which Kathleen Merritt was the conductor. On one occasion there was a contretemps about a performance in Winchester Cathedral and Steuart was furious at the action of the Dean and Chapter in cancelling a concert planned for the Cathedral. He wrote me:

"I have to go down in a minute, as soon as I can take the bread out of the oven, and stiffen the backs of my committee who are all frightened of people who say No-bow-wow. But I was bred to the noise of angry Deans and in fact you can slap their noses."

He was alone in his fury. "I flew off the handle and damned all their eyes for not having a first-class row with the Dean," he reported.

Steuart still undertook a certain amount of festival work and took a few pupils—among them our plumber, a young man with "a nice tenor voice" who showed his gratitude by his promptness in coming round to deal with burst pipes in the Great Freeze of 1963.

We had a pretty social life in London; we went out a lot with my friend, Jock Henderson (former parliamentary adviser to British Railways). Jock shared Steuart's humour and taste for limericks.* We saw a lot of Ursula Vaughan Williams, who organized a party in Frank Hollins's flat in St. John's Wood to celebrate Steuart's 75th birthday. Champagne, tributes and presents flowed in equal quantities.

Steuart became very much addicted to television. Having always refused to have a radio, he became a confirmed viewer, and was extremely catholic in his tastes. He watched news programmes and documentaries, but his favourites were BBC comedies, such as "Steptoe and Son", Harry Worth and "The Rag Trade". I remember on one occasion, he was left to entertain the small son of a Labour Party member, while we were out canvassing. We came back to find him enthralled by Dr. Who. The only programme he could not stand was Fanny Cradock, the cookery expert, with whose theories on cooking he disagreed deeply.

All in all, Steuart enjoyed his semi-retirement and was a splendid example of how to grow old gracefully. Julian Herbage, for whom Steuart did several *Music Magazine* programmes, commented:

"In later years he had mellowed greatly . . . at our last meeting when he recorded a talk on Gervase Elwes he was a Grand Old Man. He cheerfully complained that the trouble of growing old was that you had to remember to go out with your dentures, your spectacles and all your other falsies."

The only shadow over this happy life was concern about Steuart's health. I was constantly afraid for him. When I was in London, it was a great relief to me to hear him answer the telephone, because although he had been ordered to take things easy, he was extremely active—cutting wood with his electric saw, taking the car out,

---

* Just before he died, Steuart sent this limerick to Jock Henderson. I quote it as a sample of his humour:

There was a young curate of Scalisbury
Whose habits were quite halisbury-scalisbury
He walked about Hampshire
Without any pampshire
Till his Bishop insisted he walisbury

XVI. IN FOREIGN PARTS —
HONG KONG 1963

XVII. (MARGARET WILSON IN HAT) IN FOREIGN PARTS —
YUGOSLAVIA 1965

XVIII. SCULPTURE BY DAVID MCFALL R.A. – 1966

scything the nettles in the paddock or shifting furniture about. He not only had a bad heart condition; his Menière's disease grew progressively worse and he found great difficulty in walking; he got very deaf and latterly it was no pleasure to listen to music, because he couldn't hear the high notes and he could never come to terms with his deaf aid. He had frequent attacks of gout and—what was more alarming to me—the attacks of tachycardia continued. I shall never forget two very long ones—once in the streets of Warsaw and another on the Malvern Hills, which he insisted on climbing.

But I came to lose much of my apprehension as he seemed so serene and settled. The summer and autumn of 1966 were particularly full and happy, marred only by the death of my mother in June. We had a holiday in Provence, visiting Avignon, Arles, the Camargue and the fantastic walled city of Aigues-Mortes, and we were planning a trip to southern Spain, as soon as I had finished a major piece of writing I had embarked upon. Steuart was full of plans for the future. He had decided to learn to type and had become the active secretary of the Portsmouth I.S.M.

We were looking forward to a dinner with Donald Gowing, secretary of the Musicians' Benevolent Fund, and Steuart had arranged to do a broadcast on the Bach *Passions* and to give a talk on folk-music at Petersfield. He had even started to write his memoirs, after much nagging on my part. We had just installed central heating and, after a battle with the planning authorities, were preparing to build a little house on the adjoining paddock. Most days we played croquet, either on our own bumpy and hazardous patch or more professionally with Eric and Phyllis Marris on their very smooth lawn.

Steuart that summer sat to the sculptor, David McFall, who was doing a bronze of his head. Both enjoyed the sittings. Steuart told an *Evening Standard* reporter: "My capacity for sitting here doing nothing is almost inexhaustible," and David McFall said, "Two hours is normally my limit. After two hours I'm generally an emotional wreck. But Sir Steuart seems prepared to go on for ever." We collected the bronze from David's studios on 15th December, and Steuart was overcome with joy and pride at it. We planned to borrow the Great Room of the Arts Council in St. James's Square to 'launch' the head and honour the sculptor.

David McFall has recalled the sittings:

R

"Steuart Wilson stalked, rather than walked into my studio—in bald plimsolls. An impish extrovert pagan as I first remember him in July 1966. Roguish, aristocratic, intimidating, with a head like rock. It was deeply crevassed, sea-weathered and lit up from within by a brightness totally unsubdued by the ravages of time. A technical challenge for any sculptor. I set to work at once so as not to have time in which to contemplate the immensity of the problem. The two hour sittings went like lightning. Each morning my Mentor would announce an idea for discussion. I became so mesmerized by his erudition and mental agility that I very soon dropped my end of the argument and listened as best I could while applying all my concentration upon the craggy features of this indefatigable Satyr.

"He talked of many things, particularly music of course. He expounded for my benefit the secret Masonic symbolism of *The Magic Flute*. He introduced me to the *Seven Last Words from the Cross* by Schütz, for which I am eternally grateful. But he was not always so serious. One morning he pronounced a motto with wicked relish. 'Fear no man, do right. Fear every woman, don't write.' This sitting progressed with bouts of hilarious laughter and resulted in the slightly demoniacal glint of mischief to be detected, I fancy, in the eyes of my bronze portrait head."

Death, when it came, struck suddenly and silently. It was 18th December, the Sunday before Christmas, and Steuart had been preparing the menu for the Christmas dinner we were giving for Mervyn Horder—he had already bought the chestnuts for the stuffing. It had been a normal day. A good lunch of chicken, followed by a game of croquet. "I'm going to beat you," he said—we ended in a draw. Then we got down to Christmas cards. He had written three, when he collapsed at his big desk in the living-room, and I think his last words were: "Do you think the Post Office will mind if I write more than the prescribed words?" It cannot have lasted more than a few minutes and I do not think he can have felt any pain.

Steuart once spoke about death in an 'Any Questions' programme. "It doesn't matter much where you die. It's an unpleasant business, not for you, but an unpleasant business for everybody else who has to do all the doings. So perhaps you had better do it at home for convenience' sake." He typically added the story of the two old men at a village funeral. "One said to the other 'How old are you?' He said, 'Well I'm 84'—'Then it's hardly worth your going home, is it?' "

The doings of a death are indeed unpleasant, though I think that the necessary activities of notification, registration, letter-writing and making funeral arrangements are the best antidote to the shock of bereavement. Steuart, unlike his father, never left any instructions about his funeral. So we buried his ashes in Steep village churchyard, in the same grave as Canon Wilson, shaded by big yew trees and with a distant view of the Sussex downs, beside the church where his children had been christened. It was a simple service; Anthony Gillingham's choir sang, "Jesu priceless treasure" and led the singing of Vaughan Williams's "For all the Saints."

A month later, a more formal, but very beautiful memorial service was held in the musicians' own church, the Holy Sepulchre in London. Again we chose music by Bach and Vaughan Williams to honour his memory. His name is enshrined in the Book of Remembrance in the musicians' chapel and at Steep, his burial place is marked by a plain stone slab, inscribed with the words from *Pilgrim's Progress* which Steuart himself would have chosen:

"Keep this light in your eye and go up thereto."

PART FIVE

ASSESSMENT

CHAPTER TWENTY-SEVEN

THE MUSICIAN

"I SOMETIMES wonder whether I was lucky to have survived the 1914–18 War. Had I gone down in that cauldron, people would have accounted me, perhaps, as a potential singer who might have made a mark. I lived to make a mark which is hardly visible now."

In these words, Steuart Wilson, in his autobiographical fragment, summed up his own career. They were typical of his lack of self-conceit. The comments of countless friends and colleagues in the musical world give the lie to this pejorative assessment. Indeed, the flood of posthumous tributes makes one wish that people would write obituary notices before, and not after, a death.

I am not a professional musician—merely a lover of music, so I must quote the views of others who are qualified to judge and draw on the fund of Steuart's own writings, in an attempt to assess his contribution to music in England.

Gilmour Jenkins, writing in the *Folk Music Journal*, 1967 summarized it:

"His active life fell in the critical period when English music was throwing off its subservience to the Continent and was re-establishing its own proper place in the musical life of the world. Steuart played no small part in that hard and successful battle."

Of his singing, Frank Howes, wrote in the *Musical Times* (March 1951):

"Wilson had an appreciation of words and of the peculiar incandescence, generated by the dramatization of poetry in song, which appealed to cultivated audiences. In the never-ending, ding-dong struggle within the art of singing on the one hand and the sheer magic of tone and the art of vocalization on the other, it was at that time the turn of the intelligent singer to rescue the art from the partnership of triviality, banality and vulgarity which did a roaring trade in the royalty ballad of the period. 'Intelligence' in recital notices nowadays has come to be a polite euphemism for an indifferent vocal equipment. But the antithesis is not of mutually exclusive terms, and though Wilson's voice never fully recovered from its injuries it was serviceable enough to enable him to reach the top of the tree among English non-operatic singers."

Sir Arthur Bliss summed up in one short sentence: "He was a splendid soloist and an excellent musician." And Sir Thomas Beecham is reported to have said: "A dry voice, but an extremely intelligent one." Steuart, in effect, proved the falseness of de Reszke's phrase "Il est bête comme un tenor."

The variety and versatility of his repertoire has been described in earlier chapters. He was extremely catholic in his tastes. Harold Rutland remembers that in the BBC days, he, Steuart and Lennox Berkeley were listening to a broadcast performance of Rachmaninov's second piano concerto. "Their almost rapturous comments on the work pleased and also surprised me, since I had thought that the music would have been too romantic and 'impure' in style for Steuart and scarcely sophisticated enough for Lennox." Steuart once declined to be interviewed for the BBC programme *Desert Island Discs* on the ground that he didn't possess a gramophone and if he did wouldn't know how to work it. Despite the catholicity of his taste, I am sure that had he been asked to select works by two composers, he would have chosen works by Bach and Vaughan Williams, in all probability Bach's D Minor Double Concerto for Violins which he had first heard the D'Aranyi sisters play in 1913, and Vaughan Williams's *Sea Symphony*.

He himself excelled not only as the Evangelist, but in any work of Bach. Evelyn Radford, wrote in *Making Music* (the journal of the Rural Music Schools Association (Spring 1968)) that one of the great experiences of her life was hearing Steuart sing in the Bach B minor Mass in York Minster:

"As Steuart Wilson sang the 'Benedictus qui venit in nomine Domini', a reflected light from one of the lovely stained glass windows fell on him like a miracle. In my Cambridge days I had often heard him sing when he was the leading tenor in King's College Chapel and I would, on a sudden impulse, leave my studies and dash down to Evensong on my bicycle. Though his voice was variable after his severe war wound, that night at York he was on the top of his form, singing with the utmost feeling and vocal beauty."

As for Vaughan Williams, Steuart once wrote that he had revered him "this side of idolatry" from the moment when, as a schoolboy "muddling around with music" he first discovered *Songs of Travel*.

"In the days of 1909, 1910 and 1911 your music was the great excitement and stimulus of my life," he wrote to Ralph on his 70th birthday: "it has never ceased to be that but when I was young and 'exposed' to it for the first time the effect was naturally more than it could ever be in pure excitement. Do you know that you've left a more valuable thing to us of this generation than your music and that's your personal character and your integrity and 'guts'. Your 'all this' won't mean anything in 100 years unless people can divine it in your music, but it has meant everything to us, that we could admire without reserve a man who could write such music and who could stand like a rock when he wanted to. Perhaps I should have put my own rock facing a little differently sometimes, but what a thing it has been to have a rock in these days. That's the biggest service you have given to music in your generation—and in that respect we are all your pupils and should be your followers. I can't judge whether music is immortal or not and I don't care. But I do know that character in music is immortal in its influence on people, and that means you."

After Vaughan Williams's death in 1958, he wrote: "How happy I am to think of the near fifty years during which he was everything I admired in a man and in music." Steuart was one of the small party of six who went with Ursula to R.V.W.'s graveside in Westminster Abbey, where his ashes were laid. He was proud to represent Vaughan Williams's friends in the musical profession and to be at Ursula's side.

Steuart sang Vaughan Williams's music on every possible occasion, but there was no work which he performed more often, or more movingly, than *On Wenlock Edge*. Mrs. Molly Kirwan (Charlotte Monrow) recalls a performance at the Rudolf Steiner Hall on 29th May 1927: "Although I had often heard him sing Bach and was to hear him in much more, including a season of Mozart at the Court Theatre in Sloane Square, there has remained with me all my life an absolute out-of-this-world magic about that *Wenlock Edge*— the tiny hushed hall, bright warm sunlight stealing in, and above all, the sound of his voice and his spellbinding way with the piece, as if it was some deep part of him."

Professor Walter Stanton, one of Steuart's closest associates, has told me:

"As a musician, he stands in the front rank. There have been, are and always will be, a corpus of technically skilled performers, whose doings leave one utterly cold; not so Steuart, for he clothed every musical utterance with a musical perception of distinction. As a performer, he excelled in The English Singers; as a solo singer he was A plus, and not least amongst his qualities was the sense of security which any conductor could feel when he was singing. As a teacher, I did not know him personally but I am persuaded that he *must* have been an inspiration."

Very vivid impressions remain of Steuart as a teacher, and many of his former pupils have confirmed to me what a great inspiration he was. Inia te Wiata, the New Zealand opera singer, who had lessons with Steuart at Trinity College, has told me: "I feel I learnt more during my period with Sir Steuart than at any other time in my musical career—the complete fundamentals of music and professionalism in singing. I am eternally grateful to him for all the guidance and friendship he gave me."

Steuart had his own very special technique of teaching, derived from his experience with James Ley and with Jean de Reszke. He always taught with the use of Aikin's Chart,* the resonator scale of

* William Arthur Aikin (1857–1939) was a surgeon and amateur musician, who conducted a great deal of research into phonology. According to Grove's *Dictionary*, he "did not invent a new method of voice training, he merely revealed certain basic phonological principles which he regarded as constituting a sure foundation on which a good method may be built."

vowel sounds. His main emphasis was always on the words. Himself
a master of diction, he sought to impart to his pupils the same feeling
of the importance of language that characterized his own singing.
"Think the words, feel the words," he would say. He deprecated the
modern tendency—among Pop singers and others—to slur their
words.

In a talk on the BBC *Music Magazine* (1st December 1946) he
elaborated his views on how to sing English:

"We have, according to most phoneticians, thirteen pure vowel
sounds, seven diphthongs and three triphthongs, a mere twenty-
three sounds . . . We barely notice them in speech, but we have to
study them in singing because it is speech prolonged indefinitely
between consonants. Now the thirteen pure vowel sounds can be
easily memorized as:

> Who would know aught of art
> Must learn and pay his fee

Pay his fee is important! The diphthongs are such words as Hue,
High, How, Joy, Jeer, Snare, Sure; the triphthongs such words as
Pure, Sour, Fire, The debatable vowel sound is Pay, Hay takes on
a compound quality because of its final 'y', while the 'm' of name
doesn't so much modify it. All right we'll have a look at some of
them under the microscope.

> 'Who is Sylvia, what is she,
> That all our swains commend her?'

"You see we've got 11 pure sounds—who is Sil, what is she, that
all swains commend her. The doubles are a bit tricky—do we say
Syl*vier* or Syl*viah*—one sounds Camden Town and the other
Campden Hill? Well what about *our*—let's try a few ways—'that
all *ah* swains' that's pure, but wrong, 'that all *our*'. You see you
must divide your diphthongs with the right stress on each part."

As an example of how *not* to sing words, he recalled:

"When I was an undergraduate at Cambridge I sang *Israel in
Egypt* in a chorus at Cambridge under old Daddy Mann of King's,
the local variant of vowel-sounds produced 'He gave them hile-
stones for rine': add a liaison and we tenors sang 'He gave them

milestones for rine'. 'Gentlemen, gentlemen,' said old Daddy
Mann, 'hailstones were a bad enough plague, but milestones!' So
when we sing words that are in themselves beautiful, lyric poetry of
high quality and sound, we have to be rather over-careful."

I don't know if Steuart's pupils came away from a lesson with him
as alternately elated and depressed as he himself had done from de
Reszke. Steuart didn't have a green parrot to show approval or
disapproval; but he always used to say that his dog Argo could tell
whether a voice was good or bad. Argo used to curl up under the
piano stool during a lesson, and if he liked the voice, he would join
in—and the more he liked it the louder he would sing. If he disliked
the singer, he would ostentatiously get up and walk away. Argo was
not only a critic but a virtuoso—and Steuart used to get him to
perform 'Daisy Daisy' as a duet!

Steuart's other great point was rhythm. He detested slurring and
insisted that performers, whether vocal or instrumental, should
observe the full value of a note, as he himself did. He once said he
wanted to form a "society for the protection of the dotted note."

Steuart's help and advice was not limited to singing. Among his
papers, I have found a fascinating talk on concert-giving and platform appearance, in the art of which he showed consummate skill.
His main theme was the need to ensure that there were no barriers
between the performer and the audience and he said that what really
mattered was the "adaptability of the performer to *receive* an impression from the music. Are you so flexible in your music that Mozart
makes a different impression on you from Ravel? Can you distinguish between the Romantic and the merely Sentimental, and do
you stand between the music and your audience, or do you lose
yourself in the music? I can't tell you how to do that in a lecture.
But I can tell you a few things about not standing in the way of the
music so that the audience can't hear it because of *you*."

The talk was full of practical hints about getting to the hall early
to see that all the physical arrangements (lights, stage, piano, etc.)
were satisfactory and he warned: "Don't despise the whole thing and
think that you play so brilliantly that it doesn't matter how awkward
you are, how untidy or how careless." And finally—the exit. "Let
your final leave-taking be not just an acknowledgement of your own
worthiness, not just a feeling of paying what is due, but a sincere

thanks to the audience for their kindness in enjoying the music and helping you to enjoy. Audiences in this country *are* kind."

What is called Musical Appreciation in schools is often regarded as a dull subject. Steuart had the knack of making it exciting and living, whether he was talking to school-children, youth clubs or adult societies. His message was always *Enjoy* it. In an article he wrote for an Eton College publication *Orpheus* in 1965 he said:

"Let us remember Beecham's famous dictum 'The English don't know a lot about music, but they like the noise it makes.' We must add to that, 'when they become familiar with it'. Music flashes by you quicker than a film and if it holds any serious content or warrants any serious attention, it requires for most of us repetition until it becomes familiar. Then we can lean back and know what's coming and at the same time *enjoy* it when it does come. I rather go for the last point, particularly the *enjoyment*."

One of his great theories was that the whole purpose of education ought to be to teach people to *enjoy* things. He communicated his own sense of enjoyment to his audiences, and many people have told me of the thrill of hearing him sing, when they were schoolboys. Thus Duncan Wilson:

"Steuart was some kind of a force in my own life, and I'm sure in those of many school contemporaries, long before I knew him personally. In the mid-1920s he would come to Winchester to give recitals to the school. It is some indication of the vitality of his performances that after more than forty years details stick in my memory. He conveyed to us that music was full of tragedy and drama and joy, that it was not unmanly to sing it for what the words as well as the notes were worth and that it was indeed *fun* to do so."

Steuart was throughout his life concerned to encourage and stimulate amateurs. In a talk to the Gloucester Literary Club, in the autumn of 1962, he stressed the vital place of the amateur in music:

"Understanding and appreciation must come from the heart, must be stimulated by some profound emotional thought, the same kind of wonderful thought that makes you sing in your bath.

The song in the heart is something which must be there all the time. It is something which the professional player who often works 16 or 18 hours a day is not so likely to have. That is the part that we must bring to the performance; those who come to listen to the music must bring something with them other than their price tickets. They must bring the interpretation, the bearing of welcome to the sound . . . I would rather be alive and slightly dowdy than extremely fashionable and be a model dead in a shop window. I am absolutely convinced that music is a living thing and living in our hearts and minds. That is the only place it can come from."

One of his favourite subjects was the relationship between professionals and amateurs. In a talk to County Music Advisers, entitled "Gentlemen v. Players" in 1958, he stressed the need for mutual sympathy and understanding:

"The amateur can learn and enjoy what he likes, the professional has to perform what is ordered by his employers . . . In the matter of repertoire the amateurs could have it all their own way. They can meet regularly and go through all the music they desire to know—the professionals must keep up to concert pitch without fail, a very much smaller repertoire of what audiences want to hear. That is their job, but they must not despise the vastly greater knowledge of music that the amateur can enjoy.

". . . There must be the tolerance and respect especially of the professional towards the amateur. For the Pro must learn his 'symbiosis' with the amateur, and the amateur must respect the disciplined craft of the Pro."

Steuart could be kind and he could be cruel. He gave advice straight from the shoulder and without any of the usual wrappings. Many stories have been told about his caustic comments. When a hopeful young singer came for an audition, Steuart asked him "And how do you propose to make your living?" The young man replied, "I want to sing." "What with?" was Steuart's withering comment. He once said of a soprano that she sang her top notes "as if she'd had her tits caught in a mangle". And in America, he was engaged to teach the daughter of a rich lady, who complained that he wasn't making enough progress in bringing on the girl's musical talent.

"Well, Madam, you can't make a silk ear out of a sow's purse," he retorted.

It was the same with Steuart as an adjudicator. He was much in demand and probably judged as many competition festivals as any other English musician. He was sparing in his praise, but when he gave it, it was all the more welcome. Nellie Kelly, widow of Cuthbert Kelly, has told me:

"I met Steuart first in his work as an adjudicator . . . I can say that we as competitors rather hated him, for his remarks were frequently caustic and sometimes humiliating. Even so we were always delighted to see his name as judge of any class we had entered. He had great integrity and devotion to this work and a flair for picking the winners. The constructive criticism that always came from his adjudication address was a revelation to the singers and did much to raise the standard of performance in competition festivals. What we appreciated too was his whole-hearted praise when a performer merited it—coming from him we knew it was genuine and well worth having."

When Steuart detected real talent in candidates, he would spare no pains to encourage them. Many examples of Steuart's help to young musicians have been given to me. I was particularly impressed by a letter from Mr. Herbert Byard, of Bristol:

"As a boy I was mad on music. My parents were desperately poor working-class people and could not afford to give me anything in the way of a musical education beyond about 18 months' piano lessons from the local unqualified organist at 1s. a time . . . My most valuable experience was the conducting of amateur choirs in the Stinchcombe Hill Festival. At the first of these in which I took part the principal work was Bach's Cantata no 11, and the tenor soloist was Sir Steuart. The Festival secretary press-ganged me into playing the continuo. I didn't even know what continuo meant then and your husband, realizing this, very unobtrusively initiated me into the mysteries of figured bass 'realization' in the most friendly way, told me that I should shortly probably find myself grappling with the continuo in the Matthew Passion, and promised to send me something about it that I might find helpful. Shortly afterwards, I received from him a copy of 'Music and Letters' containing his famous article on that subject.

There was no need for him to have done this ... He simply recognized that an inexperienced bungler was in trouble and did me a good turn for which I have always been very grateful."

Another letter, out of the blue, reached me from Johannesburg. Francis Russell, a tenor, wrote that he had first met Steuart at a rehearsal of a Bach cantata at the Royal College in the early 1930s. "I had been told that he was austere and unapproachable, so you can imagine my surprise when he came to me and introduced himself ... I told Steuart that I was not looking forward to singing Bach, in fact I told him that it was my first Bach work and I was not happy. To my astonishment he said 'Would you like me to take you over the work?' I jumped at his offer and we went to a room upstairs at the R.C.M. In a very short time I found a musician who knew his Bach, I also found a friend whom I could always approach when I was in musical difficulty; and above all else he was a tenor, and they are not noted for their help to other tenors."

Professional musicians are not usually noted for their kindness towards music critics either, and it is rather welcome to find Steuart saying kind words about them. In a preface to the collection of A. H Fox Strangways' essays *Music Observed* he wrote:

"In the musical world we performers can seldom get the chance of criticizing our critics and indeed we hardly know them except as a black-avised gang. But they are, as the Lancashire wife said of her husband 'not so bad when you get to know them' and my friendships have taught me amongst other things that some of our critics 'know their stuff' better than we performers believe them to. Our respect for their judgment is also increased when we know that they have been in touch with any of the actualities of musical life as we performers know it."

He himself had many close friends among the music critics, and was particularly friendly with Frank Howes of *The Times* and Martin Cooper of the *Daily Telegraph*.

Steuart was a considerable scholar. For somebody who had never studied at any college or institution, or taken a degree, he had a remarkable grasp of the theory and history of music, and he was patient and persistent in his research. Nowhere perhaps has his scholarship been better shown than in the many translations which

he made, either on his own or in co-operation with A. H. Fox
Strangways. His classical education, natural wit and sense of rhythm
and language combined to produce verses in, for example, the
Schubert *Lieder*, which match the music and are masterpieces of
simplicity. Though not himself a German scholar, he tackled the
Brahms Magelone *Lieder*, Haydn's *Creation*, Mahler's *Lied von der
Erde* and a wide range of Schumann songs. No work and no language
daunted him. He even translated Welsh folk songs into English. I
have found a note, scribbled on a sheet of paper headed Angel Hotel,
Cardiff, which begins: "I am going to sing four Japanese folk-songs
in Japanese, but I must not pretend to be an authority on Japanese
music. . ."

He was an authority on church music and wrote some erudite
articles in *Music and Letters* and elsewhere on hymns and carols.

He himself wrote several carols and hymns, but the work that
pleased him most was his version of the *Benedicite*. "I think I must try
and get someone to set that as a Choral work with my words," he
wrote, "I'm not often satisfied but that was *good*."

Benedicite

O all ye works of God the Lord
We bid you now to bless the Lord,
   Angels holy
   Creatures lowly,
Ye Skies and Floods above below,
Ye Fire and Heat, ye Ice and Snow,
   Dew and Showers
   All ye Powers
Praise him and magnify him for ever.

Sing Stars of Heaven, sing Sun and Moon
Sing Beasts and Cattle every one,
   Hills and Mountains
   Wells and Fountains
Sing Winter Summer Nights and Days
Sing Light and Darkness for his praise
   Whales and Fishes
   Lightning flashes
Praise him and magnify him for ever.

s

O Winds of God, O Fowls in Air
O all ye Green Things everywhere
          Souls and Spirits
          Add your merits
O Servants of the Lord apart
O holy humble Men of heart
          Ananias
          Azarias
Praise him and magnify him for ever.

O cleansing Tide, O burning Flame
O piercing Joy that knows no name
          Heart-entwining
          All-divining
O Voice of all the Stars at dawn
O Music sound at that last morn
          When adoring
          Soul outpouring
We shall praise him and magnify him for ever.

CHAPTER TWENTY-EIGHT

THE MAN

STEUART WILSON was born in the reign of Queen Victoria and grew to manhood in that of Edward VII. There was nothing Victorian about him, though one can detect traces of the Edwardian in his taste for clothes and the gay, grand manner which he often assumed. But he cannot be pigeon-holed into any age or century. His art was universal and his personality transcended time. In later years, he described himself as "an unrepentant old square" but in fact he kept young in spirit and continued to be absorbed and fascinated by the world around him. His fund of wit and humour was inexhaustible.

How can one convey to people who did not know him the magic of his personality, the depth of his character? Or bring back the deep resonance of his speaking voice and his infectious laughter? He was big physically, well over 6 feet tall and handsome—always the 'cuddest' man as he had been in his Winchester days, and in later life, his face took on a serene beauty and nobility. When Steuart came into the room, you immediately felt that something important was happening. That much overworked word 'charismatic' can justly be applied to him.

To many, Steuart was a legendary figure—the tenor who sang on only one lung, the singer who sued the BBC and later joined them, the debonair wit and raconteur, many of whose *mots* have entered musical language. He had something of the Beecham quality of magnetism and something too, of Beecham's flair and roguishness. But there was another side to Steuart, known perhaps only to those who were close to him, his immense warmth of heart, compassion

and generosity. I hope that something of this aspect has emerged
from the foregoing pages. He was not only generous to young
musicians in time, money and advice; he would help anybody who
was in any way in sorrow or in difficulty.

Steuart suffered much during his lifetime. He waged a constant
battle against ill-health, and sustained cruel personal losses. His first
marriage broke up painfully and his second wife died a tragic death
in India; his brother Hugh was killed in the First World War, and
his elder brother Arnold and his first-born son Jonathan were killed
in the Second World War.

A colleague at the BBC told me: "Only once did I see Sir Steuart
emotionally upset. I was talking with him in his office when the
news of his elder son's death was telephoned to him. He turned pale
and for a few moments he sat looking down at his desk in absolute
silence. Suddenly he roused himself and resumed talking as if the
telephonic interruption with its tragic news was an irrelevance. He
made no comment and did not invite sympathy."

Jonathan was killed near Venloo on 20th November 1944, shortly
before his 21st birthday. He was a poet and a slim volume *Poems* by
Jonathan Wilson, which appeared in 1946, was described by G. M.
Young as "a voice of authentic poetic promise, and not of promise
only." When he enlisted, Steuart wrote to him: "I had gone into the
army in the heat and flame at the very outbreak of the last war. I
hadn't had to wait for the tide to reach me, so to speak. What you
have done is much more cold-blooded and needed far more real
courage and philosophy to face." Even after his separation from Ann,
Steuart had gone on seeing Jonathan, but after his death, the family
links snapped.

I have been moved by the number of people who have written to
tell me what a letter from Steuart meant to them after a personal
tragedy. Thus, Duncan Wilson told me: "That winter (1943) a
daughter was born to us prematurely and not without grave risk to
my wife. The child did not survive. Our hearts were sore, but a
bright ray of comfort came to us in the shape of a deeply understanding and beautiful letter from Steuart. It was typical of him.'

When the marriage of the singer Ivan Firth broke up and Kit, his
wife, was left virtually penniless to bring up a young family, Steuart
came to the rescue. "I don't quite know what our family would have
done without his friendship," their daughter Billie told me. He helped

John Firth with his schooling and when Billie got married to a young test pilot, Steuart gave them £1 a week for a full year, to help them out.

He was equally at ease with the very old and the very young. My mother, then 85, came to stay with us and Steuart looked after her most solicitously and made her 'eat'—she was accustomed to a diet of tea and porridge! He was very good with children. Lord Harewood has told me how superbly Steuart entertained his two-year-old son one day at tea at Chepstow Villas. He had scores of god-children, whom he remembered every birthday, even if he did not always fulfil the godparental duties enjoined by the prayer-book. He seemed instinctively to know what children liked; he never talked down to them, but met them on their own level. I have found a delightful letter to his godson Christopher Neame (the son of Astra Desmond) concerning a remarkable confusion over a present of Tiptree jam which arrived labelled "From Christopher."

Steuart wrote to two other Christophers before he got the right one and sent an abject apology:

"Your godfather has a strange story to tell . . . The other night he dreamed a dream. He saw an ephelant (quite clearly an ephelant, make no mistake) with a man on his back carrying a banner and on that banner was written equally unmistakeably TIPTRH, so the dreamer woke with a jump and saw what a mug he has been and here he is sitting down in Edinburgh to confess his stupidity. The moral of this story is hard to discover I'll admit but then the discovery of the moral is your godfather's business, not yours, and if you ask he'll say sagely 'You'll find out all about that when you grow up'. Now have I rubbed my forehead in the dust enough?"

Ann Pennant, Steuart's step-niece, remembers that when her mother, Rose Carver, married Arnold Wilson, she was then four and Steuart gave *her* a wedding present, as he thought she might be feeling out of it. Much later, when Ann's husband Arthur was very ill, Steuart came and sat with him for hours, not only relieving Ann of nursing duties but inspiring in Arthur the confidence that he was going to get well.

Steuart could inspire love in people—both men and women—and make deep and lasting friendships. An American friend Eddie

Weissmiller, who had known him since 1939, put it: "For more than a quarter of a century Steuart had my deepest affection and admiration and if I saw him, or wrote him, or heard from him not all that often, still I developed a sense of the world as a place the meaning of which he in part determined. I loved him and love him, for all the qualities you know so much more closely even than I."

He was, of course, enormously attractive to women. R.V.W. used to say that the reason why such and such a singer had never married was because she was repining for Steuart! He on his side was much moved by physical beauty and used rather to enjoy his reputation as a 'wolf'. But to cast him as a Don Giovanni would be a wild exaggeration.

Astra Desmond, who knew him as well as anyone, told me that there was in fact quite a Puritan streak in him.

Steuart wrote in the 1920s that he was "fearfully ambitious." Ambitious is the last adjective I would use about him. He was certainly ambitious to give a good performance and to do justice to a work—"the best for the highest" was a phrase he was very fond of using. But if he was ambitious for music, he was not ambitious for himself.

Many people have wondered why, after he had retired as a professional singer, Steuart moved in rapid succession from one official job to another and never seemed to stay long enough anywhere to make a permanent impact. George Baker, the singer, who was with him at the BBC Overseas department, put it:

"He never achieved the success his abundant natural abilities should have won for him. It is fascinating to reflect that although Steuart's obvious intellectual brilliance made him an automatic choice in a short list of selected candidates for almost any important appointment and, as events turned out, a certain winner, he never quite fulfilled one's expectations. Like many other men of his type he entered into the excitement of each new appointment with an almost electrifying enthusiasm, but this enthusiasm soon abated and his mental restlessness brought about a desire to seek fresh fields of activity. He liked to bring things up to the boil, but when they reached the simmering or routine stage, as they inevitably did, he quickly grew tired of them."

That is one assessment, by a man who knew Steuart well. I think it is a penetrating one, but less than fair to Steuart. Anybody who saw him tenderly simmering a stew or slow-cooking a joint would dispute the suggestion that he was only interested in bringing things to the boil! He certainly did not suffer fools gladly and did not like being thwarted by people he despised. Mr. Baker said: "Like many men of his extrovertial type, he never took the slightest interest in the opinions of other people whom he regarded as fools . . . His intellectual superiority aroused feelings of resentment in colleagues who claimed equal rights to speak their minds." He added, however: "I personally never had a cross word with him during the thirty-five years I knew him, maybe because both of us being fighters we had a mutual respect for each other . . . (he was) a fine musical warrior."

A rather different picture was painted by Mary Glasgow, who worked closely with Steuart at the Arts Council. She wrote in *The Times*:

"No one could have been a more loyal officer of the Arts Council. As his projects developed successfully, he saw to it that the glory went to those who carried them out and to the council which financed them; only on the rare occasions when they went awry did he refuse to remain anonymous. Then no one could persuade him not to take the blame himself—as publicly as possible."

This readiness to accept responsibility was part of what some have termed his Saint Sebastian complex—his willingness to be shot at and to shield his subordinates. Other, less friendly, critics have described him as a Don Quixote and many of the causes he espoused as windmills.

He was fearless, impetuous and decisive and would make snap decisions on matters of greater and lesser import. I shall never forget how he suddenly decided we would go over to Brockham to dig up the asparagus bed, before the sale of my house there had gone through. The asparaguses were duly dug and put in the boot of the taxi he had hired, but they never survived transplantation. There was no glory—and no asparagus either! But it was a splendid thought.

Steuart was very fond of quoting Dr. Jowett's dictum "Never explain—never apologize," and he once thought of making it the title of the Memoirs he never completed. Yet he was the first to admit it if he made a mistake; he had no sense of false pride and never took the attitude that he was 'Sir Oracle'.

Mary Glasgow said of him: "He was single-minded, generous and gay; he was a bewildering mixture of sensitivity and toughness. He had greatness of mind and heart." I think her phrase "a mixture of sensitivity and toughness" is very true. And so was Frank Howes' assessment in his beautiful tribute to Steuart at the memorial service in January 1967:

> "His art was a projection of the man himself and in these days of muddle-headed egalitarianism it is encouraging to remember him as an Englishman, an individual, of the greatest distinction. He had fortitude and brains; generosity and wit: gaiety and charm. All of us here know too that there was a thread of steel in his make-up which he inherited from his father. This could hurt and sometimes did. And he did not shrink from navigating in stormy waters. It was said of Canon Wilson that his frank acceptance of Darwinian evolution fluttered the theological dovecots and the Close at Worcester. Steuart fought a good many similar battles in his time, but I don't think he was capable of rancour or malice."

Keith Falkner summed him up: "Steuart became uncle, friend, guide and whetstone to me throughout the years"—the word *whetstone* is a particularly telling one.

Steuart had a highly developed bump of irreverence, first noticed in the 1890s when his Dame school mistress Miss Boycott had lamented his lack of respect for authority. He said what he thought and if people didn't like it, that was their affair. As W. K. Stanton said:

> "Fear of unpopularity was unknown to him. He would include remarks which he realized would be unpalatable to some of his audience, but he would 'lace' such remarks with a sudden spot of wit, or with an apposite story, which would both lessen the unpalatability and also make the moment more memorable. He would then glance round perhaps with a wink at someone who was worth such, and simultaneously gauge the effect of what he had said, and if it was not what he had intended, he would plunge in again—possibly with a more unpalatable sentence or two—but followed by a more subtle dose of wit and a more pointed story."

Many examples have been given me of occasions when Steuart's audible asides—and he had a very carrying voice even *sotto voce*—caused consternation. E. Arnold Dowbiggin recalls sitting next to him at a performance of Britten's *Rape of Lucretia*. "When Reginald Goodall, conducting the chamber orchestra, came into the pit to open with Britten's first bizarre arrangement of the National Anthem, the audience, not quite realizing what was happening, slowly straggled to its feet. Sir Steuart leaned down to me and said in a very audible voice 'The Rape of the National Anthem?'"

His ready wit and forthrightness made him a highly successful spontaneous broadcaster. His remarks on the "Any Questions" programme often got him into trouble and once when he aired his views on teen-age drinking, he met with a torrent of abuse. "We have a proverb about sowing your wild oats," he said. "If you get really well tanked up when you are a teenager, you may possibly be unable to stop it, but to my mind it is a great deal more likely that you won't do it again, and I am all for getting these things over young . . . Getting tight is an occasional spree and I am all for an occasional spree."

On another occasion, he confessed that cricket was one of his pet hates. "I've always been bored by playing cricket and I'm much more bored by hearing about it." And to the two politicians, James Callaghan and Stephen McAdden who were on the programme, he said: "It doesn't matter whether Mr. Callaghan makes the rules or whether Mr. McAdden makes them, I object to the whole damn lot of the rules and I would rather be annihilated than have to live under either of their rules."

Steuart was an extrovert, who liked to impress—that was the performer in him. Even when he became a semi-civil servant, he refused to wear conventional clothes. His outsize hat, his waistcoats, his tie-rings, his sponge-bag trousers and his red apron were not so much part of an act, as part of the man. Keith Falkner said:

"His grandfather's Passion trousers, vivid broad black and white check and much too big for him; his tight knee golfing breeches, he refused to count strokes until he reached the fairway; his carpet slippers at the Musicians Benevolent Fund dinner. All added colour to the life of a great man and a great character."

Not only his trousers, but everything about Steuart was somewhat outsize, and living with him was rather larger than life. All his equipment was big and solid. His huge desk, the enormous waste-paper basket, the heavy luggage, the big music-case, the vast fur-lined coats . . . Until we bought a Mini, he always drove very large cars. David McFall has said that driving with him in London was a highly unnerving experience. "By the time traffic lights had mercifully halted us at Oxford Street, I was terrified out of my wits and was emboldened to ask if he didn't find town driving 'a bit nerve-racking.' 'LOVE IT' he retorted with one hand ready on the trigger and a bleak eye on his starting competitors." I must confess to similar feelings when we were negotiating the hairpin bends up Mont Salève, outside Geneva, but knowing how furious he would get with a backseat driver, I refrained from comment.

Steuart was very proud of his electrical equipment—which included a washing-machine, an electric saw and hedge-clipper—and would spend hours tinkering with it. But he despised such modern gadgets as Biro pens and carried his bottle of ink wherever he went. He also despised pre-cooked vegetables, canned soups and other time and labour-saving devices in the kitchen.

He was a superb host, generous in his helpings and measures. Entertaining friends at the Garrick Club, he would order a Jeroboam of red wine. At the same time he was an extremely economical cook, to the point of parsimony, using up left-overs and scraps. He was as much at home in the local pub or fish-and-chop shop as in the Savoy. Although in some senses he was a patrician—he would always travel first-class and had an account at Fortnum and Mason's—he was utterly unsnobbish and mixed easily with people of widely differing social backgrounds. The members of the local Labour Party adored him and more than once he offered hospitality to an evicted farm worker or some other victim of local tyranny. There was no 'above or below' stairs at Chepstow Villas or his Newcastle home—everybody in and about the house ate communally at the long refectory table. He was, by birth, breeding and character, a natural gentleman* in the best sense of the word.

Quite apart from his music, Steuart was at home in every branch

---

* Steuart's own definition of a gentleman: "One who is never rude to anybody except on purpose."

of Art. He knew his Shakespeare intimately and was familiar with
all the English poets. In 1955 he delivered an authoritative address
on Wordsworth, when he re-opened the poet's house at Cocker-
mouth. His concluding words were: "Here in the country which
was Wordsworth's, which is dear to me by five and fifty years of
association, whose hills and dales, mountains and streams reflect
my youth and my lost comrades, in this country where my earliest
forebears lived their simple lives, I am proud to lay my humble
tribute at the feet of a great man, a great poet and a great patriot."
He was widely read—Jane Austen and Thomas Hardy were perhaps
his favourite writers, while Dickens and Scott passed him by. He had
a deep appreciation of painting and architecture, and a sense of the
historical continuity and universality of art.

Steuart had a conventional education and was brought up as a
strict church-goer—Sundays at Rochdale to hear his father preach
and compulsory chapel at Winchester and King's. I don't think
there can have been any layman in the world, with the possible
exception of his brother Arnold, who knew his Bible better, and he
would always find the apposite text to illustrate a point in his letters
or minutes. Although no scientist, he had inherited from his father a
restless questing mind and intellectual independence that made him
increasingly suspicious of dogma. He did not like organized religion
and he did not like the Church Establishment. Deans and Chapters
were a favourite target for his wit and many of his best stories were
told about clergymen.

In 1965, Steuart was invited to give away the prizes at the King's
School, Ely. The ceremony was held in the cathedral, after a short
service in which the lesson was Philippians 4. Steuart told the boys
to pay no attention to St. Paul's advice about "whatsoever things
are of good report." Don't bother about what people think of you, he
said, and added that he was delighted to see that so many boys had
chosen Bertrand Russell's *Autobiography* as their prize. Bertie Russell
was hardly the man whose career the Dean and Chapter would
have advised the boys to take as a model, and their blank, set faces
showed their disapproval.

Steuart's most savage attack on the Church Establishment was
contained in a letter to *The Times* in February 1959. At Vaughan
Williams's funeral service he had been angered by the words in the
prayer "We give thee hearty thanks for that it has pleased thee to

deliver this our brother out of the miseries of this sinful world," and he wrote:

WHAT THE WORDS MEAN

"Sir,

"Dr. Leslie Weatherhead in your issue of January 29th bids us stop and think what we sing at special occasions. Will the Church of England stop and think what the occasional attender at funerals is asked to participate in? Are 'the miseries of this sinful world' to be our last thought of a noble life of threescore years and ten? Must we give any credence whatever to the statement that God will end life on this world as soon as 'He has accomplished the number of his elect'? And should we still pray that He do so as soon as possible?

"Birth, marriage and death are all noble, natural things. The Church of England seems to wish us to regard birth as the entry to sin, marriage as a means of avoiding one aspect and death to be the welcome relief whereby we can sin no more. No wonder we don't go to Church.

Your obedient servant,
"Steuart Wilson"

His letter provoked a bitter controversy in the columns of *The Times*. He received many personal letters, too, including one from his old friend Dr. Fisher, then Archbishop of Canterbury. "You have no doubt had things in your life liable to make you bitter," Dr. Fisher wrote, "Few people have not. If you do not now go to church, I am sure it is not in any real sense due to occasional infelicities in the English language contained in the Book of Common Prayer: there must be some deeper cause."

Steuart penned another letter to *The Times*:

"Several correspondents are enthusiastic that such comments should be made publicly and that *The Times* should print them. Others have regarded me as cynical or embittered by the fact known to them that as a divorced person re-married I am not a communicant member of the Church of England. That is true, but I think I can still speak for the average layman who is not a churchgoer nor an adherent of the Church, but yet professes himself to be a Christian."

About the same time, he said in an 'Any Questions' programme:

"A Christian does not mean a person who has accepted the tenets of a particular sect or who believes in every inspired word of the Bible—a man who is a Christian is baptized with a certain faith which does not include the literal acceptance of the Old Testament or of any Testament at all—it merely includes the fact that he would follow the teachings and the precepts of Christ."

Steuart's own articles of faith "What I believe," are reprinted as an Appendix to this book. But I would like to conclude with an extract from a letter he wrote to Grace Hutson, after Mary's death. He was referring to his translation of the *Benedicite*:

"I feel sometimes ashamed that I can write such things when I don't believe them in the way that people think I must—or I couldn't write them! It was the same with singing the *Matthew Passion*: the full detail of the story is so true and so moving, that I *am* moved by it as I am by the Death of Socrates as told by Plato, but I can't accept the super-natural side as being necessary or as being 'Religion'. We occupy ourselves so much in Xtian faith with the after-death. I see the mental advantages of belief in it, but I can't accept it. I got a long letter from a friend who is deeply religious about 'accepting God's pattern'. I completely shy off that and I don't think death is a religious topic at all. Your relations with your neighbour are religious, because you accept those deliberately. The accidents of Life and Death are no one's Plan— it would be too cruel to expect it, but they should not alter one's fundamental relations to one's neighbour, which ought to be the basis of our following of Christ's teaching, whether you accept him as a master-teacher of Principles or as the mysterious embodiment of a mysterious Divine something.
Here endeth the Sermon!"

Whatever his views about the church and religion, Steuart showed by his very life and being, his humanity, charity and his neighbourliness, that he was a Christian in practice, if not in dogma.

He was, to use the words which he himself applied to Ralph Vaughan Williams, a Christian agnostic, and his faith had its roots in humanity and love.

LIST OF DECCA RECORDS

Folk Songs

Rio Grande ⎫
The Crocodile ⎭   4.1655

Spanish Ladies ⎫
Mowing the Barley ⎭   F.1836

Keys of Canterbury ⎫
Oh No, John   ⎭   F.1835

Classical

This Joyful Eastertide ⎫
A Benedicite   ⎭   F.1645

My heart ever faithful (Bach) ⎫
Total Eclipse (Handel)   ⎭   F.1833

Phillida flouts me   ⎫
Song of the Flea (Moussorgsky) ⎭   F.1830

Schubert

Maid of the Mill   ⎫
Miller's Song/The Brooks ⎭   F.1831

The Name   ⎫
Brook's Lullaby ⎭   F.1832

Schumann

Two Grenadiers   ⎫
O Lovely Star/The Blacksmith ⎭ F.1834

Vaughan Williams

On Wenlock Edge (3 records)   4.1649–1651

"A song recital 1929–30" Decca Mono ACL 303, issued 1968.

TABLE OF EARNINGS
(copied from Ledger)

	£	s.	d.
1912	16	5	6
1913	31	10	0
1914 to July 27	66	16	3
Total pre-war	114	11	9
July 27 1914—Jan. 22 1919	–	–	–
Feb.–Dec. 1919	159	15	6
1920 net	241	12	11
1921 ,,	556	4	9
1922 ,,	640	15	3
1923 net to Oct.	690	14	3
1924 net Sept.—Oct.	103	14	5
1925 June–Dec.	362	14	5
1926 gross	1,137	3	8
1927 ,,	1,042	16	1
1928 actual	1,279	12	6
(approx with work given up)	1,615	–	–
1929 gross and U.S.A.	1,306	11	2
1930	1,241	1	10
1931	1,737	4	4
1932	1,027	4	11
1933	797	3	9
1934	790	9	6
1935	630	15	–
1936	769	14	2
1937	725	3	3

ON WAISTCOATS:
ARTICLE IN THE TAILORS AND GARMENT WORKERS' JOURNAL', 1965

I think I got my first notion that waistcoats could be, and should be, gay from my experience at my school. The only boys to wear any kind of uniform were the scholars, of whom I was, remarkably, one and we wore an early medieval broad-cloth gown, below knee length and a sleeved waistcoat, a real "waist-coat" with a cloth back, the same weight and stuff as the front. But the rest of the school were free in their choice and when you rose to a certain dignity, freedom became manifest in your knitted, or flowered, waistcoats: certain rather senior and old-fashioned masters affected moleskin in the winter and elaborate tie-rings. I vowed that one day I would follow their example. It took me a long time to establish myself.

My first attempt was soon after I left the University, which was in those days not imaginative in its dress, took the form of a plum-coloured velvet dinner-jacket and a flowered silk waistcoat rather high cut with lapels. I remember the snort of disapproval with which it was greeted at the first conventional party at which I dared to wear it.

My working life was spent in a profession which virtually insisted on the conventional evening dress of white waistcoat and tails (I was not a head-waiter so guess what!) I had to wait for my chance. While I was—waistcoat-wise—in my "formative years" as they say I met a distinguished evening dress waistcoat decorating a well known slightly eccentric actor, and as I congratulated him he told me it was made out of his mother's—or maybe grandmother's—wedding dress, a lacey affair. That gave me an idea. My niece was being married and going to South Africa. I saw that her wedding dress had a small train; I told her that when she cut the train off, I would be glad to make an evening waistcoat out of it. My father-in-law in those days knew all the craftsmen in the hosiery and haberdashery lines and he got a wonderful creation, wide lapels of blue and gold brocade—the substance of the wedding gown with a thin line of piping for the pockets and the body of the waistcoat a splendid white satin. I

T

heard later that the brocade had been the end of a lot which had provided some part of the present Queen's wedding trousseau and that the white satin likewise had had a similar honourable past. One of my waistcoats was bought from an Indian trader in Bulawayo, who told me that the pattern of scarlet and gold was a revival of that which had been woven for Queen Victoria as a Durbar offering.

A treasured possession is an antique Austrian waistcoat of great dignity, embossed velvet with a calico back which certainly is a hundred years old.

Now these are pomps and vanities, I must turn to my workaday covers. Leading the field is a noble affair of "hunting pink" provided at the end of the war again by my cunning father-in-law who could wangle his way into the pink which couldn't be rationed. The moleskin was advertised in the local Portsmouth papers, both of these have specially warm backs to keep the kidneys warm! I had for many years a corduroy fellow but he dated back so far that I had long out-girthed him and he had to be given to a slimmer chap than I. Am I just vain or am I rightly proud of my waists? Do you know the difference, given by a small child in the language of Bunyan?

MR. VAIN says: "I wonder what you think of me."

MR. PROUD says: "I don't care what you think of me."

THE RECITATIVES OF THE
ST. MATTHEW PASSION

It may be convenient at the outset of this article to indicate the problems of these Recitatives: first of all the matter of Translation, secondly the question of Accompaniment, and lastly, once the two previous problems have been in some measure solved, the more difficult problem of Performance. If I may make at the start a general and comprehensive apology for the intrusion of my personal views and tastes, it will save repetition. I will also ask for an indemnity against wrath if I recount the stages by which I personally was led to the point of view which I now hold.

My first acquaintance with the *St. Matthew Passion* was in 1909, when, as an undergraduate at Cambridge, I sang in the chorus, when the narrator was Gervase Elwes and the words of Christ were sung by Francis Harford. I heard it again in 1911 at the Worcester Festival with Gervase Elwes and Campbell McInnes. I must confess that up to this time I was not an enthusiast about it. There had never seemed any dramatic continuity, the short outbursts of chorus were not enough to "get your teeth into" (I compared them with the Mass in which I had also sung in Cambridge) and the arias, though beautiful to the ear, had never brought conviction to my mind. And, most important of all, I regarded the Narrator's Recitatives as a necessary evil which had to be got over in order that we might get to the choruses. In 1913 I got my first chance of singing those Recitatives myself in the chapel of Guy's Hospital, where the organist, that much-lamented genius, Denis Browne, had an excellent little choir. After the performance the chaplain said he had never heard anything sung or said so quickly in his life, and it reminded me then of Augustus Trollope's account of the Minor Canons of Winchester in the 1840s, one of whom boasted that "he could give any man to Pontius Pilate in the Creed and beat him." I was perhaps influenced by the amazing speed and articulation with which one of the Minor Canons of Worcester Cathedral—my home at that time—would career through the Prayer for Parliament.

After the war there was a performance at the Worcester Festival of 1920, when Gervase Elwes sang the Narrator, and as I was actually singing in that performance I could follow his way very closely and, indeed, discussed it with him. My impression is that he still regarded it as not intrinsically interesting, either melodically or dramatically: the story had to be told as unobtrusively as possible in order that the comments on the story in the shape of aria and chorus might be made: but the emphasis was not on the story itself.

During the next few years I sang it occasionally, and it happened that in 1928 I had the opportunity of singing it several times, and I began to grow somewhat dissatisfied both with the manner in which the accompanying chords were arranged in any edition to which I had access, and also with the actual melodic outline of the notes as given in the various standard editions; and I discovered that the passages in which it was difficult to pitch the right interval were generally those from which the editors had removed one or more notes as written by Bach. But up to this time I had never taken what should have been the first step of all—I had never learnt it thoroughly in the original German. I took pains to do this, and during the autumn of 1928, when I was forced to spend three months in bed, I spent many hours of time in going over and over the German text and the various English versions, and at the same time I decided that I would go and study it from the beginning with Madame Wanda Landowska in her school outside Paris. I knew that her knowledge of such music was unrivalled and that she had many scores of times played the continuo for Willem Mengelberg's famous performances in Holland. To achieve what I wanted it was necessary also to study the accompaniments, and for that purpose Miss Jean Hamilton also came with me, and for some three weeks we worked with Mme. Landowska nearly every day, transcribing exactly her methods of accompaniment and learning from her the countless varieties of expression in the actual voice-part which had so long been unrevealed to me.

On returning to England, Miss Hamilton spent more time in making a version specially suitable to the piano rather than to the harpsichord, and I myself in rewriting entirely the recitative text to fit the Authorised Version words.

So much for the personal history with which I have felt it necessary to begin.

I. THE PROBLEM OF TRANSLATION

The syllabic method of setting the text which was traditional for recitative was seldom departed from by Bach except to illustrate with definite melismata such words as *gekreuziget, begraben, krähen,* and in the quite definite *arioso* passages at the words of the Institution of the Eucharist. Thus it may be stated that the syllabic method was definitely in Bach's mind and his departure from it justified almost entirely by some pictorial idea.

The difficulty of translation as a general rule is to find suitable English words which will as a whole, and not syllable by syllable, articulate—*i.e.,* divide the words and have cæsura—in approximately the same manner as the German. For the *Passion* we have in existence an English version with which most listeners are familiar and which is an incomparable masterpiece of language. It is this text of the Authorised Version which alone rings true to our ears, and if we make up our minds to use it we must not hope to be able to use also in their entirety the notes that Bach wrote for the German version. It may seem superfluous to emphasize this, but I have often received letters from listeners who refer to one or other of the standard versions as "the correct text", and I have been reproved by a music critic for making "departures from the text". It cannot be made too clear that all existing English versions are a compromise between the musical text of Bach and the verbal text of the Authorized Version or other versions.

There are three possible methods:

1. To take the musical text and to write to fit the musical phrase a deliberate paraphrase of the A.V., or a new translation from the Greek, in the manner of Dr. Moffatt's translation of the New Testament in Modern English, or the Twentieth Century New Testament.

2. To take the A.V. text and to rewrite the music to fit it syllabically as Bach might have been expected to do had he known English as well as his native German.

3. To compromise between the two extremes, and to endeavour to secure a general conformity with Bach's syllabic treatment without any rigid adherence to that principle, while being still at liberty to rewrite boldly any musical passage that proves intractable.

There is one method which I myself cannot tolerate as a solution, that is to adopt the A.V. as a basis and to 'pad' it when extra syllables are required, or to use inversions when the accentuation is inconvenient. This seems to me to argue an insensitiveness to literary style which is more serious than any departure from the exact notes of recitative. For example, such inversions as "He that his hand with me in the dish hath dippèd" and "Thou shalt me thrice deny," and such dangerous padding as "Peter remembered *sore* the words of Jesus," or "The Son of Man is *about to go* as of him it hath been written", or such assonances as "although all shall be offended", or the failure to notice the characteristic usages of 'unto' and 'to', all these to most ears detract more from the object of the narration, namely, to present a vivid story, than any departure from the exact notation.

Of the three former methods, the first so far as I know has never been seriously attempted, nor has the second, with sufficient boldness to distinguish it from the third method, of compromise.

The editors' prefaces present their dilemmas and their solutions very briefly, as will be seen by some extracts.

Novello, 1899.* "The adaptation of the narrative of the Evangelist, a task rendered perhaps somewhat less difficult and hazardous by the aid of the Revised Version of the New Testament, has been carefully reconsidered and rearranged so as to preserve unaltered, *as far as may be*, the musical text of the original." (Troutbeck.)

Stainer and Bell, 1910. "The recitatives have been considerably revised in order to reproduce *as far as the English version will allow* the declamation of Bach" (Stanford.)

Novello, 1911. "Our aim has been to retain the words of the Authorized Version, and at the same time to reproduce Bach's declamation *as closely as the English words allow*." A further note states it has been thought well in a few cases *to alter the sequence of the words* in order to preserve some characteristic point." It is noted that in one recitative there has been "*a slight re-arrangement* of the musical passage." (Elgar and Atkins.)

Breitkopf and Härtel, 1906. "The chapters of St. Matthew are here reproduced without alteration." (Claude Aveling.)

Boosey, 1877. "The Biblical text has been faithfully followed—at the same time the accent and rhythm of Bach's melody has been so closely adapted that *no material change* has taken place—while in no instance has the harmony suffered misplacement." (John Oxenford.)

Oxford Press, 1931. "We have followed the simple but instructive rule, so to order the declamation that the composer, *were he to hear his work in English*, would be as little conscious as possible that it was being sung in a foreign tongue." "The assurance is hardly necessary that the task has been undertaken with the intention to vary *as little as is necessary* a text hallowed by tradition and usage." (C. Sanford Terry.)

The italicised words show the hesitations of the editors—"*as far as may be*,'" or their re-assurance to themselves, "*no material change*" "*as little as is necessary*"—but they none of them grasp firmly the real nettle, namely, that the rhythm of English is entirely different from the rhythm of German, and it will not suffice to keep the notes of Bach and lose the rhythm of English. Let us take two examples to show how this matter has been treated.

In No. 54 the German text is as follows:

* Novello 1862 (Sterndale Bennett) makes no mention of any difficulty or compromise.

ORIGINAL TEXT

Ex.1 : Er halte aber zu der Zeit einen Gefangenen, einen son-der-liche vor andem der hiess Barabbas

This is bound to present a difficulty as the A.V., "And they had then a notable prisoner called Barabbas," has fifteen syllables compared with twenty-eight in German.

The solutions of the puzzle are as follows:

NOVELLO 1894

Ex.2 And at that time there was among the prisoners a no-ta-ble one called Barabbas

This is a fairly free paraphrase, but notice the slowing up of pace on the "notable one", the two crotchets running are impossible in this style of Recitative.

STAINER BELL 1910

Ex.3 And they had then a prisoner and a not – a-ble one called Barabbas

We are nearing a solution as far as the first half of the sentence is concerned, but the rhythm limps badly in the second half.

NOVELLO 1911

Ex.4 And they had then a not – – a-ble pri – so-ner called Bar – ab-bas

The dotted crotchets give a bigger limp still.

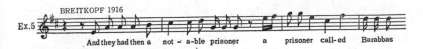

BREITKOPF 1916

Ex.5 And they had then a not – a-ble prisoner a prisoner call-ed Barabbas

Three crotchets running and the text altered despite the preface— see above.

BOOSEY 1877

Ex.6 And they had then a not-a-ble pri-so-ner call – ed Barabbas

Here the two minims top the lot for an impossible passage in recitative.

These are from the versions whose editors and translators claim that they have "reproduced the declamation of Bach". I consider that there is a considerable limitation to this claim, in that they have neglected the vital question of rhythm.

The following example is from the Oxford Press Edition:

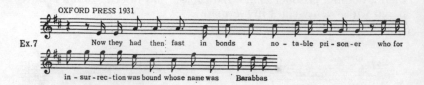

Ex.7

This is the method of free paraphrase, and is a successful example of that method.

All these solvers are, however, "tied by the leg" so long as they insist on keeping the exact number of bars of the original without regard to the rhythm of the contents. If there are only fifteen syllables to divide among the bars which have previously held twenty-eight, it is obvious that what must happen is a complete slowing up of the rhythm somewhere.

I have ventured in my own version to cut this knot by 'paraphrasing' Bach and collecting into *one bar* the melodic phrase that Bach spread over two and a half bars.

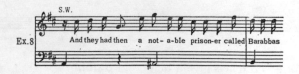

Ex.8

The continuo also changes its position to back up, not the first change of the harmony from tonic to diminished seventh, but the most important moment in the phrase based on that harmony.

Another important aspect of English rhythm is its tendency in sentences as well as in words to throw the accent back as far as possible: this is particularly noticeable when the sentence ends with a personal pronoun which it is not desired to emphasize. Such sentences as in No. 64:

> And after that they had mócked him
> They took the robe óff from him
> And put his own raiment ón him,

are all paroxytone or proparoxytone (*i.e.* accent on the penultimate or antipenultimate), which correspond with a German text:

Und da sie ihn verspottet hátten
Zogen sie ihm den Mantel aús
Und zogen ihm seine Kleider án,

two of which are strongly oxytone (accent on the last syllable). The only way of securing an English equivalent which is truly English-rhythmical instead of German-rhythmical, is to treat it as follows:

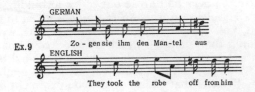

But no editor up to date has printed such a solution.

The question of ligatures *versus* syllabic style must not be shirked. But again it is a question of compromise and of personal taste. Sometimes the omission of one note in a melodic line, as for example the B in the last example does not seem to hamper the line of the phrase, whereas to remove the last A seems quite out of the question. The importance of preserving the natural English proparoxytone sentence-rhythm seems to me to be as essential as preserving the verbal accent correctly, and when Professor Terry states that his object is to make a version which would sound like German, he is forgetting that it cannot then sound like English.

From all this my deductions are that one cannot too boldly grasp the nettle of rewriting Bach in order to preserve the language and rhythms of the noblest prose in the English language. It may be unlike Bach to use ligatures freely, but we are not writing German recitative, we are attempting to write English recitative.

One more small point before the problem of translation is left. It has been considered a reverent and traditional manner of speech in church to sound wherever possible the final -ed of the past tenses of verbs. An analysis of Elizabethan and Jacobean music, and of contemporary poetry, shows that both usages were concurrent (the spelling being sometimes altered, as 'vexed' or 'vext') as in the similar cases of words ending in -tion, which were apparently pronounced 'tempta-ti-on' or 'tempta-tion' according to circumstance. Throughout my own version I have left the final -ed mute in every case, as the old-fashioned ecclesiastical pronunciation now sounds somewhat affected to most ears and detracts from the straightforward dramatic value of telling the story in simple language.

II. THE PROBLEM OF ACCOMPANIMENT

The bass of Bach's recitative was played by a stringed instrument, and filled in with harmonies by a keyed instrument: this was the universal practice, except in England during the period 1800–1850, when Lindley the 'cellist and Dragonetti the bass-player—sitting at the same desk in the opera for fifty-two years—evolved a system of the double-bass sustaining the continuo, while the 'cello played arpeggios to support the voice. Rockstro agreed that this custom was confined to England, and Sir George Smart recorded that the only musical quarrel he ever had arose out of his forbidding Lindley to play thus in a Handel oratorio. An example is given in *Grove*, third edition, 1928, vol. iv, p. 337, *s.v.* Recitative. The writer of this article condemns the practice—which he never could have heard—as being "entirely at variance with the effect intended by the composer". The writer in the first (1880) edition—who might well have heard it himself—says that "Lindley's accompaniment of recitative was perfection". Let us incline our hearts to remember that Taste and not Rule governs Performance.

In operatic *recitativo secco*, as opposed to *recitativo stromentato*, the *basso continuo** was written in long notes, semibreves and minims, and it is so written invariably in Handel oratorios, the church cantatas and the *St. John Passion*. But in the *St. Matthew Passion* the recitative bass is printed in the Bach-Gesellschaft in crotchets only,† the notes of longer value being reserved for the string orchestra that accompanies the words of Christ. I do not think that the inference is that Bach intended here to depart, for the only time in recorded music history, from keeping the bass virtually continuous in recitative. I will admit that a contrary opinion could, in theory, equally well be established, but I believe that in practice it is easier to listen to and easier to sing when the accompaniment is in sustained minims and not in detached crotchets. In support of this, Dr. J. E. Borland kindly allows me to tell this story, which he once told me. Dr. Borland as a young man played the piano for Otto Goldschmidt, the founder of the Bach Choir, and in playing recitative did not "revive the bass". Goldschmidt told him that his teacher Schneider had laid it down that Carl Philipp Emanuel Bach had said that the bass must always be 'revived' as long as the bass note continued to be the harmonic bass of the melody of the recitative. This Johann Gottlob Schneider was organist at Dresden and had the reputation of having the direct tradition of John Sebastian Bach himself. This

* The term *continuo* or 'thorough-bass' properly implies a bass which is literally continuous, but the word is used with reasonable looseness to describe such a bass, figured or unfigured, as we are now discussing, which has rests and is not therefore continuous.

† I have unfortunately not been able to verify this fact from the actual MS.

living chain of evidence is worth more to me than many books of theory.

This is also the firm conviction of Madame Wanda Landowska, to whom, as I have already said, both my collaborator in this work, Miss Jean Hamilton, and I myself owe all our inspiration. We boldly tackled the first recitative in the *St. Matthew Passion*, which opens in Bach's own MS. with a single crotchet G on the first beat. N.B.— In all these examples Bach's bass, with any figuring of his, is given in brackets.

Ex.10

This treatment challenges many hitherto received methods of accompanying recitative: first, it lengthens and repeats the bass note; secondly, it does not wait for an indication of figuring to change to 6/4 7/5 as necessary; thirdly, it places the notes of the chord in a widely spread position, starting from the G below the bass clef, which a harpsichord could not play, and rising to the D in the treble clef above the limits usually assigned to accompanying chords and, finally resolves in the chord played by the orchestra.

The first point, to lengthen and repeat the bass note, must be stretched to include, where necessity of translation arises, putting the bass note at any beat in the bar where the words require it, not being necessarily the beat at which Bach placed it to suit his German text, as in Ex. 20 in Part III of this article. It must also cover the rare occasions when the exciting rhythm of the crowd, in No. 32, surging into the garden to arrest Jesus, seems to need a bass, and Bach has left the bar empty.

Ex.11

The second point, to change the figuring as needed, must follow as an obvious corollary once the first is conceded.

The third point is important and novel, for it implies that we are definitely writing for a modern piano where the sonority of the lowest octave is far greater than that of the harpsichord; where notes in such octaves must be widely spaced, whereas in the harpsichord they must be close, to be effective; and moreover we will boldly write an arpeggio over five octaves in order to emphasize "then all the disciples *forsook* him and fled".

Ex.12

One must not forget that the sustaining powers of the piano are so much greater than that of the harpsichord that it was all the more necessary in Bach's day to "revive the bass", with arpeggios, repeated notes, or contrapuntal devices, and in actual fact John Sebastian himself must have done far more "filling-up" than a modern pianist would require (or dare) to do. The greater resonance of the piano also permits of another device, namely, to lift the damper of the string with the gentlest touch of the note and to allow the voice to cause that string to vibrate in sympathy. (See Ex. 16 in Part III below.) Again, the more continuous sounding power of the piano causes the silences in the rests to be not mere accidents but definite planned functions in the whole scheme, as, for example, the sudden silence in No. 32 at the words, "and kissed him". (Ex. 19 in Part III below.)

The theory that the accompaniment should be kept low in position is no doubt based on C. P. E. Bach's "Versuch", but the qualities of a modern piano must be allowed for in modifying the strict rule for harpsichord playing. Lastly, it is the habit of Bach in the *St. Matthew Passion* to introduce the words of Jesus by a note on the bass before the upper strings play: it is to fill in this gap that the keyboard instrument is also useful. There is every reason to believe, both from general custom and from the fact of the bass being figured throughout while the strings are playing, and further from C. P. E. Bach's statement that "no piece can be performed satisfactorily without a keyed instrument", that the harpsichord would have played throughout in Bach's own performance.

The ordinary view held even today of the function of the continuo player in recitative is to set the key by a staccato chord at the beginning, to end with an 'Amen' cadence, and to interject by the way an occasional, unavoidable, and usually unrelated, chord. Our own view differs widely from this, as has already been shown, not only in its main principles described above, but in the following subsidiary characteristics. First, the maintenance in the right hand of a definite melodic line in conjunct movement; next, the importance of definite contrapuntal inner parts where they may be required, and last, attention to providing variety in the formal cadences according to their importance in the dramatic scheme.

First—a definite melodic line:

Second—definite contrapuntal inner parts:

Third—cadences. Variety in these can be obtained in several ways:

(a) Suspensions.
(b) Spacing of notes in the chords.
(c) Elaboration of parts either in continuation of the melody of the recitative or independently:

(a) Suspensions will be only used for the same reason as appoggiaturas (see below in Part III of this article) for increasing emotion. This example is from the end of the words "and began to be sorrowful and very heavy".

(b) The open fifths are the cadence which follows the words "and when he had scourged Jesus he delivered him to be crucified". The bare octave at the words "Then came they and laid hands on Jesus and took him".

(c) Pilate's wife "suffered many things in a dream because of him". In the second exquisitely simple cadence "many false witnesses came, yet found they none".

Another way in which variety can be obtained during the run of the recitative—i.e., neither by the introductory chord nor by the cadences—is by altering the position of the chord to suit the mood of the moment. In such a passage as the end of No. 15, "and they were exceeding sorrowful and began every one of them to say unto him, Lord is it I", the accompanying chords are kept low in the sombre key of B flat minor. In No. 59, when Pilate cheerfully disclaims responsibility, "I am innocent of the blood of this just person, see ye to it", the accompaniment sustains this atmosphere (see Ex. 13 above), the rhythmical contrasting chords at "one upon the right hand, and another on the left", are placed in a high and low position respectively.

We do not wish to let the impression remain that it is only by a few dramatic or obvious touches that the perfect accompaniment will be achieved: it is rather by the persistent and scrupulous care with which each cadence is considered, each chord spaced in the most effective style, and the value of each touch adjusted to fit the surroundings. Finally, the pianist must enter into the spirit of the performance, as described in the next part of this article, no less than the singer. The quality of touch is supremely important as well as the actual notes sounded; the pianist must back up the urgent rhythms calling the chorus in, must slow down the long sorrowful cadences that mark each poignant moment in the story, responding to the elasticity of each living phrase so that the curved steel of the melody bends but never breaks. tempered to express every degree of imaginative utterance.

III. THE PROBLEM OF PERFORMANCE

The Narrator must consider himself as the story-teller-in-chief; although he does not himself utter the spoken words of the various characters, he prepares the stage for them and "calls them on" in their various degrees of importance and in their separate character. The *mise-en-scène* of the drama is his care—and no man can neglect so important a feature. How is this care to be undertaken? Principally, I think, by attention to the broad principles of story-telling—variation in pitch of the voice, in pace of narration, in intensity of feeling. The pitch of the voice is already determined by the music—but the pace is left entirely to the discretion of the singer, who can vary it episode by episode and sentence by sentence, keeping in mind always the one object a story-teller has in view, to interest his listeners, now by one mood and now by another, never maintaining the same mood for too long. Musical rhythm must always be considered, and though it may be perfectly legitimate to sing one phrase twice as fast as another, yet in that one phrase a definite rhythm must exist. The characteristic English word cadence—proparoxytone as we have said already—must be preserved if possible with a dotted rhythm, to suit such words and phrases as "Gethsemane", "Golgotha", "Field of Blood", "multitude", "óff from him", and sometimes in a continuous rhythm, such as "rólled a great stóne to the dóor of the sépulchre", which constitutes a long 12/8 rhythm. There is also another most important factor, that of silence; the slight pause before the telling word, the time to be allowed for the dramatic moment to enter into the listener's mind, the silence that closes one episode and introduces another; all these are part of the framework of the larger rhythm that encloses the picture which has been painted by close attention to the smaller rhythms.

Bach himself has assisted the singer by writing certain passages in an obvious though not directly indicated arioso: the best known are the melismata on the words "wept bitterly" in No. 46 after Peter's denial, and "to crucify him" in No. 64. Less conspicuous are such passages as "and poured it on his head as he sat at meat" in No. 6, or "and began to be sorrowful and very heavy" in No. 24. But in fact there are many more, some of which gain their significance from the fact that the phrases before have been very freely uttered, and thus the strictly measured time has a certain gravity, as in No. 24, "Then cometh Jesus with them unto a place called Gethsemane, and saith unto the disciples", which, if put under the microscope, yields the following qualities. The introductory words, "Then cometh Jesus with them", are one unit spoken in absolutely free speech-rhythm which defies exact musical notation; then the next unit, "unto a place" slight pause "called", another comma, to introduce the solemn word "Gethsemane" in strict dotted rhythm, and in the same slow tempo the grave musical phrase that introduces the words of Jesus, "sit ye here while I go yonder and pray", a simple phrase concealing its beauty and dignity. Note the treble of the accompaniment touching gently the E flat to accentuate the pathos.

A great deal might be written on each recitative to attempt to explain by words what words can no more exactly convey than musical notation. Each word is a jewel that can be polished, each sentence has its rhythm, and each episode its peculiar dramatic value. The character of Judas, for example, gradually unfolds itself: first, the quickly muttered agreement that thirty pieces of silver was a fair price, through the sad avowal that this was the beginning of the treachery (in a characteristic 'sentimental' jump of the dominant seventh and with the melancholy of its cadence carried on by the continuo):

The parentheses (I have actually inserted the brackets) which follow the future mention of Judas' name, in No. 17 sharply anticipating the tragedy, in No. 49 poignantly recalling the misery of the treachery:

all seem to make more heart-searching still the actual moment of betrayal.

"And forthwith he came to Jesus and said, Hail master; and kissed him."

The very fact that this dropping seventh is unique among the Passion cadencies emphasizes the icy chill of the traitor's salute, emphasized by the cessation of the accompaniment.

The Narrator must be alive to the steady growth of the emotion in the scenes of the Agony in the Garden (Nos. 24–31), beginning with Christ's request to his Disciples to watch with him, which leads to the exquisite lullaby for tenor, oboe and chorus; through Christ's increasing intensity of prayer that he might be spared the final humiliation, through the bass aria in G minor treading an infinitely solemn dance-measure (as so often in the Passions—*e.g.*, the

U

Institution of the Eucharist in minuet-rhythm), again returning to the scene in the garden with growing passion as the Narrator's voice rises:

No.30

Ex.20

He went a-way a-gain the second time and pray — ed say — ing

GERMAN

be — te - te und sprach

(N.B.—In the original German Bach permits himself the unique emphasis in these recitatives of a dotted crotchet on the D# for the first syllable of "Betete und sprach" which gives some grounds for turning the phrase into a melisma.)

And finally the congregation, taking up the last words of Christ, "Thy will be done", joints itself into the drama and adds not a comment, but the individual identification of each person present with the agony of mind described in those scenes.

No discussion of Performance can omit the vexed question of the appoggiatura. For a fuller dissertation on this the reader is referred to a Symposium in *Music and Letters*, vol. V, No. 2, April, 1924, in particular to Mr. Herman Klein's contribution. To summarize his argument here briefly: The appoggiatura is a note added in order to arrive more gracefully at the following note, whether rising or falling. These passing notes were never written into vocal parts as it was deemed a reflection upon the personal taste of the singer to indicate to him what was so obvious. In Italian music its omission is unthinkable. The only question for us to decide is how far Handel and Bach expected to hear the Italian style used in their music. Of Handel it may be said at once that he could not have expected to hear any other style, and therefore to remove *all* appoggiaturas from the *Messiah* recitatives is an unscholarly, unimaginative, piece of pedantry. The question can never be solved in its entirety—what did the composers expect to hear? But when—as in the soprano-alto duet of the *Matthew Passion*, No. 33—the instruments have a written out appoggiatura and the voices singing an identical and sometimes simultaneous phrase have none, one must infer that the singers did not need reminding of this necessity. An instance which I believe has not been quoted in this argument before is that of the instrumental bass in the Choral Symphony *versus* the vocal bass in two identical passages, where it was clearly necessary to insert for the instrument the appoggiatura which the singer would sing by instinct.

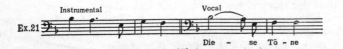

Herman Klein summarizes Spitta's view, that the omission of the appoggiatura in church music was designed to give the recitatives a non-theatrical style, but that this omission is directly contrary to the contemporary tradition of Bach, where the universal rule was to treat church recitative in a melodious rather than a declamatory manner, whereas in opera the reverse was the case.

My own personal opinion leads me to use the appoggiatura mainly for emotional purposes, as a strong suspension. Where no emotion is needed it can be omitted. Thus, in two similar musical passages: the first is not emotional, but in the second every legitimate device to strengthen the pathos of the word 'forsaken' must be employed.

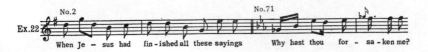

I have no hesitation in using appoggiaturas to avoid a repeated note in a cadence where the pace is quick and conversational, thus obeying the age-long convention of the operatic secco:

I must apologize for the intrusion of a personal opinion into the middle of learned opinions, justifying myself by an adaptation from H. W. Fowler's *Modern English Usage*: "Some singers certainly need advice upon it and few have time for the inductive process required, in default of perfect musical instinct, to establish sound rules."

Out of many more characterizing touches that might be mentioned

I will only give one. The very last recitative which the Narrator sings, "So they went, and made the sepulchre sure, sealing the stone, and setting a watch", must be made to contain, in the voice, the qualities which it seems to me to contain in the music directly, and by implication in the narrative: the first is the half-mocking touch of the word 'sure', the formality of the seals and the watch, so pompous, so useless, so like official man attempting to imprison the Spirit; and the second is the feeling of suspense, as we know very well that the story is not ended, but indeed only begun.

Such is the nature, it seems to me, of the Recitatives in the Passion, and such are the qualities for performance which they demand, that it has been truly said of this music that it can only show "how great and satisfying Bach is, and how little fit we are to be in his company."

STEUART WILSON

"THIS I BELIEVE"
BY STEUART WILSON

I am one of those many people who can no longer say with complete confidence "I believe" (and the words must be in quotes), in the sort of way that belief is implied in the creeds of the Christian churches, or in the statements and affirmations of non-Christian religions. But among those people like me, many are deeply religious by nature, in so far as they can accept the idealism and the social philosophy, if one may use such a word, which the teaching of Christ and other great idealists contained, while they find it impossible to belong to any close corporation which excludes others who think slightly differently about administrative church matters, while they have overlooked the two things that should be a human bond between us all, namely: Do you care for Truth above all things, and Will you never do unto others that which you would not wish others to do unto you?

If you really care for truth passionately you will have a mind that is perpetually enquiring and alert, a mind that is unable to hold strong convictions without examining their truth, and to examine is not the same as to repeat the same identical statements over and over again.

Again, if you care for other people as you care for yourself, you simply have to *act*, not just look for truth. And when you have made up your mind that "something ought to be done"—and how often have we said that—you must put forward some very good reason indeed why it should not be YOU that does it.

The great Saints felt like that: how else can you explain St. Francis, St. Ignatius on the one plane; General Booth of the Salvation Army or the Abolitionists on another plane? They felt a burning sense of duty to prevent the doing unto others of that which they would never in any circumstances wish, or indeed allow, others to do unto them; and they could not rest quiet until they had "done something".

Truth does not live at the bottom of a well. Truth is much more like the Sleeping Beauty surrounded by a high quickset hedge. Truth has to be fought for by a living person as a virtue which must be brought back to life by personal struggles. Surely it is this fighting which gives us the right to hold the truth, and equally the credit in maintaining it.

The purpose of life can be said to consist in two words: Truth and Love. How can we attain any objective so grand, so remote as these? Let me quote the obstinate, determined visionary thinker, John Bunyan. Christian, the Pilgrim of *Pilgrim's Progress*, is seeking information from Evangelist as to how to find the way to the Celestial City and escape from the City of Destruction. This is the dialogue:

EVANGELIST: Do you see yonder wicket-gate?

CHRISTIAN: No.

EVANGELIST: Do you see yonder shining light?

CHRISTIAN: I think I do.

EVANGELIST: Keep this light in your eye and go up thereto.

PUBLICATIONS

Published works of Steuart Wilson include:

James M. Wilson, jointly with Sir Arnold Wilson. Sidgwick and Jackson, 1932.
Schubert's Songs Translated, jointly with A. H. Fox Strangways. Oxford University Press, 1924.
Music Observed, preface to A. H. Fox Strangways' collected essays, Methuen, 1936.
Haydn: The Creation, jointly with A. H. Fox Strangways, Oxford University Press.
Schumann Songs Translated, Oxford University Press.
Brahms Requiem Translated, Oxford University Press.

Articles in Music and Letters:

April 1922, Church Music
October 1924, On being taught singing
July 1925, A lesson with the Master
July 1929, Vocal and unvocal
October 1930, Olympic Music
July 1935, The Recitative of the St. Matthew Passion

Royal Society of Arts, Cantor Lecture "Music and the audience", April 1949.

SELECT BIBLIOGRAPHY

James M. Wilson, 1836–1931. Sidgwick and Jackson, 1932
Letters of H. S. Wilson. Cambridge University Press (privately printed), 1919
Late Victorian (life of Sir Arnold Wilson) by J. Marlowe. Cresset Press, 1967
R.V.W., a biography of Ralph Vaughan Williams, by Ursula Vaughan Williams. Oxford University Press, 1964
The Works of Ralph Vaughan Williams, by Michael Kennedy. Oxford University Press, 1964
Gustav Holst, by Imogen Holst. Oxford University Press, 1938
Heirs and Rebels. Correspondence between R. Vaughan Williams and Gustav Holst, edited by Ursula Vaughan Williams and Imogen Holst. Oxford University Press, 1959
Jean de Reske, by Clara Leiser. Gerald Howe, 1933
Memoirs of an Amateur Musician, by Dr. E. H. Fellowes. Methuen, 1946
Immortal Hour, by Michael Hurd. Routledge and Kegan Paul, 1962
Rupert Brooke, by Christopher Hassall. Faber and Faber, 1964
The Hallé Tradition, by Michael Kennedy. Manchester University Press, 1960
Two Centuries of English Opera, by Harold Rosenthal. Putnam, 1958
Glyndebourne, by Spike Hughes. Methuen, 1965
John Christie of Glyndebourne, by Wilfrid Blunt. Geoffrey Bles, 1968
Basso Cantante, by David Franklin. Duckworth, 1969
Portrait of Elgar, by Michael Kennedy. Oxford University Press, 1968

The Birmingham and Midland Institute, by Rachel Waterhouse. Birmingham, 1954

Myra Hess by Her Friends, edited by Denise Lassimonne and Howard Ferguson. Hamish Hamilton, 1966

Hatred, Ridicule or Contempt, by Joseph Dean. Constable, 1953; Penguin Books, 1968

Grove's Dictionary of Music and Musicians, 1954 edition. Macmillan

Who's Who in Music. Love and Malcolmson, 1949–50

The Oxford Companion to Music, Percy A. Scholes, Oxford University Press

INDEX